COMING DOWN THE MOUNTAIN

Other Titles by Brian Kennedy

Growing Up Hockey
Living the Hockey Dream
My Country Is Hockey
Pond Hockey

Coming Down the Mountain

RETHINKING THE 1972 SUMMIT SERIES

EDITED BY BRIAN KENNEDY

WOLSAK
& WYNN

Cover and book design: Julie McNeill, McNeill Design Arts
Typeset in Adobe Caslon
Printed by Coach House Printing Company, Toronto, Canada

The publisher gratefully acknowledges the support of the Canada Council for the Arts, the Ontario Arts Council and the Canada Book Fund.

Canada Council Conseil des Arts
for the Arts du Canada

ONTARIO ARTS COUNCIL
CONSEIL DES ARTS DE L'ONTARIO

Canadian Patrimoine
Heritage canadien

Wolsak and Wynn Publishers Ltd.
280 James Street North
Hamilton, ON
Canada L8R 2L3

Library and Archives Canada Cataloguing in Publication

Coming down the mountain : rethinking the 1972 Summit Series / edited by Brian Kennedy.

Includes bibliographical references.
ISBN 978-1-894987-86-8 (pbk.)

1. Canada-U.S.S.R. Hockey Series, 1972. I. Kennedy, Brian, 1962-, editor

GV847.7.C66 2014   796.962·66   C2014-902528-9

For my sister, Sandra,
who shared the moment with me in 1972,
and my brother-in-law, Phil,
who shares it with me now.

Contents

The Series as Cultural Artifact

What about Now?

Introduction:
"Yeah, I've Got That, Too":
What's Left (Over) from the Summit Series?

♣

BRIAN KENNEDY

The Fraught Quality of Memory

Forty-plus years on, the Summit Series exists for Canadians as a set of what might appear to be uncomplicated facts. It was "us" versus the big "evil other." Our guys banded together, despite early setbacks, to win. "The goal" was a never-to-be-forgotten moment of triumph that united a large and politically fractious country. Access to this set of commonplace beliefs is as close as the nearest Internet-connected computer, DVD player or library bookshelf. Maybe it's as close as the nearest Tim Hortons, where the question "Do you remember September 1972?" is likely to spark recognition, discussion and camaraderie, even amongst those too young to have witnessed it in person, or those who lived elsewhere at that time.

This volume exists, in large measure, to ask *what else* there is to the Summit Series. Aside from the familiar tropes of enmity, triumph and nostalgia that live on in its wake, what else can be seen as its enduring legacy in Canadian life and elsewhere? Many of these essays look at topics not discussed previously, from the influence on the women's game to various international reactions to the series. Others turn familiar themes upside down, reexamining received opinions. But before embarking on these topics, it might be worthwhile to give some thought to the idea of memory itself and how it is preserved into the present. As such,

I want to consider the ways in which human memory is supplemented and expanded, with some particular attention to the detritus of consumer culture, which clings to past events, like the series, or even – depending upon one's point of view – looms larger as a legacy than the actual historical events and witnesses' reactions to them.

Let's start with an irony: over time, the Summit Series has grown to be both more than it was in 1972 and different than it was in its historical iteration. For instance, it is documented on DVD and thus can be replayed at will. Further, over the past twenty years an industry of souvenir commemoration surrounding the series (and sports and other popular culture more broadly) has grown up. Add those two things together, and you have an event that is both sacred and profane, if those two poles can be suggested by, say, the average person's memory of Henderson's goal on the one hand and the bobblehead doll version of Henderson himself on the other.

And yet memory itself is contradictory and multi-dimensional. "Do you remember where you were when the goal was scored?" seems like a simple question. Common recollections involve kids leaving classrooms and being herded into cafeterias or auditoriums to watch games. Usually, because of the limits of technology at the time, they would watch on a nineteen-inch black-and-white TV mounted on an AV cart. Those who were adults might remember skipping out of work and going to a Simpsons or Eaton's department store and catching parts of the games on the TVs displayed for sale.

But even those who did not have these experiences have a reference point for the series. For example, Andrea Doty, who was an elementary school student in St. Catharines, Ontario, when the series happened, is sure that her class was not given the option of seeing the games. She is adamant that it's not just that she doesn't remember the moment. Her memory, then, exists as a product of the *absence* of doing something. Measured against the presence of the event – the fact that kids in other schools did see the games, particularly game eight – the day has significance for her, but in the negative. It's like the black spot one sees in front of one's eyes after a camera flash has gone off.[1] Such a memory (of something that never happened) can exist only when the opposite, or what might have happened, is significant. It's like someone in the US saying, "I don't remember where I was when I heard that Kennedy got shot." That in itself becomes a memory, and important.

Paul Henderson, in the introduction to his and Jim Prime's *How Hockey Explains Canada*, says that people ask him about "the goal" all the time, but he says that they also tell stories about missing the goal. One man was denied the chance because his high school chemistry teacher hated hockey and would not release his students to watch game eight in their school's gym. "I've hated that teacher ever since. I missed one of the greatest sports moments in Canadian history because of this SOB," the man exclaimed to Henderson (xiv). Likely he has thought about that moment as many times, or more, than some people who actually got to see the winning goal live on television.

The same is true for Prime, who talks about having missed the goal because he was driving an American colleague to the airport in Halifax. He got so excited while listening to the end of the game on the radio that he almost lost control of his car, giving himself a nosebleed in the process (xxiii). Is that a better story than one of sitting in the living room and jumping up when the goal was scored on TV? I think so, though what's more important is to note that both of these accounts point out how the series often becomes reducible to the goal, or the goal becomes synonymous with the meaning of the series, and that when the goal is recalled, other, more complicated and fraught aspects of the series are erased.

Lingering Memory and Meaning

The function of memory is described by cultural critic Norman Klein in *The History of Forgetting: Los Angeles and the Erasure of Memory*. He describes memory as being like a portrait of a person recalled from one's childhood. This, labelled an "imago" by Klein, is more like the outline of the face than the actual features of the face itself (3–4). In time, new memories come to supplement the original one, and in a moment of "distraction," one imago quietly replaces the other (13). Indeed, cultural critic Andreas Huyssen reminds that "Freud already taught us that memory and forgetting are indissolubly linked to each other, that memory is but another form of forgetting, and forgetting is a form of hidden memory" (27).[2] For Klein, it's not the precision of the memory that

11

matters. Indeed, his point is that memory is always inexact. In fact, he says that often all that remains is the "trace" left behind of the original experience (4). Observing that points one back to what ought to be remembered but cannot be in its pure form.

It seems a cultural commonplace that Canadians mention "the goal," or the series more broadly, whenever they get the chance. In the foreword to the Henderson and Prime book, Stephen Harper raises the series as an example of how two worlds collided, the systems so different as to be irreconcilable. "It was an event that reminded Canadians of why we were in the Cold War. It was a pretty important moment in history," the prime minister comments (xi). Canadians gladly share this myth with others, especially newcomers, and then take pride in those (select few?) who make it their own. Henderson talks about an "Asian gentleman" who didn't come to Canada until 1975 but became interested in the Summit Series via videotape, seeing it almost as if he had known about the series when it happened (xiii).

The series also exists all over Canadian literature and popular culture. Writers like David Adams Richards and musical groups like The Tragically Hip have ensured that future generations will know about the series, at least if their readers or listeners want to understand the nuances of reference in these artists' works.[3]

Further, Canadians lay this myth over subsequent experiences as a template to measure meaning. It is recreated in the Subway Super Series between Major Junior players from each country, and it lingers in the minds and on the tongues of commentators whenever Canada and Russia meet in international play, such as in the IIHF World U20 Championship (the "World Juniors") played at year's end. This fact, for instance, is cited by TSN personality Gord Miller in Dave Bidini's book *A Wild Stab for It: This Is Game Eight from Russia:* "The myth of '72 is still very strong. You notice this during the World Junior tournament, or whenever the two countries meet. This is in spite of the fact that Russian players are [now] everywhere in the West" (48–49).

The Canada-Russia dichotomy was used most notably as a measuring rod against which to gauge the importance of the Olympics of 2010, with Sidney Crosby's winning goal put up against Henderson's as a cultural marker to be remembered forever; the difference being, of course, that the "evil other"

Russians had, in this instance, been replaced by the "looming other" Americans. Harper, however, tells the truth when he says that moment was important, but that anyone from an older generation (i.e., one who had seen the Summit Series live) would argue that it was different (by which he means "better," but he's doing a delicate dance so as not to offend the young or the Crosby fanatics) (Henderson and Prime, x).

The Summit Series and Vimy Ridge are perhaps the two defining moments of Canadian history, aside from Confederation and the introduction of the Charter. The value of the series as a historical event was only heightened with the creation of the physical monument outside the Hockey Hall of Fame in Toronto in 2000. The monument commemorates what has come to be called "Canada's Team of the Century" and might be interpreted as a miniature version of the Vimy Memorial. The image it offers is of an event fixed in time and memory. And yet, as Klein points out, memory work is not an uncomplicated process. New facets accrue to memory as the event is melded into one's personal experience over time, and old ones are lost (3–4).

With reference to the series, memory is supplemented with documentary retellings that exist on the border between souvenir commemoration and history. Added to that are tangible "collectible" objects that give the series a kitsch quality but that nonetheless may feel authentic to the collector. The ways in which all of these things meld together with the devout fan's reliving of the series via contemporary media (DVDs of the games) serve to sediment the series into memory in ways that both supplement and supplant the original moments. This accretion of memory and its integration into one's life become as significant as the original moments the memories are based on, until the two can no longer be separated.

Do You Have the Goods?

Consumer kitsch related to the Summit Series has been issued in an ever-increasing variety of late, and it is here that a critical eye might be levelled as we ask the question, "What's left of the Summit Series?" Replica sweaters, bobbleheads, cards, pucks, souvenir coins, books, DVD versions of the series – all of these have been offered to fans since the first meaningful anniversary in

1992. "Meaningful"? Why that word, and why especially should it be used for the twenty-year mark and beyond? Because that was the first year that modern kitsch culture caught up with the Summit Series.[4] The simple reason for this was that the players' desire to capitalize on their efforts on the ice coalesced in that year, starting them on a trajectory to make money from the series – or, as I will get into presently, from nostalgia for the series. The impulse is described by player Ron Ellis in response to my question about how the series has worked its way into commercial culture of late, something that surely wasn't anticipated in 1972:

> I think it was our 20th anniversary, or maybe it was 25.... Rod Seiling and I...with the help of a couple of sponsors...were able to bring the fellows into town. We had a little fun game at Maple Leaf Gardens. We had a dinner with our wives.... During dinner, we just said to the guys, would you like to continue this? Everybody seemed to really enjoy themselves, and they said sure. Because what was happening at that time was, Hockey Canada owned the rights to the jersey, the film footage, and so on. And every once in a while, we'd see a clip of us on TV in a commercial. We'd say, "Hmm, everybody's making money on this." That caught our attention because it was happening more and more, and so we decided as a group to incorporate ourselves. And then we started negotiations with Hockey Canada, and they were wonderful. They said by all means, you guys deserve the rights. An agreement was put in place, and we now, the team, the players, we own the rights to the jersey, and the footage, and so then we said "OK, none of us are in a position or have the time to market the team properly, so we hired a firm." That...was a process.

There had been prior celebrations, and even a replica series (three games) played in 1987 at the fifteen-year mark, but never the commodification of the series as Ellis describes it.[5]

Three responses come to mind. For one thing, Ellis's description seems to reflect modern commercial capitalism in a way that parallels Fredric Jameson's characterization of the postmodern moment, albeit without mirroring the critic's pessimism. Production of "stuff" in this view is inevitable, given the larger context of the day, a point to which I will return. For another, I feel for the players, who by modern standards were not paid well. Finally, as a fan of hockey and the Summit Series, I am all for kitsch. My collection of it is bordering on large. Thus my goal in what follows is not to take the players of Team Canada 1972 to task for their impulse to capitalize (pun intended) on their success over the Russians. Rather, I want to digest and analyze the fact that the products that have resulted, no matter how much they appear to enhance the contemporary fan's experience or enjoyment of the series, also alter it in a way that is impossible to retreat from because they ensure that the series can't ever be remembered in an uncomplicated way again. That alone would not be a problem, and indeed might be inevitable, as Klein's formulation on memory suggests. Yet the issue with souvenir kitsch is that it can create an illusion of authenticity, offering consumers the feeling of being closer to the series than they otherwise could be while leaving them unaware of the layering between them and their original experience. As Huyssen dissects the phenomenon of the contemporary craze for memory studies, he suggests that one critique leveled at "the turn toward memory and the past" is that it can create a "culture of amnesia" that is itself couched in critique of media, which "make ever more memory available to us day by day" (27).

The most authentic Summit Series collectible would appear to be the DVD set of all eight games. But think about that. Fans who buy the games in reproduction can see the series over and over. For those who have memories of 1972, this practice makes the original moments distant, or somehow forces them out to arms' length, the opposite pole to their videotaped version. The moment when fans experienced the goal, for instance, was singular, yet the current experience of the series when watched repeatedly in reproduction multiplies itself ever outward, and when that is added to all aspects of "stuff," from replica sweaters to souvenir coins, the proliferation threatens to render the pure moment of the series invisible. Thus the choice, in the age of the souvenir, seems to be a surplus of mediated memory versus an atrophied experience of original memory. Most fans, judging by the success Ellis and the team have had in marketing kitsch, have voted for the former. To take the most pessimistic view of this leads one to conclude that one day the series will be impossible to disentangle from the bobblehead version of itself.

Fredric Jameson, in his towering work *Postmodernism; or, The Cultural Logic of Late Capitalism*, offers insight that might help us position the Summit Series and its later appearance in consumer culture. Jameson, remarking on the divide between modernism and postmodernism, argues that the cultural products that come out of the postmodern moment, itself a simulacrum for the late stages of capitalism, are commodifications, recyclings of older images, but ripped from their contexts. As such, the actual ties to the past, to history, to, if we can extend this to the Summit Series, an event itself are lost. What remains are the kitsch, the souvenir, the detritus, but because these fragments have reference to the past – some past, albeit an unrecoverable one – they retain a trace of meaning. To say it another way, borrowing from Huyssen, this is "the standard Adornean argument that commodification equals forgetting…that the marketing of memory generates nothing but amnesia" (31).

Listen to Jameson's language as you contemplate the volume of Summit Series merchandise currently being sold: "Aesthetic production today has become integrated into commodity production generally: the frantic economic urgency of producing fresh waves of ever more novel-seeming goods…at ever greater rates of turnover" (4). In context, he's talking about art and architecture and the ways in which these are tied up with funding provided by commercial interests, but the words sound like an accurate diagnosis of a situation in which the Summit Series becomes a good argument for buying a new, "authentic" souvenir to treasure. That piece becomes superseded by the next. As soon as those in the marketing department determine that one product's market is exhausted, they offer another.

As Jameson describes the postmodern moment in which he writes, he is not trying to urge that the past be retained in some pristine state. Indeed, his project is one of diagnosis more than "treatment." He is looking at post-modern culture as a given, as acting in his present moment (the early 1990s), not as something to be resisted, transcended, or reversed by reaching back to the moment of modernism (if indeed it could be resisted at all). Warhol has come, and he is all, in Jameson's point of view. The problem is that the product has become indistinguishable from its reference point outside itself (or in the event, in the case of the Summit Series). "Distance in general (including 'critical distance' in particular) has been very precisely abolished in the new space of

Postmodernism," Jameson says. "We are submerged in its henceforth filled and suffused volumes to the point where our now postmodern bodies are bereft of spatial coordinates and practically (let alone theoretically) incapable of distantiation" (48–49).

His point of view is bleak as he goes on to argue that nothing (in the world) is outside the postmodern. Using that as a lens with which to view the Summit Series, one might adopt a similarly pessimistic attitude if one were to see the series as inevitably and entirely covered over with its post-1992 and post-1997 consumerist baggage. However, taking Jameson's point in a minor key allows us to rescue meaning out of the contemporary version of the series by understanding its function as a combination of original memory, later commentary, reproduced versions of the original moment, and souvenir memorabilia.

Jameson offers a way to rescue meaning as he describes that there might be "a certain authenticity in these otherwise patently ideological productions" such as postmodern art or architecture. He claims that "postmodern (or multinational) space" can have authenticity if the cultural products that occupy it are not simply "a cultural ideology or fantasy" but have "genuine historical (and socioeconomic) reality" (49). Hence, a useful approach might be to forge a compromise between attempting to recapture the original (authentic) series and becoming entirely distracted (to return once more to Klein) by the consumerist detritus that exists in its wake. Huyssen describes the compromise that might be struck by suggesting an alternative to giving up when faced with a choice between the failure of modernity and the amnesia of commodification: a process of remembering that is "active, alive, embodied in the social – that is, in individuals, families, groups, nations, and regions" (38).

We must find a way to negotiate, in other words, between late capitalism's totalizing embrace as seen in the proliferation of Summit Series commemorative souvenirs and an always impossible ideal of restoring the Summit Series to its originary moment by "rescuing" it from the space it now occupies in the Canadian imagination and in pop culture and consumer culture. The attitude I'm suggesting admits that kitsch has happened but finds ways in which the series is still worth analyzing and rethinking – from a post-celebratory point of view. There is no pure series anymore (indeed there never was), but the fact that other stuff has also come in to cover over the events of 1972 is not tragic;

it's inevitable. We must claim the series as the artifact it is, bobbleheads and all, and make of it what we can.

What Do Bobbleheads Cost Us?

We must come to the recognition that no matter how much we think we are in touch with the primary moment of the series when watching the DVD set, for instance, we are not – we know the result of the games even as we watch the contests unfold. Huyssen says, "There is no pure space outside of commodity culture," but "that does not mean that each and every commodification inevitably banalizes" what it replicates (29). The moment of tension is past, as is the shock of what the Soviets were able to do to our best players. And the DVDs don't have attached all the other cultural artifacts that made the series what it was in its first moment – commercials, for one, and the features that showed the Soviets and how they lived, which added a layer of interpretation to the "reality" of the games as we were seeing them. To cite Huyssen again, "We do know that the media do not transport public memory innocently. They shape it in their very structure and form" (30).

Let me illustrate what is lost by putting this in personal terms: like many others, I *think* that I remember the Summit Series, because I have a version of two key memories – the games being shown in my school's cafeteria and the moment of celebrating Henderson's goal – stored in my head. Those reside alongside other memories, including the way Trudeau looked as he dropped the ceremonial first puck (I wouldn't have noticed that, except my father brayed so loudly at how the rose in Trudeau's mod-style wide-lapelled jacket looked that the moment has stuck with me) and the triumph-turned-disappointment that hit me as the events of period one of game one unfolded. That was perhaps more poignant because I lived in Montreal as a child, and I knew the Forum well as the home of the Canadiens. My grandmother lived a few blocks from there, and we passed it all the time. That, added to my adoring worship of Ken Dryden in the playoffs of 1971, made Dryden's utter failure to stop pucks, both in the first game and the series as a whole, unforgettable.

But before I offer the boast that because of these memories I "own" the series in a way that many Canadians think that they do, I must admit that there are things I also do not recall. I had no idea Phil Esposito had made a speech to conclude game four until I started to research the series for an article I wrote in 2004 (Kennedy, 53). And personal memories have also escaped me. A few years ago I featured a friend in a hockey book I wrote, and when he and I got back in touch via email after twenty or so years of each not knowing where the other was, he excitedly told me a story of our getting postcards from an Esso gas station and filling them in with messages of encouragement for our favourite players. We did this at my kitchen table, he said. I had no recollection of this, and I still don't, though I can imagine it's exactly correct because it's precisely like me to have done this.

Those details are forgotten. But if my memory of the series is selective, and partial, it is also layered over with other elements, post-1972. The times my brother-in-law and I have watched the eighth game on DVD late into the night during my biannual Christmas visits to Toronto. The Ken Dryden bobblehead that sits on my bookshelf. My "the goal" commemorative coin, forgotten and then rediscovered when I rearranged my hockey memorabilia. The moment of pure joy when I discovered that my sister had found the "it" gift for me a few Christmases ago – the replica Team Canada 1972 hockey sweater. The series is all of these things to me, and more, and much of what it means to me in the present has only tangential reference to the distant past (i.e., 1972).

Of course, it may be that I collect what I do because I'm irredeemably addicted to pop culture kitsch. It might be that once I got on a roll, my interest in this stuff gave my family easy shortcuts to pleasing me at Christmas. Or it may be that I, like everyone else, want the Summit Series, if it is the pivotal moment in Canadian history many believe it to be, to be a happy, triumphant moment (and what could suggest that more accurately than a commemorative coin with Henderson jumping into Cournoyer's arms after scoring the winning goal embossed on one side?). In fact, while the win was grand, the series did more to wake Canada up to its shortcomings as a hockey nation than it did to reaffirm the country's sense of itself and its superiority, a fact often now overlooked, although a detail that I remember.

If there is any criticism one might level at the collector, it is that he or she comes unaware to moments of Kleinian "distraction" because of the seeming authenticity of the stuff collected. But that feeling is a lie. My Summit

Series sweater, for instance, while it resembles the one Team Canada wore and is trademarked by CCM and made in Canada (surprise!), bears no relationship to the ones the players wore. Because it is made of modern, breathable material, its similarity to theirs is only a trace, to go back to Norman Klein's word. And yet when I wear it, I feel like I'm part of something. Should that be read as naïve, the "cultural logic" of kitsch having fooled me into thinking that there is a traceable line between my experience of the sweater and Team Canada's experience against the Russians? Or even between my experience and the Russians' of Team Canada, albeit that this was received by me through the medium of television?

To ask it another way, am I, like others, drawn to Summit Series commemoratives because they stand in for the memories I know I should retain but do not? Even if that's not the case, what do these souvenirs really cost – that is, not in monetary terms but in terms of one's memory (bank)? Are my contemporary experiences with my souvenirs a gain, as they seem to be, because they create novel ways to celebrate an important moment in my life as a Canadian, or a loss, because with each new item that appears on my shelf some old but authentic memory is sacrificed?

So Why the Souvenirs?

Perhaps if Jameson is right, there is no going back. The point, then, is not to rescue my "real" memories of the series at all. But neither should I view my experience/memory of the Summit Series and its contemporary manifestations in consumer culture as ruined (by kitsch). It simply is. The series has become to me as a Warholian soup can painted on canvas, and it cannot be otherwise. Thus I simply accept that the series as I have it forty-plus years on is what I have. It is that which must be analyzed, not some imagined "authentic" series of 1972.

Jameson says, "What we must now affirm is that...this whole extraordinarily demoralizing and depressing original new global space...is the 'moment of truth' of Postmodernism. What has been called the postmodernist 'sublime' is only the moment in which this content has become most explicit, has moved the closest to the surface of consciousness as a coherent new type of space in its own right" (49). It would be tempting, following Jameson, to see the proliferation of Summit Series souvenirs as "demoralizing" because they totalize one's experience. His diagnosis claims that even when one believes he or she is close to a postmodern version of Kantian sublimity, all that is truly happening is that the ubiquity of the (totalizing, capitalist) system is breaking through the margins of consciousness. In terms of the Summit Series, having passed through the gate into collecting kitsch, there is no going back to the original moment, to the events of the series itself (again, said without valorizing the notion that pure experience of the past can be or ever could have been recreated). But what one can do is to analyze the experience of the series as it exists on a continuum from (in my case) hearing a radio call of Henderson's goal on my school bus on September 28, 1972, to wearing my replica sweater while I watch game eight on TV where I live now – in California. What rescues one from futility is recognizing that it is possible to enjoy Warhol's soup can without assuming that one could eat from it.

Perhaps it is useful in this regard to understand the motivations of those who produce (or sanction the production of) the goods in question. At the time of the games themselves, former player Ellis said, not much was available as mementoes, even to the players themselves: "We were given one sweater. And, uh, I think Paul [Henderson] got both of his, which makes sense to me. We all got one and I think Al [Eagleson] took the rest of them." He also kept a pair of gloves, of which he said, "I had them a long time, then I gave them to my kid brother. But that's it; we didn't get any other equipment. The memorabilia back then, it wasn't really a big deal. I really have very little from my career, as I look back now, not like the guys today, who keep everything."

He adds, "There was very little [souvenir artifact material]. I remember we did get a watch. I think it was given to us before we went over, sort of thing. It wasn't a gift. It said 'Team Canada' on it. There was very little in the way of gifting; there was no trophy, of course. We do have a Team Canada ring now, but it wasn't given then. This is the ring that denotes us as being the team of the century." He also explained that he has some of the things that the players exchanged during the opening ceremonies of the games. "I've got some of that. The dolls…. An autographed stick. I've got a few of those things. There might be a few of them here [at the Hockey Hall of Fame in Toronto], too, that have been donated. But there wasn't a lot of gifting back then." In creating consumer goods for consumption, the team supplements this lack, and not just for fans.

As for the stuff that he and his fellow participants have, through their licensing agreements, been responsible for creating, Ellis says, "I have a signed set [of the trading cards produced in 1991–92], a gold set signed by the players; I have a set signed by every player that has a lot of value." He also has a DVD set of the games; however, here is where Ellis's great personal irony comes in: "I know where it is, but I don't look at them. But I think, it's interesting why I haven't sat down and...watched the games. I [have] it very handy, but I want to do that at the right time. Almost like I want to rent a cabin in the woods and do it properly and not be disturbed, not be interrupted." Since 1972, he has never seen himself play the Russians, except in clips, never having watched the games whole. But he can, and will. And in offering fans the chance to do the same, perhaps he believes that he has contributed to their memory and enjoyment of the series, a much less sinister reading of the souvenir industry than what Jameson's approach might suggest. To look at it another way, while Ellis has been a part of creating the record of the series that the DVDs and souvenirs represent, he leaves it up to the fans whether they will watch, or wait, their memories undisturbed, as his are. The irresistible logic of late capitalism may be to produce the goods, but it does not extend, in the case of the Summit Series, to compelling anyone to consume them.[6]

Any marketing efforts aside, the events of the Summit Series form a story that still matters, even though it has become layered over – if not to say burdened – with intention as time has passed. For most, learning and sharing that story costs nothing. Ellis described Canadians' genuine feelings of affection for the series:

> We knew at the time that this was a special series, because it was the first time we were playing the Russians with our Canadian pros. But did we think people would still be excited about it forty years after? Definitely not. And we are...honoured that the memory of this series is still front of mind. And parents or grandparents are passing it down to their kids. It's amazing. Sometimes I'll run into a young person at the Hall of Fame who (and you know it's because of the grandfather passing this down)...has taken the time

> to go on the Web and read all about our team, and…this
> twelve year-old knows everything that happened, already
> has a good knowledge of it…. That's one of our goals now,
> as a team. I chair our players committee, so I'm very involved
> in our anniversary this year [2012]. But as a team, we now
> want to leave a very positive legacy. We want to work with
> school boards. We want to make sure this becomes part of
> history, because it is such a special Canadian moment.

He's not talking about doing that by selling the kid a replica game sweater, nor a print of Henderson jumping into Cournoyer's arms. Rather, he's talking about documentary history, the passing on of information that is free. Sure, the kid may later want the bobblehead, and so what if he does?

The point is that, despite the clutter of things that the series has spawned, underneath it all is a story. Over time, that story has taken on new emphases, become something other than what it was to begin with. But that's the fault neither of poor memory of original events nor of boosted memory that exists as the product of capitalist accumulation, and the goal is not to seek some absolute version of the truth about the series within any one set of data. Rather, we must examine all expressions of this narrative, understanding that the series will never be what it was in 1972, but that its meaning is no less powerful, nor any less authentic, for that. Perhaps Huyssen is key once more here: "Memory is always transitory, notoriously unreliable and haunted by forgetting – in short, human and social" (38). If we put our emphasis less on worrying about what is lost and more on what is gained and offered down to the next generation, who can't have original memories themselves, perhaps we have an instructive mode for moving forward.

What We Did Not Learn

The series will, one assumes as a point of departure, always be with us. Even kids celebrate it – as I write this, my nephew is twelve, and he knows all about it and watches the games. But forty years of hagiography is enough, and if the series is to maintain a prime place in Canadian history and culture, it must do so not because it is viewed in singular and unchanging contexts but because it can stand up to critical scrutiny, even if, at times, that scrutiny puts it and its mythological quality under pressure. The goal of this collection is not to retrieve a "pure" series from the rubble of consumer culture that surrounds Team Canada '72 and their victory. Neither this book nor any other could accomplish that, because any approach to the Summit Series will always take place in a complicated, crowded context where "authentic" memory combines with post-1972 revisions, and revisiting, of the series. Rather, the idea here is that forty-plus years after the end of the Summit Series, it is time for a new look.

As a culture, Canadians have forgotten a lot of the lessons that the Summit Series taught them at the time. The shock of how good the Soviets were. Canadian hubris, the classic mistake that Sun Tzu warned about millennia ago, that one ought never to underestimate the enemy. Canadians' appalling ignorance and superstition about these Soviet "others" with their robotic looks and their absolute love of ketchup, a sort of simulacrum for our entire way of life. This, after all, was the era when people believed that the Russians seeded our clouds in order to alter rainfall patterns, and fathers, particularly, ranted about why we sold wheat to the commies at highly subsidized prices when their economies survived by the forceful suppression of competing ideas and were, as a result, dismal failures.

Not forgotten, but perhaps repressed by many, is one key moment in the series, one of the more ugly moments in hockey: game six and the slash by Bobby Clarke on Valery Kharlamov. The Summit Series existed in the first place to redeem the image of Canadians – not of Canadian hockey players only – as a violent bunch of sore losers who would take their frustrations and embarrassments out on others when they lost. This slash, as Brett Kashmere discusses in the present volume, is a key legacy of the series, making a lasting impression on hockey fans and players and setting a course of hockey violence that continues to the present. But where does pop culture commemorate this moment? Of course it does not, although one can imagine an ironically intentioned T-shirt that might say something like, "Watch it, or I'll go Bobby on your ankle." (A joke successful with only a certain audience, naturally.)

The present volume, itself an artifact of the Summit Series, intends to retrieve some of these other aspects of the series while recognizing that knowledge about it now exists in a marketplace crowded with everything from books to commemorative postage stamps. The idea, likely obvious by now, is not to pile on another collector's must-have, but rather to do the opposite – to nudge readers away from the fetishization of the series, whether due to consumer kitsch or whatever else, and to urge a new appraisal of the events and contexts of the series, not uncomplicated but also not one that takes the default approach that the series' story is the singular one of Canadian victory over the "evil other" (Russians). There's more than enough of that already. Bidini's aforementioned recent book, for instance, talks about the mood going into period three of game eight in the usual mythological terms: "It looked as if they were about to be defeated by a country of dark shadows.... You'd have excused us for feeling like all was about to be lost. Without hockey to define us, we would have nothing. We would cease to exist" (87).

Maybe it did feel like that, in that moment of 1972. And maybe to cite that feeling is to be historically accurate. However, no matter what happened in that hockey game, Canada wouldn't have ceased to exist. Nor would it have ceased to be a hockey country. A loss would simply have accelerated the change to hockey's being viewed, not the least by Canadians, as a world sport. More likely, the series would have faded into obscurity the way the 1974 series between the World Hockey Association all-stars and the same Russian squad has, and none of the discussions about the mythological nature of the engagement would even have taken place in the four-plus decades from then until now.[7]

The reality of the Summit Series, in other words, would have been constructed differently because, after all, events gather meaning in a social context, not as absolute in themselves. Because of the ubiquity of consumer culture under late capitalism, souvenirs would still have been sold, just not ones that commemorate 1972. Yet as long as "Sammit Series"[8] souvenirs do exist, the twenty-seven days of the series will be thought about and argued over. Hopefully, this book adds some dimensions that enhance those arguments by bringing to light what we did not learn at the time or may have forgotten since.

---

[1] See the later discussion on Norman Klein and how memory is constructed.

[2] Note that while Huyssen does invoke Theodor Adorno and Walter Benjamin and their critique of postmodern commodity culture, many of the examples he uses in his discussion are more weighty than sports or other iterations of popular culture.

For instance, he speaks of the Holocaust at some length. My use of his ideas in the present context in no way suggests my blindness to what he discusses nor to its relative gravity compared to a hockey series.

[3] See, for instance, David Adams Richards' novel *Nights Below Station Street* (78) and the Hip's song "Fireworks."

[4] This is not to say that souvenirs were not available before 1992. See n. 5 for detail.

[5] In fact, the history of Summit Series collectibles (using the term broadly) takes an obvious trajectory. What follows is not an exhaustive list of what's come out, but an indication of the trends over the years.

In 1972–73, there were half a dozen or so books on the series, some of them large-format picture volumes intended more as souvenir than history. 1972–73 also saw O-Pee-Chee produce a set of twenty-eight cards that were given as inserts in regular NHL packs. During this time, there were also souvenir pennants produced, and a record album called *The Canada-Russia Hockey Series* with game commentary and explanations of strategy by Coach Harry Sinden. Following this initial burst, only the occasional book came out in the next twenty years, including *The Days Canada Stood Still* by Scott Morrison in 1989.

Except for a set of 101 cards issued by Future Trends in 1991–92, things went quiet until the twenty-fifth anniversary, when the Canadian government issued a silver dollar proof of Henderson after the goal. At this time, a documentary set of interviews plus game eight in its entirely came out as well. The defining book on the series even until now, MacSkimming's *Cold War* also dates from this time, with a release date of 1996.

Perhaps in anticipation of the thirtieth anniversary, 2001 saw more books released. The one with the most suggestive title for my purposes was Brian McFarlane's *Team Canada 1972: Where Are They Now?*, which detailed the players' lives and careers since the series. Interestingly, this year also saw the release of a kids' book (*The Greatest Goal* by Mike Leonetti) and a spoof (*Shadrin Has Scored for Russia* by Kevin Sylvester). But perhaps the greatest game-changer in terms of memory was that all eight games became available on DVD for the first time that year. It was also during this era that the replica jersey became available. Fans could now relive the moments – all of them – of the series while creating the fantasy that they were a part of Team Canada. At this time also, players, including Dryden, Henderson, and others, became immortalized as bobblehead dolls.

The thirty-fifth anniversary passed relatively quietly except for 2006's airing of the CBC television drama *Canada Russia '72*. Between then and the forty-year anniversary, a fanciful book called *Hockey Gods at the Summit* was released (2011). It tells the story of ex-NHLers watching the series from heaven and intervening when needed. Also in 2011, a small volume that repeats the myths of the series for an audience of younger readers (I presume) was published (*Summit Series '72* by Richard Brignall).

The fortieth anniversary of the series prompted another flurry of activity. ITG (In the Game) issued a trading card set in 2009–10 called "1972: The Year in Hockey," and another in 2011–12 called "Canada versus the World Summit Series." An interactive history of sorts was created with the inauguration of the '72 Project, which allowed people to submit their memories of the series online. A book was produced as a result, *The Goal that United Canada: 72 Amazing Stories by Canadians from Coast to Coast*, and was launched at the Hockey Hall of Fame in Toronto on September 5, 2012 (www.72project.com).

In addition, a number of books – enough to rival what had been written in the time immediately after the series – were issued, including Bidini's *A Wild Stab for It*, Leonetti's *Titans of '72* and the official fortieth anniversary volume put together by Podnieks. The Russians may have produced books in their language. They certainly produced a dual-language magazine-style souvenir program for the anniversary meeting in Moscow (*Anniversary of the USSR-Canada Summit Series 1972–2012*), with introductions by the mayor of Moscow, the minister for sports, and the president of the Russian Ice Hockey Federation, Vladislav Tretiak.

Souvenirs also became available, including a bottle of wine with a specially etched label. Combining "history" and salesmanship, the website offering this product (www.heritagehockey.com) also has original photos of each of the players for fans to look at. Names are scrolled below images for those who otherwise wouldn't know one Esposito from the other.

No accounting of the kitsch produced to commemorate this series would be complete, however, without a mention of the greatest souvenir of them all: the watch produced by the Russian company Molniya. This came out on an anniversary, though whether for the twentieth or thirtieth I have not been able to determine precisely. It's large in format, originally having been the case for a pocket watch, and on the face are the Russian and Canadian flags and the names of the stars (Henderson and Esposito for Canada, Kharlamov and Tretiak for Russia). Also appearing are the numerals 59:26 for the time of the goal and 5:6 to represent the score, as well as other lettering and graphics. But perhaps the most touching and ironic are the words "Sammit Series," spelled exactly that way.

[6] And just to note: there is no Ron Ellis Summit Series bobblehead.

[7] Interestingly, there is a DVD set of this series that has more recently become available. And in the same vein as the "Sammit Series" watch commemorating 1972, a Molniya watch is on the market. It lists the games as 4–3–1 for the CCCP against the WHA, and it, too, says "Sammit Series."

[8] See note 5 and note 7.

Works Cited

Anniversary of the USSR–Canada Summit Series 1972–2012. Russia: February 25, 2012.

Bidini, Dave. *A Wild Stab for It: This Is Game Eight from Russia*. Toronto: ECW Press, 2012.

Brignall, Richard. *Summit Series '72: Eight Games That Put Canada on Top of World Hockey*. Toronto: James Lorimer, 2011.

Canada Russia '72. DVD. Directed by T.W. Peacocke. Montreal: Maple Pictures, 2006.

The Canada-Russia Hockey Series. LP album. Arthur Harnett Entertainment, n.d.

Canada's Team of the Century: 1972 Canada vs. USSR. DVD. Produced by Robert MacAskill. Willowdale, ON: Universal Studios Canada, 2002.

Cosentino, Frank. *Hockey Gods at the Summit: How the 1972 Canada-Soviet Hockey Summit Became a September to Remember*. Illustrations by Gary Frederick. Renfrew, ON: General Store, 2011.

Dick, Ernest J. "Remembering September 1972." In *Putting It on Ice*. Vol. 2, *Internationalizing "Canada's Game,"* edited by Colin D. Howell, 45–50. Halifax: Gorsebrook Research Institute, 2002.

Doty, Andrea. Telephone interview with author. July 12, 2013.

Dryden, Ken. *Face-Off at the Summit*. With Mark Mulvoy. Toronto: Little, Brown, 1973.

Ellis, Ron. Personal interview with author. Toronto: D. K. "Doc" Seaman Hockey Resource Centre, July 25, 2012.

Gault, John. *The Fans Go Wild: Paul Henderson's Miracle*. Toronto: New Press, 1973.

Henderson, Paul. *How Hockey Explains Canada*. With Jim Prime. Chicago: Triumph, 2011.

Hoppener, Henk W., ed. *Death of a Legend: Summer of '72, Team Canada vs. USSR Nationals*. Montreal: Copp Clark, 1972.

Howell, Colin D. "The Layering of Identities: Hockey's Personal and Public Meanings." *Canadian Sports Studies* (March 2004): 22–24.

Huyssen, Andreas. "Present Pasts: Media, Politics, Amnesia." *Public Culture* 12, no. 1 (2000): 21–38.

Jameson, Fredric. *Postmodernism; or, The Cultural Logic of Late Capitalism.* Durham, NC: Duke University Press, 1991. http://flawedart.net/courses/articles /Jameson_Postmodernism__cultural_logic_late_capitalism.pdf.

Kennedy, Brian. "Confronting a Compelling Other: The Summit Series and the Nostalgic (Trans)Formation of Canadian Identity." In *Canada's Game: Hockey and Identity*, edited by Andrew C. Holman, 44–62. Montreal: McGill-Queen's University Press, 2009.

Klein, Norman M. *The History of Forgetting: Los Angeles and the Erasure of Memory.* New York: Verso, 1998.

Leonetti, Mike. *The Greatest Goal.* Illustrations by Sean Thompson. Vancouver, BC: Raincoast, 2001.

———. *Titans of '72: Team Canada's Summit Series Heroes.* Toronto: Dundurn, 2012.

Ludwig, Jack. *Hockey Night in Moscow.* Toronto: McClelland & Stewart, 1972.

———. *The Great Hockey Thaw; or, The Russians Are Here!* Toronto: Doubleday Canada, 1974.

Macfarlane, John. *Twenty-Seven Days in September: The Official Hockey Canada History of the 1972 Canada/USSR Series.* Canada: Hockey Canada-Prospect, 1973.

MacSkimming, Roy. *Cold War: The Amazing Canada-Soviet Hockey Series of 1972.* Vancouver, BC: Greystone/Douglas & McIntyre, 1996.

McFarlane, Brian. *Team Canada 1972: Where Are They Now?* Etobicoke, ON: Winding Stair, 2001.

Mitton, Sean, and Jim Prime. *The Goal that United Canada: 72 Amazing Stories by Canadians from Coast to Coast.* N.p.: Sean Mitton & Jim Prime, 2012.

Morrison, Scott. *The Days Canada Stood Still: Canada vs. USSR 1972.* Toronto: McGraw-Hill Ryerson, 1989.

Podnieks, Andrew. *Team Canada 1972: The Official 40th Anniversary Celebration of the Summit Series.* Toronto: Fenn/McClelland & Stewart, 2012.

Richards, David Adams. *Nights Below Station Street.* Toronto: McClelland & Stewart, 1997.

September 1972: Collector's Edition. VHS. Markham, ON: Polygram Canada, 1997.

Sinden, Harry. Hockey Showdown: The Canada-Russia Hockey Series. Toronto: Doubleday, 1972.

Sylvester, Kevin. *Shadrin Has Scored for Russia: The Day Canadian Hockey Died.* Toronto: Stoddart, 2001.

Team Canada 1974: The Lost Series. DVD. Produced by Jonathan Gross. Toronto: Video Service, 2006.

Terroux, Gilles. *Face-Off of the Century: The New Era.* Translated by Yvon Blais. New York: Collier-MacMillan Canada, 1972.

The
Series
as Myth

Da, Da, Canada; *Nyet, Nyet,* Soviet: From Hagiography to Reality in the Canada-Soviet 1972 Hockey Series[1]

🍁

DON MORROW

> I believe that imagination is stronger than knowledge –
> *That myth is more potent than history.*
> I believe that dreams are more powerful than facts –
> That hope always triumphs over experience –
>
> – Robert Fulghum's credo and his
"storyteller's creed" (VIII–IX)[2]

What fascinates me about the famous/infamous and fabled '72 Summit Series is the latter adjective: fabled. It was and is legendary, epic, extraordinary, remarkable, impressive and outstanding – it was nominally a summit, connoting top, pinnacle, zenith – in so many ways, certainly in the manner it played out and in the way it is remembered. In fact, if the series had been scripted – and it has in its aftermath – it could not have been contrived to be a better story. For those Canadians over forty, it was a defining moment of their generation. Similar to Fulghum, I too, believe that myth can be more potent than history, and even that myth is vital to writing about our past. By myth, I don't mean in the sense of untrue or supernatural story; instead, I use myth as a concept to invoke the idea of a story of meaning, something that informs our sense of who we are as a culture, a set of truths about – in this case – Canadians.[3] This essay examines the notion of myth connected to and created by the series as evidenced through the lens of representativeness. What is it that makes this set of hockey games mythic? There exists a mythos, a pattern and a recurrent narrative that began during the series and is echoed resoundingly in the forty years since the actual events. The series encapsulated a whorl of deeply consecrated elements that coagulated into making the series mythic in proportion, whether deservedly so or not. It may be that nostalgia has enshrined the meaning of the series out of all proportion to its reality. Nevertheless, we continue to celebrate the event, to walk around it, and to revere and cherish it. If hockey is our Canadian drama, then the 1972 Summit Series is, at the very least, a mythic-series spinoff replete with narratives and narrative richness,[4] speeches, dramatis personae, archetypes, video representations and analyses, a voice and voices, a heroic journey, recreated texts and discourses – in short, a cascade of elements, embedded in cultural contexts, that makes the series' myth more potent than history.

Setting the Stage of 1972

Every narrative and every drama needs a venue, a time and place for the theatrical to play. The organizational events leading up to the contrived series are not germane to this essay. However, some important points about the cultural and temporal milieu are most relevant and pertinent to the 1972 setting. Hollywood movies produced two blockbusters that year: *Deliverance*, starring Burt Reynolds and John Voight; and Mario Puzo's *The Godfather*, featuring Marlon Brando, Al Pacino and Robert Duvall, among many other stars. Both movies were grand narratives in their own rights, and both were blockbuster stories that were literally projected onto our imaginations in the months immediately preceding the series. The duelling banjos refrain from *Deliverance* was embedded lyrically in our minds, as was the fascination with an all-powerful, unscrupulous godfather who could make offers people couldn't refuse.[5] Deliverance-as-theme (not the movie) became the unspoken Canadian chorus when the nation realized Team Canada had lost three games, tied one, and won one after the fifth game in Moscow. And the "don" of Puzo's thriller became The Eagle (Alan Eagleson), in all his manipulative machinations,[6] of the series' suspense.

The year 1972 itself was a year of intrigue – it was pre-AIDS and pre-baby boomer angst, and it was a year filled with conflict and atrocities such as the Watergate scandal, the prolonged Vietnam War, the Burundian geno-cide against the Hutus, uprisings and deaths in Northern Ireland, floods, hurricanes and the Munich massacre during the Summer Olympic Games, the latter event occurring coincident with game six of the series. Overall, Western nations lived in abject, often unspoken fear of "the Bomb," the what-if-ness of nuclear warfare. Even though Richard Nixon and Leonid Brezhnev signed the SALT I treaty in May, the spectre of the bomb loomed in the global collective unconscious. Parachuting a hockey series into the 1972 maelstrom of events created a new and parallel narrative that mirrored conscious and unconscious fears and provided a literal arena or arenas in which the hockey story could be played out. Canada, a nation of perceived values and attributes like ones associated with being polite, peacekeeping, apologetic, non-American, bilin-gual and inventors of the game of hockey, was pitted against the Red Machine, the Communists, and the presumed and dreaded terrors that we all "knew" lay *behind the Iron Curtain.* The latter vivid metaphor created by Churchill after the Second World War instilled a cold conception of an impermeable barrier between western and eastern European ways of life and political ideologies.

In some ways then, the series became a kind of reiteration or encapsula-tion of good versus evil, Canada-the-good versus USSR-the-evil. In fabled terms – and fables feed the human imagination at all age levels – in our minds' eyes, Canada as a nation had a hibernal version of the "Snow White and the Seven Dwarfs" tale. Canada was anthropomorphically Snow White, pure and pristine, while the Evil Witch clearly lived behind the Iron Curtain, Rasputin-like in appearance and presumed madness, easily mirrored on each visage, menacing under every red-bucket-helmeted Soviet player. The "dwarfs" of the Summit Series served Snow-White-Canada as Eagleson the Shyster, Dryden the Intellectual, Esposito the Braggart and Victim, Ferguson the Vulgar, Cournoyer the Shy, Sinden the Skinflint and Henderson the Hero.[7]

The Script

In many respects, the series' set-up was an odd – or better, even – set of games, eight games in total, four to be played in different Canadian cities and four in Moscow at the famed Luzhniki Ice Palace. (What better place in which to play out a fable or fairy tale than a *palace?*) The script, in brief:

In Canada:

Game/Act	Date	Title	Canada	USSR
1	Sept. 2	We Lost!	3	7
2	Sept. 4	Redemption	4	1
3	Sept. 6	The Win that Got Away	4	4
4	Sept. 8	Canada Booed off the Ice	4	5

In Moscow:

5	Sept. 22	Buried in Moscow	4	5
6	Sept. 24	The Slash	3	2
7	Sept. 26	Canada Forces Game Eight	4	3
8	Sept. 28	Henderson Has Scored for Canada	6	5

For those of us who lived during 1972, and from the mountain of descriptions and accounts written during and long after the events, we felt then and have heard ever since that everything was set for a great Canadian victory party. Before Eagleson conspired with the NHL to prohibit Bobby Hull, who was at the time the World Hockey Association's paragon player, from playing, I smirked and opined to my friends and relatives that Hull's slapshot alone would at once terrify, shatter and overpower Soviet netminders. In fact, there was an ethereal Bobby-ness about the series itself. For example, Bobby Orr, arguably the dominant player – and clearly Canadian, with his Parry Sound, Ontario, roots – in the NHL, could not play because of his knee injury issues. American Bobby Fischer beat Boris Spassky for the World Chess Championship title in Reykjavik less than one month before the series began. For some reason, likely to do with the Cold War aura of the era, that chess event and its outcome was widely followed in the Western media and competitively, if not politically, foreshadowed or set the stage for the hockey series. And Team Canada player Bobby Clarke, the Master Carver from the Philadelphia "Broad Street Bullies," perhaps another of the archetypal dwarfs, was poised to play his special role in the series. It was as though "Bobby" was in the arena and media air as much as the certainty of victory seemed at the forefront of the minds of the one hundred million worldwide television audience for game one.

When Canada lost 7–3 in the first game, it was as though the expected, prewritten, preordained script had to be rewritten. It was perceived by the media, and by extension, the Canadian nation, as the catastrophe of the century, a shock of gargantuan proportion, hockey humiliation. It became a time of alibis and yes-buts – but, of course, Bobby Orr and Bobby Hull are not playing, our best were not even there! Sportswriters' rhetoric was critical of everything deemed to be "wrong" with the series as the narrative seemed to take on a life of its own in reinventing meaning after the drubbing. In terms of perceived vindication and a reinvigoration of the myth of Canadian superiority, game two was heralded by the Canadian media as a pivotal game of the series, very likely because of our decisive victory. The game was preceded by a banquet replete with speeches about Canadian hospitality. Juxtaposed with the ensuing game, wherein Cashman "worked the corners" and the Soviet players complained of Canadian "stickwork," the pre-game platitudes of friendliness sounded hollow and the narrative seemed to sully in its undertones of goons that foreshadowed even more questionable, if not unethical and injurious tactics. Consider one "tactical" example, that of famed sportswriter Ted Blackman:

> Wayne Cashman's number flashed all night. So did Jean-Paul Parise's, Gary Bergman's, Pete Mahovlich's. But it was Cash most of all, tapping the Soviets on the back of their helmets with his stick and throwing every limbs [*sic*] at them in the corners.

> He set up Phil Esposito's goal with a highly-representative
> act of aggression. Taking Vladimir Luchenko down in a
> heap, he snapped the big defence man's stick and eventually
> grabbed the puck to set up Espo as the Russians tried in
> vain to clear it with his [*sic*] skates.

Followed by the Soviet reaction: "In defeat, the Soviet coaches were as ungracious as Team Canada was after Game 1. Bobrov accused the two referees, Americans Frank Larsen and Steve Dowling, of letting the Canadians get away with murder, in particular, the rough play of Wayne Cashman. Andrei Starovoitov, head of the Soviet Hockey Federation, was so outraged that after the game he burst into the officials' room, kicked over chairs, and screamed: 'The American referees let the Canadian players perform like a bunch of barbarians!'" (Kish).

In Winnipeg, for game three, the shadow of the decision to ban Bobby Hull – the Winnipeg Jets was his WHA team – loomed in the media with clever epithets like, "To Russia with Hull" and the Bobby-ness chorus redoubled its perceived importance in the storied circumstances. Preceding the prairie game, the arena, and by extension the viewing audience, was invited to observe thirty seconds of silence in honour of the victims of the Munich massacre. The intended respect was genuine, and the unintended but very real impact of the reverence was only to heighten the dramatic tension of the series. And, as if to underscore that tautness, the observation of silence was one slice of the game sandwich that was completed by the 4–4 outcome and Coach Sinden's later representation of the significance of that game when he quipped, "Someone once said that a tie [in sport] is as exciting as kissing your sister. Well for the last ten minutes tonight, that hockey game looked like Raquel Welch to me."[8]

Almost every play and therefore every screenplay features at least one monologue, and in this series' script, Phil Esposito delivered his nationally televised speech to Canadians after Team Canada's loss in game four. In part and abbreviated, he exhorted,

> To the people of Canada, we tried. We gave it our best.
> To the people who booed us, geez, all of us guys are really
> disheartened.... We're disillusioned and disappointed. We
> cannot believe the bad press we've got, the booing we've got
> in our own building.... I'm completely disappointed. I can-
> not believe it.... Every one of us guys – 35 guys – we came
> out because we love our country. Not for any other reason.
> We came because we love Canada. ("davey boy phelan")

Beyond the heroic implications of Esposito's speech, what is interesting
for the mountainous myth-machine that is the '72 Series is the comparison
of what is now known as Esposito's "rant" to King Henry V's speech to his
troops before the walled town of Harfleur – though not a monologue – in
Shakespeare's *Henry V.*

> Once more unto the breach, dear friends, once more,
> Or close the wall up with our English dead.
>
> ....
>
> Dishonour not your mothers; now attest
> That those whom you call'd fathers did beget you.
> Be copy now to men of grosser blood,
> And teach them how to war. And you, good yeomen,
> Whose limbs were made in England, show us here
> The mettle of your pasture; let us swear
> That you are worth your breeding, which I doubt not;
> For there is none of you so mean and base,
> That hath not noble lustre in your eyes.
> I see you stand like greyhounds in the slips,
> Straining upon the start. The game's afoot!
> Follow your spirit, and upon this charge
> Cry, "God for Harry! England and Saint George!"
>
> (*Henry V*, 3.1)[9]

While Esposito's exposition was nowhere near the elegance of the
Shakespearean character's oration, the point is that the association of the two
speeches underscores how much the series' narrative was played out, literally
and figuratively, and represented in events such as this one, even to the point

of perceiving the nationalistic fervor parallels, Canada to England, to the highest forms of drama.

The Heroic Journey and the Monomyth

In *The Hero with a Thousand Faces*, mythologist Joseph Campbell describes a basic pattern in the hero's journey that is at the core of many, if not most, narratives. In stages, the hero departs his or her home; encounters "fabulous forces" in a new land in the second stage; and in the third phase, returns home to bestow what s/he has learned or gained during the heroic adventure. In the series, Canada's team-heroes, albeit scarred and underdogged from the first four games, ventured to Moscow and experienced yet another defeat from the CCCP "forces" in game five. As every good drama has its chorus, 2,700 Canadian fans at game five in the Palace chanted, "*Da, da,* Canada; *nyet, nyet,* Soviet,"[10] in group effort to encourage the players. In game six, the script's "the slash" pricked the heroic bubble when Bobby Clarke viciously stick-slashed Soviet star-player (some say the best player, both teams included) Valery Kharlamov's lower leg, rendering him, euphemistically, "ineffective after that." Team Canada's assistant coach, John Ferguson, later said of the attack, simply, "It was necessary." Brett Kashmere – who noted the preceding Ferguson comment – quite brilliantly, has represented the incident in his 2006 video essay, *Valery's Ankle*.[11] The incident occurred behind the play and off-camera to the television audience. Soviet outrage was vociferous, as it should have been. I watched the game, and even after the game, I was oblivious to the event. We heard about it in the news, and its significance, sadly, was overshadowed by the 3–2 score in favour of Canada. Clearly it was an unheroic act, but in the mythology, as Kashmere noted, the slash still engenders public disgust and private gratitude in the Canadian psyche. It was a miasmic blight, a subterfuge that happened in the background, a highly improper slaying of the Soviet dragon by the Master Carver ignited by his coach's fervor for victory at any cost.

Going into the eighth game, the Super Series' script seemed incredible. What were the chances of an eight-game series – how does one team "win" a best-of-eight-game series? – becoming boiled down to such a power-ful climax? Each team had won three games and tied one; the outcome of the eighth game would determine the outcome of the series. It is estimated that fully two-thirds of Canada's population watched or listened to game eight, a vast audience for this theatre of sport. There could not have been a greater buildup of uncertainty (the *sine qua non* of all sport), anxiety and excitement that reached its pinnacle when the voice of hockey, Foster Hewitt, screamed, "Henderson has scored for Canada!" Hewitt's exclamation might be likened to Canada's "shot heard round the world,"[12] as unassuming and quiet as Canadians are perceived to be compared to Americans and their reverence for baseball. For the mythic and the heroic, Team Canada went through Campbell's journey paradigm from the public and media embrace of "our" team, to disgrace and falling out of the national embrace, and then back, after game eight, to be "our team" again. Team Canada completed their heroic journey home, "victorious" and embraced by eighty thousand fans in Nathan Phillips Square in downtown Toronto the Good. The series was, and con-tinues to be, characterized as Canada's iconic sporting and cultural moment. Famed sports writer Dick Beddoes effused its significance in one of Canada's national newspapers, the *Globe and Mail*: "In Canadian history, we had the FLQ crisis in 1970, the taking of Vimy Ridge in 1917, and we had VE Day in 1945. VE Day and the celebration in 1972 were the biggest this country has had."

Books abound from and about the series: *Twenty-Seven Days in September* by John Macfarlane; *Face-Off at the Summit* by Ken Dryden; *Hockey Night in Moscow* by Jack Ludwig; *The Days Canada Stood Still* by Scott Morrison; *Hockey Showdown* by Harry Sinden; and *Shooting for Glory* by Paul Henderson are some of the more acclaimed narratives that recount, repeat and perhaps even reify the events of the '72 Series. In the latter regard, the series wasn't in any way abstract and made tangible, as the word "reify" would suggest; how-ever, perhaps no event, certainly no sporting event, has been raised to near hagiographic proportions as was the Summit Series. Just as films like *The Godfather* pervaded in the cultural air in 1972, so filmic versions of the series have lingered in our cultural space down to the present. Possibly the most realistic representation of the events is the CBC documentary-snapshot-styled film *Canada Russia '72*. Shot in Fredericton, New Brunswick, it comes across as realistic, poignant and well-researched, and is punctuated by off-ice narratives that seem to level the impact and importance of the series some thirty-four years after the actual event. The characterization, the periodization and the music (such as the song "Signs" by Five Man Electrical Band being played after game one's re-enactment) all serve to make the film work. And yet, as realistic as this film is, and as accurate as textual and scholarly assessments of the Summit Series might be, the actual narrative, and all of its mythic and monomythic representations, underscore the potency of myth and the cornucopia of sub-myths, meanings and narratives in Canada's cultural and hockey history.[13]

---

[1] An earlier version of this essay was published as "Le mythique et le mono-mythique: Les représentations de la Série de hockey Canada-URSS 1972/The Mythic and the Mono-mythic: Representations of the 1972 Canada v. USSR Hockey Series." *Canadian Issues* (Winter 2012), 52–60. Most of that version is republished here with full permission. In addition, this text, in part, was presented under the same title as an academic paper at the North American Society for Sport History, Halifax, Nova Scotia, May 2013.

[2] Emphasis added. Fulghum offers that this credo stems from his Storyteller's License. See Robert Fulghum, *All I Really Needed to Know I Learned In Kindergarten: Uncommon Thoughts on Common Things* (New York: Ivy Books, 1988), viii-ix. On his official author's website, it is his front page credo; his credo ends with two more lines: "That laughter is the only cure for grief / And I believe that love is stronger than death." (See http://robertfulghum.com/index.php/fulghumweb/credo.)

[3] I am fully aware that hockey itself is replete with myths related to our culture; myths emanate from the debates about hockey's rightful birthplace to our hibernal "happy naturalism" hockey myth. This chapter is selective in looking at representations of the '72 Series myth.

[4] I use the term "mythic-series" in comparison to the term "miniseries." The '72 Series was anything but mini in proportion, at least in terms of the meanings and remembrances attached to it.

[5] The exact line from the movie was, "I'm gonna make him an offer he can't refuse," a line that has been copied many, many times in sketches, comedy routines and other movies since Brando's utterance.

[6] Eagleson's leadership role in the NHL Players' Association in raising players' salaries, making Bobby Orr the richest professional hockey player ever, and colluding with NHL owners are all well documented. His eventual exposure as a racketeer and embezzler make the "don" connection even more apropos.

[7] The idea of a "Snow White and the Seven Dwarfs" application to the series is not mine in original concept. It was an idea connected with the 2006 CBC documentary production of *Canada Russia '72*. My intent here is not to make the comparison a literal one but to show how archetypal the series as narrative was to our collective psyches.

[8] Raquel Welch was an American actress and sex symbol; the title of her 2010 autobiography, *Raquel: Beyond the Cleavage*, is indicative of her renown and the intention of the citation provided by Sinden. See, http://www.1972summitseries.com /kish2game3.html, accessed April 5, 2014.

[9] This version is Kenneth Branagh's famous rendition of the Harfleur speech from the 1989 British drama film adapted for the screen and directed by Kenneth Branagh, based on the William Shakespeare play of the same name.

[10] The intent, very likely, was to mix words from both languages, most assuredly so that Soviet fans would realize the taunt of "Yes, yes, Canada; no, no, Soviet."

[11] See Kashmere's "Valery's Ankle: The Break and Its Consequences" later in this essay collection.

[12] The reference is to the now-famous line taken from a Ralph Waldo Emerson 1837 poem about the American Revolutionary War and applied to the walk-off home run hit ("shot") by the New York Giants' Bobby Thomson during the 1951 National Baseball League series against the Brooklyn Dodgers.

[13] The hoopla of the fortieth anniversary of the series produced a wide variety of myth reverberations. See, for example, the *Toronto Sun*'s "40 Things You Don't Know about the Summit Series" at http://www.torontosun.com/2012/09/17/40-things-you-dont-know-about-the-summit-series. Also, the *Globe and Mail*'s extensive "The Story of the Summit Series, as It's Never Been Told Before" at http://www.theglobeandmail. com/sports/hockey/the-story-of-the-summit-series-as-its-never-been-told-before/ article4546471 is replete with narratives and sub-narratives in the form of nearly one hundred interviews conducted over five months, edited and condensed by Patrick White, a national correspondent.

Works Cited

Beddoes, Dick. "The Story of the Summit Series, as It's Never Been Told Before." *Globe and Mail*, September 15, 2012. http://www.theglobeandmail.com/sports/hockey/the-story-of-the-summit-series-as-its-never-been-told-before/article4546471 (accessed March 2013).

Blackman, Ted. *Gazette* (Montreal), September 5, 1972.

Campbell, Joseph. *The Hero with a Thousand Faces*. New York: New World Library, 2008.

"davey boy phelan." "1972 Game 4 Phil Esposito Rallies the Nation." Phil Esposito's speech after game four of the Summit Series, plus later commentary; original footage filmed September 8, 1972. YouTube video, 2:26. Posted July 15, 2007. http://www.youtube.com/watch?v=_2v4rHgRyUo.

Fulghum, Robert. *All I Really Need to Know I Learned in Kindergarten: Uncommon Thoughts on Common Things*. New York: Ballantine, 1988.

Kish, Bruce. "The 1972 Summit Series: A 4-Part Series." 1972 Summit Series.com. http://www.1972summitseries.com/kish2game2.html. First published August and September 1972 by *Gazette* (Montreal).

Sinden, Harry. *Hockey Showdown: The Canada-Russia Hockey Series*. Toronto: Doubleday, 1972.

Valery's Ankle. Independent digital video. Directed by Brett Kashmere. 2006.

Pluralism and the 1972 Summit Series

❦

MICHAEL BUMA

It isn't often that hockey upstages Shakespeare at the Stratford Festival. On September 28, 1972, a production of *King Lear* was playing to a full house in Stratford, Ontario. At the same time, another drama was unfolding halfway around the world in Moscow: the tie-breaking game of the hockey Summit Series between Canada and the Soviet Union. When news of Paul Henderson's game-winning goal arrived backstage, the actor playing Lear finished his famous storm soliloquy with the news that Team Canada had won. Pandemonium broke loose among the two thousand festival attendees, and the stagehands left the thunder and lightning effects on to complete the celebration ("Canadians Flip").

This uncharacteristic outburst in Stratford was emblematic of the broader reaction to Team Canada's victory. Henderson's goal inspired an arguably unparalleled expression of Canadian popular nationalism that was made all the more potent by the Cold War political and ideological context in which the series was played. Taken together, the themes of clashing civilizations and national pride comprise what Stuart Hall might call the "preferred reading" of the Summit Series.[1] The term "preferred reading" refers to the dominant interpretation of a particular text, the one that the majority of readers will see as obvious and commonsensical. Most Canadian hockey fans know and probably subscribe to some version of the following reading of the Summit Series: that although the Soviets surprised us with their skill, Henderson's dramatic goal in the dying seconds of game eight managed to salvage Canadian pride, prove that hockey is "our game," and assert the superiority of democratic and free market values.

While this understanding certainly isn't wrong, Hall points out that "it is always possible to order, classify, assign and decode an event within more than one 'mapping'" (98). Because of this, Hall allows for the possibility of two other interpretive positions: a "negotiated" position, in which the interpreter accepts the preferred reading as legitimate but modifies or augments it somewhat based on an alternative frame of reference or experience, and an "oppositional" position, in which the audience understands the preferred reading but rejects it in favour of an alternative code (102–3). I would like to identify a "negotiated" reading of the Summit Series that a small but noteworthy number of commentators have put forward: the idea that the series signifies to some extent within the larger narrative of Canada's centennial-era shift toward cultural pluralism. Throughout the 1960s the Canadian government undertook a series of cultural initiatives attempting to move Canadian identity away from the traditional British/colonial framework and position it instead as being characterized by multiculturalism and pluralism. In keeping with Hall's framework, this reading shouldn't be seen to supersede or replace the dominant narrative but to function as a complementary sub-theme that enriches the meaning of the series and its lingering importance in Canadian society.

From Ethnocentric Nationalism to Multicultural Pluralism

The Summit Series is one of Canada's most iconic expressions of popular nationalism. For instance, Ken Dryden and Roy MacGregor refer to it as the only "wholly Canadian event" to have "made time stand still" (193), and – writing in 1993 – Richard Gruneau and David Whitson suggest that the victory "mobilized patriotic interest among Canadians like no other cultural event before or since" (249). But the Summit Series is by no means the first time hockey became associated with Canadian identity. One of Canada's most prominent founding nationalist mythologies was that of the Canada First movement, which emphasized northernness as the prime determinant of Canadian character. Northernness was seen as being "synonymous with strength and self-reliance," a desirable alternative to southern climates that bred "degeneration, decay, and effeminacy" (Berger, 5). It was believed that only certain races – hearty, strong, industrious races – could survive in a demanding climate such as Canada's, and that consequently Canada would be spared from the "negro problem" that plagued its southern neighbour (Berger, 9). This early version of Canadian nationalism, then, was founded on the idea that "because of the climate and because Canadians are sprung from...the 'Aryan' family, Canada must be a pre-eminent power, the home of a superior race, the heir of both the historical destiny of the ancient Scandinavians and their spirit of liberty" (Berger, 7).

As a game played on ice and snow, hockey came to be seen as an extension of the rugged Canadian landscape, a hearty game to be played by hearty (white) Canadian men. Throughout the late nineteenth and early twentieth centuries, the cultural meanings of hockey often worked to further the ethnocentric assumptions of the Canada First movement, a point nicely illustrated by the Canadian Government Motion Picture Bureau's film *Hot Ice: The Anatomy of Hockey, Canada's National Game* (released in 1940 and circulated until 1964). In the words of Christopher Gittings, "*Hot Ice* represents white male possession and domination of hockey and represses the raced other's enjoyment of this national Thing, although the historical record indicates that Blacks in Canada were participating in organized hockey as early as 1899" (34).[2] Gittings goes on to point out that the ethnocentric beliefs of Canada First manifested themselves in actual policy well into the 1930s: Herb Carnegie, a top-ranked black Junior B player, was prohibited from moving up to the Toronto Maple Leafs because of the colour of his skin. Conn Smythe, the founder and coach of the Maple Leafs, commented, "I'd take him tomorrow if somebody could turn him white" (quoted in Gittings, 36).

In the decades following the Second World War, Canadian governments began to envision new ways of formulating identity and nationhood. This shift was prompted by growing anxiety over the increasing Americanization of Canada and the perceived need to articulate a distinct and differentiated Canadian culture in order to maintain political sovereignty. In the years that *Hot Ice* enjoyed circulation, then, the Canadian government put the steps in motion that would lead to the undoing of the film's ideological assumptions. Between 1949 and 1963, Parliament launched four major commissions with a mind to protecting Canadian culture from the threat of American imperialism; one of these, the Massey Commission, paved the way for the subsidies to Canadian hockey that would begin under Prime Minister Pearson. It was the last of these, however, the Bilingualism and Biculturalism Commission, that was to prove most influential. The "B and B Commission" (as it came to be called) essentially recommended recasting Canada's historical French-English dualism – which could be described less charitably as an antagonism – into a national virtue, emphasizing Canadian difference by highlighting and encouraging bilingualism and cultural diversity. This mode of self-definition, which has evolved into what Gerald Kernerman refers to as "multicultural nationalism" (5), remains a central part of the way in which Canadians have been asked to conceive of their national identity.

The report of the B and B Commission led to the Trudeau government's formal implementation of the "Multiculturalism within a Bilingual Framework" policy on October 8, 1971, but the shift toward cultural pluralism had been on the government's radar for several years before this. The inauguration of a redesigned nationalism, of course, warranted the refurbishment of prominent national symbols, and the Pearson government undertook this task throughout the mid 1960s. Parliament accepted the Maple Leaf flag in 1965, and in 1967, just in time for Canada's centennial, "O Canada" was approved as the official national anthem. The Pearson administration saw Canada's centennial as the perfect opportunity to stir up support for its platform of multicultural nationalism, and government money flowed unrestrainedly into centennial festivals, historical re-enactments, tree-planting ceremonies, youth achievement medals and other nationalistic pageantry. Ottawa sponsored the construction of centennial parks, concert halls, arenas and other memorial projects in countless municipalities across the country. A *Maclean's* retrospective entitled "A fond look back at our wacky Centennial year" offers a suggestive year-end tally for the celebrations: 1,020,500 Maple-Leaf flags sold or distributed; 300,000 sales of bandleader Bobby Gimby's *Canada* (making it the most successful record in Canadian history at the time); almost 600,000 sales of a centennial booklet "extolling Canada's virtues and history" (89); hundreds of citizens crossing the country at their own expense (on foot, on horseback, on roller skates, by canoe, and even by hot-air balloon); a "Centennial train" that toured the country and attracted 2,407,873 visitors; a town that celebrated by burning 33 outhouses; another town that constructed a memorial landing pad for flying saucers, etc. But the centrepiece of Canada's centennial celebration has yet to be mentioned: the Canadian Universal and International Exhibition in Montreal, popularly known as Expo '67. In the words of Eva Mackey, "Expo '67 was a site in which Canada could elaborate its emerging national identity: differentiating itself as a nation from external others as well as defining relationships between internal populations...it was a moment in which the nation 'came out' to the world, and to itself, in what was perceived as its new progressive and pluralist form" (59).

It could be argued that the rhetoric of Expo '67 helped chart a course for many subsequent articulations of multicultural nationalism. One of the pamphlets distributed by the Canadian government pavilion, *Change Comes to Canada*, makes this particularly apparent:

> Nobody knows for sure where the name Canada comes from. Some say it's an Indian word, others say it's Spanish. Canada: nobody knows what the word means, nobody knows what the country means. So everybody is free to find a private meaning of his own.... Canada is an idea, a dream, a feeling, above all, a sense of home. Every Canadian who thinks about Canada (and most of us do at one time or another) has his own idea about the meaning of that dream. But if you talk to people from one side of the country to the other, you will feel that for all its variety, the idea of Canada still has a power to bind our hearts. In all its forms, it gives us a sense of home. (Sinclair, 3)

This follows what has become a standard rhetorical formula for articulating Canadian pluralism: it expresses an overarching uncertainty about what it means to be "Canadian," tempered by a gesture toward some ineffable consensus on diversity and tolerance (which are themselves based on a vaguely articulated notion of shared geography and experience). *Change Comes to Canada* even extends the pluralist ethos of national unity without abolishing cultural differences or requiring uniformity explicitly to hockey, in that "Canadians don't fit into compartments very easily. The hockey fan also goes to the opera. The tailor is an outdoorsman on the weekend. The truck driver likes good food, and the university librarian (who put himself through college driving a truck) portages his canoe" (Sinclair, 31). By casting hockey as a component in this ostensibly diverse cultural scene and highlighting the difficulty of compartmentalizing national identity, *Change Comes to Canada* – along with hockey's prominent inclusion elsewhere in Expo '67 – suggests a repositioning of hockey from the Canada First version of nationalism to the emerging myth of multicultural pluralism.

Throughout the centennial celebrations and especially Expo '67, citizens were asked time and time again to participate in an "insurgent nationalism" (Miki, 44), a directed push to "define a Canadian past and to create a usable tradition" (Mandel, 81). Jeffrey Cormier has documented the activity of the "Canadianization movement" during this time, a social crusade concentrated mainly in the university system that attempted to "resist the growing strength of foreign, often American influences on Canadian culture and at the same time encourage, nurture, support, and foster, an indigenous Canadian culture" (8). In the same vein, Mackey estimates that the Canadian government spent more than the equivalent of a billion 1992 dollars to encourage nationalism throughout the centennial year (a figure which she compares to the relatively meagre fifty million spent on Canada's one hundred and twenty-fifth anniversary celebrations in 1992) (58). Suffice it to say that during the late 1960s and early '70s many Canadians took on board the versions of multicultural nationalism being propounded in Canadian universities and rehearsed in the pageantry of Expo and the centennial celebrations. All that was needed was a monumental event, something to anchor Canada's newfound sense of pluralist identity by evoking large-scale popular expression of "true patriot love." In the minds of at least some Canadians, the Summit Series managed to do exactly this.

Hockey Unity, Cultural Difference

One of the most frequent tropes among the newspaper articles reporting Team Canada's Summit Series win is the idea that Paul Henderson's goal created a rare moment of national unity. Take, for instance, the *St. John's Evening Telegram* headline from September 29, 1972: "Jubilation All Across Canada." The accompanying article, like others of its kind, works by anecdote, moving across the country from "St. John's to Vancouver" and thus creating the impression of a unified national response. The Montreal French-language newspaper *Le Devoir* spoke of "un grand cri, sorti de millions de gorges, a retenti dans *tout le Canada*" ["A great cry, out of millions of throats, sounded in all of Canada"] ("Le suspense se dissipe"; emphasis added). These assertions of national unity must have been, at least to some extent, animated by the spirit of multicultural nationalism. Many such suggestions of national unity specifically cite Canadian "diversity" as the backdrop for this rare moment of togetherness, which of course is both the language of pluralism and the thematic message of Expo and the centennial (i.e., we may be different in many ways but have our Canadianness – in this case, expressed through hockey – in common).

For instance, an editorial in the Quebec newspaper *Le Soleil* resonated with the official government policy designation for cultural pluralism, Multiculturalism within a Bilingual Framework: "les memes reactions se firent sentir chez les Canadiens des deux langues, dans les villes de l'est et de l'ouest du pays. Pour un fois nous atteignions l'unité nationale...les Canadiens admirèrent partout leur esprit d'équipe et les applaudirent meme plus que leurs propres jouers. Cette ouverture d'esprit est l'honneur des Canadiens" (Boyer, 4).[3] Similarly, one of Canada's assistant coaches, John Ferguson, Sr., suggested that he'd "been through Stanley Cups before but they were for Quebec. This was for Canada" (quoted in Proudfoot). Paul Henderson also struck the "unity in the face of diversity" chord in one of his retrospectives: "There was no such thing as a Francophone or a Westerner, or anything else. We were all Canadians. The series brought us all together. It brought an entire country together. It was Canada playing, not Team Canada. It was us against them and every Canadian somehow seemed to have a sense of ownership of that team. I guess war is the only thing that could bring a country together like that series did" (quoted in Pelletier, "1972 Summit Series Quotations"). Other commemorative accounts make similar gestures to hockey's ability to create unity in a culturally and geographically diverse country. Michael P.J. Kennedy recalls travelling from Ottawa to the Maritimes for a late summer camping trip during the Canadian leg of the series: "Before there was the euphoria of victory, there was the pall of defeat across the land. Indeed, as I ventured into the East, all that people discussed was the series. At a campground in Cape Breton or a service station in

PEI the feelings were the same. We were all Canadians whether from Ontario or Nova Scotia, farmer, fisher or student, we shared in our collective shock, sadness, and perhaps anger at the early success of the Soviet team" (20). Although geographically speaking Kennedy's account doesn't include all of Canada, it does portray the series as a moment of national unity that cut across regional and professional lines – both in early defeat and eventual victory. Similarly, CBC news anchor Peter Mansbridge wrote on the fortieth anniversary of the Summit Series that the win "kind of united the country.... You could pretty well point to anyone across the country and you knew they were all watching the same thing. That doesn't happen very often in our country, as big as we are and as diverse as we are" (Mitton and Prime, 99). Again, the Summit Series is seen as a rare moment of unity in a country defined predominantly by difference, distance and diversity. This point can be argued in hockey terms as well: in the words of Bruce Dowbiggin, "going into the series people were still, you're a Habs fan, you're a Leafs fan. The big game was still Montreal-Toronto. And I think for the first time, really for the first time, [the Summit Series] made us all in the same boat. We were all Canadians rooting for one team" ("The Goal that Changed Canada").

Another suggestion that the Summit Series brought together Canadians of diverse backgrounds occurred in an online *Globe and Mail* discussion forum commemorating the thirtieth anniversary of the Summit Series in 2002:

> For Game 8 they let us all watch televisions set up in the school auditorium.... [When] Paul Henderson scored the goal...the place erupted like we'd all won a million dollars.... I felt, and I firmly believe everyone else in that room felt, that it was CANADA as a country that scored that goal.... As corny as it sounds, I loved Canada more than I ever had at that moment, as if we had won a war, not some game on frozen water.... To sum up the whole experience, from that series on, I took a whole lot more interest in Canada, as a country, and my role in it. The way guys with diverse names like Savard, Henderson, Esposito, Makita, and Bergman could be kicked and down, but work together, dig down and struggle back, and show what they were made of on the other side of the world. Now that's Canadian! (Jennings)

Jennings echoes the idea that *all* Canadians had a personal stake in Team Canada's victory, but also proposes the team as a sort of pluralist model for nationhood and citizenship based on intercultural unity and co-operation that doesn't seek to eradicate difference. (Jennings' point about the ethnically diverse range of names is important too, but this will be returned to later.) More explicit than Jennings' assertion that hockey can create a common bond among people of diverse ethnic backgrounds is Nova Scotia Minister of Economic and Rural Development and Minister of Tourism, Culture and Heritage Percy Paris's fortieth anniversary reflection on the Summit Series. Paris begins by mentioning that like "millions of other people" he would not leave the TV set while the series was on, and goes on to suggest that "this demonstrates for me the power of the game of hockey. I am an eighth generation person of African descent. I'm a Canadian. Hockey is that sport here in Canada that doesn't look at you in terms of where you are born, what religion you are, what the pigmentation of your skin is. You grow up in Canada loving the game of hockey and for many of us, it is a way of life" (Mitton and Prime, 124).

In addition to Paris's suggestion that hockey has the potential to transcend race, religion and background, we might also add the category of age – at least when considering an essay on the Summit Series written by Krystal Yee, a (then) eighteen-year-old Canadian of Chinese descent, for a website she created in honour of Team Canada's Summit Series victory.[4] According to Yee, the Summit Series "naturally bonded us together as a nation…. When Henderson scored that goal, all of Canada watched. You really realize the impact of 'the goal' when children of an entirely different generation are talking about it. I wish I could have been there to see the goal live, but I feel I know as much about the series as someone who was alive at the time. It holds such a special place in our hearts, something that can never be taken away from us." Again, Yee puts forward the familiar suggestion that the Summit Series contributes to Canadian unity, and her status as a person of colour and a young Canadian who didn't witness the series firsthand implicitly testifies to the series' intercultural and intergenerational appeal. That a young Canadian woman of Chinese descent who wasn't even alive in 1972 would go out of her way to create a commemorative website suggests the extent to which the Summit Series helped move hockey beyond its traditional white and male parameters and into the multicultural pluralist value system that has become the dominant paradigm in which Canadian identity is understood.

Canada's Changing Face

Aside from tapping into the language and ideas of multicultural nationalism that Canadians were encouraged to take on board in Expo '67, the centennial celebrations and the Canadianization movement in general, the Summit Series also provided a way for Canada to see itself more fully in a pluralist light. As Dave Bidini notes in *Tropic of Hockey*,

> [Phil Esposito] was the first Italian. Before him, you never saw Italians on television in Canada. It was all British and Irish. Tommy Hunter. Juliette. "Front Page Challenge." The closest you got was Stan Mikita. Stan was a man of colour. He was Czech, but he looked Asian. But that was it. Until Espo became the de facto captain of Team Canada, hockey was all Conachers and Smythes and Clancys. But Espo was no cake Loyalist. No: he looked and sounded different and, by seeing him every day on television and in the newspapers, you could tell that Canada's face was changing. (193–94)

The face of Canada *was* changing in the 1960s and '70s, and the suggestion that Team Canada reflected the nation's emerging diversity is by no means unreasonable. Bidini makes this connection again in a fortieth anniversary retrospective, noting that in 1972 "the front page of the Sept. 1 edition of the *Toronto Star* had a story about multiculturalism in schools, citing a necessity for other cultures – they named three: Italian, Polish and Hebrew – to be recognized. A few pages in, the news is all about hockey; about how Team Canada is gonna destroy Team Russia" ("Forty years later"). Admittedly, the range of ethnic and cultural difference in both examples is relatively limited (Bidini's suggestion that Stan Mikita looked Asian notwithstanding). But, for Bidini at least, Esposito's prominent role in the Summit Series and especially his emotional speech to the nation after game four – "we came because we love Canada" (quoted in Pelletier, "Esposito Addresses the Nation") – changed everything about being Italian-Canadian: "He was the first. The first Italian. Afterwards, no one in Canada could deny that we Italians existed" (*Tropic of Hockey*, 197).

Bruce Dowbiggin makes a similar point reflecting on the symbolism of Henderson jumping into the arms of a French Canadian, Yvan Cournoyer, after scoring the final goal: "You couldn't have scripted it better. And I think it begins the era of Canada looking on itself internationally in a different way as well, not only that we can do it but that we can do it together" ("The Goal That Changed Canada"). The image of Henderson and Cournoyer celebrating together – which, significantly, was captured in what is probably the most well-known photograph from the series – offers a concrete image of the pluralist ethos: that people of different cultures and backgrounds might come together and co-operate as citizens to accomplish shared goals. Bidini makes a similar suggestion about intercultural co-operation between Henderson and Esposito by noting that "Espo carried the team on his back. Him and Henderson, the God-fearing Leaf who was born in a sleigh" (*Tropic of Hockey*, 197). Unless Bidini is aware of some little-known anecdote about Henderson's birth, he seems to be gesturing to the fact that Henderson represents the white Anglo-Saxon Protestant model of Canadianness that prior to the cultural shift of the centennial era, at least in theory, held sway as the Canadian ideal. The joke about being born in a sleigh gestures to the longstanding connection between Canadian identity and northernness, a narrative in which hockey is often imbricated because of its purportedly "natural" connection to ice and winter. As noted earlier, these ideas have historical connections to the ethnocentric nationalism of the Canada First movement, which believed Canada's northern-ness (symbolically embodied in its icy northern game of hockey) would ensure that it remained an Aryan nation.

The Summit Series images of Henderson alongside Esposito, Cournoyer and other players from backgrounds outside the traditional Canadian identity mould must have confirmed to some extent the pluralist narrative of tolerance, respect, co-operation and intercultural unity that the nation was slowly beginning to take on board. Furthermore, Esposito in particular illustrates the extent to which the barriers between hyphenated Canadian cultures had already become somewhat permeable by 1972, in that his Italian background doesn't seem to have been an impediment to becoming a fan favourite and the team's undisputed leader. One fan's sign at a rally welcoming Team Canada home after the big win sums up this indiscriminate adulation with a poetic turn: "Roses are red / Violets are blue / Phil you were perfect / and Paul you were too" (quoted in Beaufoy). Part of the message here, though surely not explicit, is that in modern Canada *anyone* can excel and contribute, and that the nation is well-served when people rise above differences of background and culture in order to work together.

While the idea that the Summit Series brought about unity in the face of diversity connects implicitly to Expo '67 and the centennial-era transition to multicultural nationalism, several observers have made this connection more explicitly. Joanna Dawson, for instance, has suggested that during the Summit Series "Canada was still riding a tide of nationalism – fuelled by the country's centennial birthday, Expo '67, a new national flag, and its renewed obsession with Canadian identity…. On the world stage, Canada was eager to show a united front." In addition to reflecting the new face of Canada back to itself, then, the Summit Series (like Expo before it) presented an opportunity to showcase this new identity to the world. Michael P.J. Kennedy similarly notes that 1972 "was a year that most Canadians alive at the time will never forget. It was a year not unlike 1967, the year of Canada's centennial and Expo '67, which defined for many of us who we were within the global community" (19).

Far more than showcasing Canadian pluralism to the world, however, the Summit Series encouraged the nation to become increasingly pluralistic.[5] One outcome of the series that is often remarked upon is the way in which it changed the Canadian style of hockey, ultimately resulting in a "cross-fertilization process" that led to "the opening up of the NHL to Europeans: Swedes, Finns, and Czechs at first, eventually Russians" (MacSkimming). As a result of the Summit Series, then, according to Roy MacSkimming, "we've learned to share our game with the world, just as we've learned to share our country with people from many cultures. The globalization of our national sport has become a key aspect of our multiculturalism." As Jack Ludwig put it while eating humble pie about his initial assessment of the Russian players in 1972, "I…assumed, as I think most Canadians did, that people who don't speak the Queen's English can hardly be expected to keep up with those who do" (26). Ludwig's realization here, of course, is that people who don't speak the Queen's English actually *do* have something valuable to contribute, and so in this sense the lesson of the

Summit Series is thematically the same as the lessons Canadians were learning at the time about how to exist as a multicultural society.

The Semiotics of Hockey Sweaters

At the risk of making too much of a design that was essentially thrown together at the last minute, it is worth suggesting that Team Canada's iconic jerseys can also be read as contributing to the pluralist signification of the Summit Series – and illustrating its limitations.[6] Roland Barthes defines myth simply as "a system of communication…a message" (109), suggesting that this message exists apart from the form or object of its conveyance and can consist in any mode of representation, even something so seemingly unobtrusive as a hockey sweater. For Barthes, myth is a "second-order semiological system" (114) in that it functions using another linguistic system as its basis (which Barthes terms the "language-object"). Barthes uses the terms form, content and signification to connote a signifier, signified, sign pattern in the metalanguage of myth, recognizing that the form of a myth system exists as a sign (or meaning) of the language-object it discusses.

To work the Summit Series through in Barthesian terms, the form might be said to be the hockey itself: the rhythms of the game, the efforts of the players, the ice, the roar of the crowd and so on. The meanings of these things are delivered a priori, embedded in pre-existing patterns of expectation and knowledge (the NHL careers of the players, the rules of the game, the Canadian anticipation of easy victory, etc.). The content, nationalism, is supplied through the visual symbol of Canada's newly adopted maple leaf, proudly emblazoned on the players' jerseys. In the cultural context of the late 1960s and early '70s, the maple leaf had been loaded with pluralist freight by the centennial celebrations and Canadianization movement, the push to establish a distinct cultural identity and usable Canadian tradition. In other words, nationalism inevitably came to the Summit Series with Canada's emerging pluralist identity in tow. Again, the jerseys provide a semiotic clue: rather than displaying the names of individual players (as was the case with some NHL teams at the time) they simply read "CANADA" across the back.[7] This fairly unobtrusive visual sign points toward the signification, the essence of the myth itself. In Barthes' framework, the signification forces a particular field of content (nationalism) into the hollow specificity of form (hockey), producing "myth-meaning" by distorting its subject.

To display the players' names would reveal the diversity of their cultural and ethnic origins: British, French, Italian, Czechoslovakian and Jewish, to name only a few. In a sense, the players are deprived of their cultural diversity (though not of their actual origins and traditions) when they put on their uniforms. They continue to hail from diverse ethnic and cultural communities, but carry on their jerseys the visual tags of purported unity: the maple leaf on the front, and the word CANADA across the back. At the same time, the markers of the players' diversity are not completely divested; their names are circulated widely in the press and announced at the start of every game. During the game, these markers of difference remain subsumed beneath the overarching intimation of national unity but are not symbolically effaced or eradicated. Consequently, the members of Team Canada appear to represent a nation that respectfully accommodates diverse ideas and traditions under the common banner of shared experience (i.e., hockey itself, with attendant ideas of unity by setting). This is, of course, as noted earlier, a cultural identity that Team Canada could not fully exemplify: despite hailing from a diverse array of ethnic and cultural backgrounds, its members were without exception white males.

This is not the only limitation of the pluralist reading. As Brian Kennedy notes, there is danger that "those who keep the series alive do so in wistful remembrance not just of a Canada that at that moment had a clear sense of who it was but also of a Canada that is no longer, culturally and ethnically, what it was" (60). Seen this way, the Summit Series signifies more as a marker of the "old" Canada than as a representative of a still-emerging multicultural pluralism. Dowbiggin makes a similar point in *The Meaning of Puck*: "Even as the puck nestled behind the fallen Vladislav Tretiak, there was a sense of new possibilities in the country. But now, thirty-six years later, the moment is remarkable more as the culmination of the national myth that existed since the Second World War rather than the start of another. Even as Prime Minister Trudeau greeted the beer-soaked heroes of Team Canada as their plane returned to Canada in 1972, the deconstruction of the post-war Canada that the hockey players defended so fanatically was well under way" (16). The danger, then, is that continually hearkening back to the Summit Series might actually be a way of avoiding the challenge of "[forging] a new definition of Canada" that recognizes the nation as "a place that has its others *within* its boundaries" (Brian Kennedy, 60).

As Kelly Hewson notes, "the sentimental constructions of national unity" that found expression in the Summit Series were "on the verge of collapse" even as they were happening (190). Multicultural pluralism was and is, in practice, far more messy and conflicted than the momentary unity of the Summit Series may have made it seem. Indeed, the centennial-era drive to create a "usable [Canadian] tradition" abated throughout the mid 1970s and '80s to the point that many recent entries in the identity debate recognize crisis or instability as their starting point. Perhaps more than anything else, then, the endurance of the Summit Series as a national icon testifies to Canada's perennial identity crisis, our persistent desire for an all-encompassing principle of belonging, and our obdurate drive to find that fixed point on which we may once and for all hang our national identity.

---

[1]   Hall's theory refers specifically to the ways in which meaning is encoded and decoded in television, but has often been applied to other cultural texts as well. Obviously the Summit Series is an event rather than a text, but for anyone beyond the immediate participants it is an event that is (and was) necessarily mediated in some way by a vast range of texts: television and radio broadcasts, newspaper and magazine articles, books, documentary films, websites, etc.

[2]   For an in-depth account of early Black Canadian involvement in hockey, see George and Darril Fosty's *Black Ice: The Lost History of the Colored Hockey League of the Maritimes, 1895–1925*.

[3]   The same reactions were felt by Canadians of both languages, in the cities of the east and the west of the country. For once, we attain national unity…. Canadians everywhere admired their team spirit and applauded it even more than their own players. This opening of spirit is the honour of Canadians. [My translation.]

[4]   Yee was eighteen years old at the time of our correspondence in 2000. Although her Summit Series website no longer exists, her article still appears at Joe Pelletier's *A September to Remember* website (www.1972summitseries.com/krystalsreport.html).

[5] Donald Macintosh and Donna Greenhorn have argued that a major reason for the series was the desire of the Department of External Affairs to rehabilitate Canada's status in international hockey, where in the years leading up to 1972 Canadian players had acquired a reputation of being "brutish and reprehensible" (100).

[6] According to Ken Dryden, "they had to come up with a team jersey design within 24 hours. They had no jersey, they didn't know what it was [going to look like], and they gave it to the ad agency of Vickers & Benson and said give us a jersey by tomorrow.... To me that is the best looking Canada jersey we have ever had" ("The Goal That Changed Canada").

[7] The NHL mandated all teams must display player names on the backs of jerseys for the 1977–78 season, though according to the unofficial NHL Uniform Database, the California Golden Seals, Los Angeles Kings, New York Rangers and Pittsburgh Penguins had been doing this already before the time of the Summit Series (see http://www.nhluniforms.com/1970-71/1970-71.html).

Works Cited

Barthes, Roland. *Mythologies*. Translated by Annette Lavers. New York: Hill & Wang, 1972.

Beaufoy, John. "Wet Fans Jam City Hall Square to Cheer Team Canada Players." *Globe and Mail*, October 2, 1972.

Berger, Carl. "The True North Strong and Free." In *Nationalism in Canada*, edited by Peter Russell, 2–26. Toronto: McGraw-Hill, 1966.

Bidini, Dave. "Forty Years Later, the Canada-Russia Games Still Ring with Emotion." *National Post*, September 1, 2012.

———. *Tropic of Hockey: My Search for the Game in Unlikely Places*. Toronto: McClelland & Stewart, 2000.

Boyer, Gilles. "La Série Canada-URSS." *Le Soleil*, September 29, 1972.

"Canadians Flip as Russians Slip – WE'RE THE CHAMPS." *Calgary Herald*, September 29, 1972.

Cormier, Jeffrey. *The Canadianization Movement: Emergence, Survival, and Success*. Toronto: University of Toronto Press, 2004.

Dawson, Joanna. "'72 Summit Series." *Canada's History* (blog), September 27, 2012. http://www.canadashistory.ca/getdoc/aa3502fb-6138-4357-99d7-d349b732bec9/default.aspx.

Dowbiggin, Bruce. *The Meaning of Puck*. Toronto: Key Porter, 2008.

Dryden, Ken, and Roy MacGregor. *Home Game: Hockey and Life in Canada*. Toronto: McClelland & Stewart, 1989.

"A Fond Look Back at Our Wacky Centennial Year." *Maclean's*, December 1967.

Fosty, George, and Darril Fosty. *Black Ice: The Lost History of the Colored Hockey League of the Maritimes, 1895–1925*. Halifax, NS: Nimbus, 2008.

Gittings, Christopher. *Canadian National Cinema*. London: Routledge, 2002.

"The Goal That Changed Canada." *The Agenda with Steve Paikin*. TV. Hosted by Steve Paikin. Toronto: TVO, September 27, 2012.

Gruneau, Richard, and David Whitson. *Hockey Night in Canada: Sport, Identities, and Cultural Politics*. Toronto: Garamond, 1993.

Hall, Stuart. "Encoding, Decoding." In *The Cultural Studies Reader*, edited by Simon During, 90–103. New York: Routledge, 1993.

Hewson, Kelly. "'You Said You Didn't Give a Fuck about Hockey': Popular Culture, the Fastest Game on Earth and the Imagined Canadian Nation." In *Now Is the Winter: Thinking about Hockey*, edited by Jamie Dopp and Richard Harrison, 187–203. Hamilton, ON: Wolsak and Wynn, 2009.

Jennings, Harry. Comment on *Globe and Mail* online discussion group. http://www.globeandmail.com/series/72summit/responses.html (accessed May 27, 2005).

"Jubilation All Across Canada." *St. John's Evening Telegram* (St. John's, NL), September 29, 1972.

Kennedy, Brian. "Confronting a Compelling Other: The Summit Series and the Nostalgic (Trans)Formation of Canadian Identity." In *Canada's Game*, edited by Andrew Holman, 44–62. Montreal: McGill-Queen's University Press.

Kennedy, Michael P.J. "I Am Hockey." In *Going Top Shelf: An Anthology of Canadian Hockey Poetry*, edited by Michael P.J. Kennedy, 19–22. Surrey, BC: Heritage House, 2005.

Kernerman, Gerald. *Multicultural Nationalism: Civilizing Difference, Constituting Community*. Vancouver, BC: University of British Columbia Press, 2005.

Ludwig, Jack. *Hockey Night in Moscow*. Richmond Hill, ON: Penguin, 1974.

Macintosh, Donald, and Donna Greenhorn. "Hockey Diplomacy and Canadian Foreign Policy." *Journal of Canadian Studies* 28.2 (Summer 1993): 96–112.

Mackey, Eva. *The House of Difference: Cultural Politics and National Identity in Canada*. Toronto: University of Toronto Press, 2002. First published 1999 by Routledge.

MacSkimming, Roy. "Hockey Put Canada's Cold War Perceptions on Ice." *Globe and Mail*, August 31, 2012.

Mandel, Eli. "Modern Canadian Poetry." In *Another Time*, 81–90. Erin, Ontario: Porcépic, 1977.

Miki, Roy. *Broken Entries: Race, Subjectivity, Writing.* Toronto: Mercury, 1998.

Mitton, Sean, and Jim Prime, eds. *The Goal That United Canada: 72 Amazing Stories by Canadians from Coast to Coast.* N.p.: Sean Mitton & Jim Prime, 2012.

Pelletier, Joe, ed. "1972 Summit Series Quotations." *A September to Remember* website. http://www.1972summitseries.com/quotes.html (accessed March 30, 2014).

————. "Esposito Addresses the Nation." *A September to Remember* website. http://www.1972summitseries.com/espospeech.html (accessed March 30, 2014).

Proudfoot, Dan. "From Russia with Glory." *Globe and Mail*, September 29, 1972.

Sinclair, Lister. *Changes Comes to Canada: Challenge of the Changing Times.* Ottawa, ON: Queen's Printer, 1967.

"Le Suspense se Dissipe à 34 Secondes de la Fin." *Le Devoir* (Montreal), September 29, 1997.

Yee, Krystal. Email to the author, September 18, 2000.

Canadian *Iliad*: The Summit Series as Canadian Epic Poem

♦

RICHARD HARRISON

Great stories of the past reappear in the great stories of our lifetime. Not because history repeats itself, but because great stories tell alike: accounts of pivotal events in the life of a people are framed by the myths – religious or otherwise – that establish for them the pattern of Story itself. Thus an analysis of those accounts, considered as artifacts, can reveal both what a culture sees in itself as well as what it does not. Applying the phrase "Canadian *Iliad*" to a hockey series makes sense to us because the epic poem of the Trojan War, written down some twenty-five hundred years ago, taught European-born cultures one way to sing of the kind of protracted, surprising and suspense-filled conflict that the Summit Series became between the two great powers of hockey in 1972. In the drama of that ice rink showdown between Canada and the USSR, the form of Homer's great work becomes filled by the events of the modern contest, even as its medium changes from verse recited millennia ago into years of excellent radio and TV for a twentieth- and twenty-first-century nation.

Canada has many such stories. Hockey fans and promoters often speak of the Stanley Cup playoffs in terms of Arthurian legend, with the winning team as one of mythology's greatest committees fulfilling its holy task because each man endured his pain and did his duty; each resisted the temptations that draw others off their course; each sacrificed individual glory for the glory of the group. And while there are things that myth puts in that have nothing to do with the present, and things that appear in any team's run to the Cup that have no echo in *Le Morte d'Arthur*, that isn't the point. The worth of the mythic interpretation is dependent on the connection desired (consciously or otherwise) between the story already written and the events that the story lends its shape to. The question to ask of such interpretation isn't whether it is right or not, but whether or not it *fits*; whether it casts an ancient light on the modern subject that lets us see it in a new and satisfying way.

Consider, then, the emotional investment and political intrigue involved in the construction of the Canadian Summit Series team. Add the shock of Canada's stunning early reversals and the popular despair when Canadians found themselves staring at their team's impending defeat at the hands of the dreaded Soviets. Then see Canadians' seeming loss of hope transformed – literally at the last minute – into the triumphant surge of victory through the bravery and cunning of the men in the field who embodied everything the nation wanted to be true of itself (and some of the things that it did not). All these taken together say that this story can repay a reading as the Canadian *Iliad* – a civilization-level conflict of Us versus Them – Self versus Other – in a test of national character, strength and will.

Like the Greeks in *The Iliad*, most Canadians of the time (and I was one of them) misjudged the other side. They thought their opponent's political system couldn't possibly produce a team of warriors as mighty as their own. Troy, too, was seen as a fundamentally incoherent and unnatural body politic held together by subordination to a single throne. And Homer is pointedly clear in his choice of metaphor for this political structure:

> But not the Trojans, no...
> like flocks of sheep in a wealthy rancher's steadings,
> thousands crowding to have their white milk drained ,
> bleating nonstop when they hear their crying lambs –
> so the shouts rose up from the long Trojan lines
> and not one cry, no common voice to bind them
> all together, their tongues mixed and clashed,
> their men hailed from so many far-flung countries. (4.502–9)

Where the independent-minded Greeks all spoke – and debated – in the same language, the sheep-like Trojans didn't even understand each other. Canadians saw the Soviet Union as many peoples held together under tyranny, and used then (as now) many different terms to refer to them: "The Russians,"

"The Soviets," "The Communists," "The Red Army" or just "The Reds," shifting, sometimes ironically, between these overlapping but not synonymous terms. Whatever could be said of them, "they" were not, unlike us, representative of a people who, though we often squabbled – like the Greeks amongst themselves at Troy – did so in the spirit of a people willing to work out their differences the way free people do.

It is easy to see in that portrait of ourselves an image that either willfully ignores the tensions between French and English, the violent form of which had only recently been subdued in October 1970, or symbolically tries to heal them. But that image of on-ice solidarity was reinforced by hockey's use of English as its apparently politically unifying language – every player on that team could speak it – and by the unifying nature of Team Canada itself for the nation: French-speaking players and English alike *volunteering* to play dressed in the country's colours. Perhaps then, in national sentiments that became more pointed as the series wore on, Team Canada was emblematic of the Canadian desire to put the divisions between Canadians behind them in the face of a common opponent on a field of play that symbolized the country itself. And though it is just the result of the play at the time, it is one more happy accident made possible by the team's composition that the final, triumphant and iconic image of series victory *because* the team pulled together as one is that of an ecstatic Henderson, the English Canadian scorer, held aloft by Cournoyer, his French-Canadian brother-in-arms.

In the beginning, though, Greeks and Canadians both thought their battles would be swift, decisive and few. It was like that for the first ten minutes on the beaches of Troy and on the ice in the Montreal Forum. Then things changed. By the end of the long and wearying contest, the Canadians, like the Greeks before them, their backs to a foreign wilderness, found the weak spot in the enemy's lines and won. And even though the Greeks at Troy and the Canadians at the Luzhniki Ice Palace were victorious, each of them, dazzled by victory, embedded their own self-affirming interpretations of events (at least some of which led to their early defeats in the first place) into their mythic accounts of their nations' character and glory.

Myth: the word's meaning is clarified only with knowledge of the speaker's history and intent. In nineteenth and early twentieth century Western thought, myth meant the opposite of truth, and truth was the province of scientific method. Myth became a label of discredit and disdain, applied to the ideas from other, less sophisticated cultures or held by those within our own who did not toe the party line: myth was either a fiction, whose tellers were too ignorant to know was false, or a kind a of con job whose listeners were. But fuelled by nineteenth-century Romanticism (and its rejection of modernity), and arguably the influence of myth-centred thinkers like Martin Heidegger, myth became revalued. Instead of flights of fancy, or primitive religious gestures, the stories that formed the body of myth came to be seen as a condensed, perhaps even pure, form of a people's philosophy, science, religion, language and social practice expressed in a way both teachable and deeply affecting. Instead of a kind of deception, then, a myth became a metaphorically dense code passed down from generation to generation to ensure the survival of a people. The mid twentieth century offered a revised view of myth as key to cultural survival and personal enlightenment in the work of anthropologists like Marvin Harris (*The Rise of Anthropological Theory*) and literary and psychological theorists like Joseph Campbell (*The Hero with a Thousand Faces*) and Bruno Bettelheim (*The Uses of Enchantment*). The century also gave us an unsettling sense that science could neither explain us nor control our own often horrific behaviour not only towards each other but also to the planet. (In the latter sense, I'm thinking of books that sounded an ecological alarm like The Club of Rome's *Limits to Growth* and Rachel Carson's *Silent Spring*, the *Inconvenient Truth* of its time.) Both academic and popular movements either saw greater wisdom in myth than in science or, worse, saw science as a practice whose practitioners were too ignorant to realize it was only one myth among many. Or, worse than that, as a kind of industrial-strength con job selling an increasingly intrusive technology to its ignorant consumers. In the mid to late twentieth century, then, myth became something far-reaching, holy and almost unquestionable.

But such reverence for myth, freeing it from critique, overstates its value and obscures its worth. Myth is still story. And story is still selection. While that does not make myth merely a form of fiction, it means myth isn't the whole truth, either. And while myths do seem to have the power to let us carry on in the world, they also change as cultures come into inevitable contact – and sometimes conflict – with one another. For instance, though there are distinctions, they are no longer relevant to the way we use the figure of Hercules in the language: when we speak of something or someone as "Herculean," we could be referring to properties found in the original Greek Herakles or his Roman remake. Or, for that matter, to his appearances in the pop culture "mythologies" of the Marvel Universe or Disney animation. On a more serious level, consider Tom Harpur's argument in *The Pagan Christ* for the identity of the biblical Lazarus and the Egyptian Osiris as one myth answering another in its own miraculous terms (132–36).

In the case of the Summit Series and *The Iliad*, there's more than enough evidence of an almost uncanny ability of the Homeric epic (with help from *The Odyssey* and other texts in The Epic Cycle [Schofield, 10] as well as, later, Virgil) to capture the course of the Canada-Russia hockey challenge. Aside from the symmetry between the two stories, the resonances within the sub-stories are fruitful as well. A narrative is believable only if its plot is driven by characters who make choices consistent with their own natures. For *The Iliad* and the Summit Series to be congruent as plots, they need at least some of their players to match up as well. We need kings and conflict. The ancient poem and the modern history provide both.

The Iliad begins with a quarrel between Agamemnon, first king among the Greeks, and Achilles, the seemingly unbeatable Greek fighter the Trojans fear most. The quarrel concludes with Achilles removed from the field. Though the dramatic language of the conflict is that of personal pride and desire on both sides – the two men are fighting over a woman prized by both but captured by Achilles in a raid – the conflict itself is that of rule-follower versus rule-breaker. Agamemnon, the head of state, demands respect for the laws that he represents and the rights they give him; Achilles, the Greeks' greatest warrior, for the qualities that make him what he *is* and the rewards that only those qualities make possible. I look at this millennia-old battle of wills, and I see Bobby Hull cast as Achilles, the superstar, with Bill Wirtz and Clarence Campbell tag-teaming the role of Agamemnon, the management.

Bobby Hull was not only regarded as the best player of his day in North America but, according to Ken Dryden in *Home Game*, also the standard against which the father of Soviet hockey, Anatoly Tarasov, "measured the progress of his own team" (200). In Hull's hands, the slapshot: the shot the Russians feared most and had least experience with. As Kent Russell notes in the online magazine *n+1*, the Russian finesse game was in part dictated by "domestic sticks too frail" to make the slapshot part of the attacking repertoire. Their players rarely took what Dryden calls in *The Game* "distance" shots (275), so their goalies were least practised at stopping them. Subsequent history supports the Russian concern about Hull, at least in part: even though he never played in the '72 Summit Series, between that summit, the '74 WHA/Soviet Summit, and the 1976 Canada Cup, of the sixteen games teams from Canada played the USSR with Tretiak in net, Hull's goal totals line up with those of Phil Esposito and Paul Henderson (nine for Henderson, seven for Hull, seven for Esposito).[1] Of facing Hull for the first time in game one of the 1974 series, Tretiak wrote, in mythic language, "No wonder people are telling legends about him. He's got some slapshot! Sometimes, I wasn't even able to see the puck!" (Tretiak). In all, though each man played in only two of the three tournaments, between the three summits in the opening era of international all-star play – 1972 and 1974 (each exclusively Canada versus the Soviet Union), and 1976 (Canada, the Soviet Union, Czechoslovakia, the United States, Sweden and Finland) – Hull's goal total was twelve, followed by Esposito at eleven, with Henderson tallying nine (Hockey-Reference.com; "Summit Series Goalies All-Time"; Anderson, 8; Chidlovski). Prior to the Summit Series, before his "legend" was proved true in the rink for Tretiak, Hull was not just one of the powers in conflict with the kings of the NHL, he was also the prize, or, more specifically, his ice time was. The debate over Hull's contract was as personal as any in the Greek poem. And, like the result of the conflict on the beaches of Troy, the individual defying the rules, no matter how important he was, lost out.

Hull desired the freedom to play where he wanted to for the price his play deserved. Much has been written about the machinations of the move that saw Hull leave the contract offered by the Wirtz-owned Chicago Black Hawks unsigned in the spring of 1972 and opt instead for Winnipeg and the WHA. But because Hull's actions in regards to his contracts affected only his relationship with the NHL, an international corporate body, and not his citizenship or connection to Canada, it was understood by the public, as well as by many involved in the creation of the team, as Gare Joyce recounts in *The Devil and Bobby Hull* (92–102), that Hull would be eligible to play for Team Canada.

The team represented the nation, and thus would, as it should, be made up of *Canadian* players on the basis of their merit alone – national good would trump corporate divisions. Such was not the case. If there are two schisms that Team Canada has yet to overcome, one of them is "the slash," which I'll consider later; the other is the roster. In his memoir, *Thunder and Lightning* (121), Phil Esposito almost spits the line "it ought to be called Team NHL, not Team Canada," an opinion he hasn't changed, repeating it from a podium in Brantford as recently as 2012 (Marion). Phil is not alone in this criticism. In an extended online version of its "Summit Series at 40" interviews, Adam Proteau of the *Hockey News* quotes Team Canada members Pete Mahovlich and J-P Parise saying the same thing – and not just about Hull, but about Howe, Sanderson, Cheevers and Keon as well. (Keon's web page on the Hockey Hall of Fame's website goes further, stating that he was left off the roster "because of the *possibility* he might leave the NHL" [italics mine].) The parallel: in *The Iliad*, though his exclusion from the field is the focus of the story, Achilles does not go alone: with him go the Myrmidons, his formidable army, from the Greek side.

As well as being the owner of Hull's spurned team, Wirtz was also chair of the NHL Board of Governors. As part of the contract that allowed NHLers to play in the Summit Series, he inserted a clause stipulating that all players on Team Canada had to be under contract with NHL teams (Joyce, 97). At the time, Hull was still in negotiations, his contract having expired in Chicago but the one waiting for him at Portage and Main still unsigned. The clause was a clear statement that Wirtz, like Agamemnon before him, was going to insist on Hull following the rules and signing with the NHL (returning the prize of his own talents to the ones who "rightfully" owned them) if he was going to get his own heart's desire – the place on Team Canada.

Canadians themselves, like the Greek commanders witnessing Achilles and Agamemnon's feud, provided the chorus. Fearing the resultant animosity, and possibly loss, all urged the king to forgive the single warrior his resistance. Famously, Pierre Trudeau himself appealed to Clarence Campbell, commissioner of the NHL, to intervene, but even that was not enough. It is possible that Campbell never had the power to overturn that clause in the agreement, even after Hull signed with Winnipeg in June 1972, and the clause, having lost its power as a bargaining tool, could only be a punishment. But Campbell, like Agamemnon, is often made the villain of the piece: the man who deprived Canada of its demigod of a champion because he couldn't overlook the rules of a body within the nation (the NHL) for the good of the nation (or the game) as a whole. Yet I would venture that Campbell was probably used to the role, even proud of it. In 1955 he had banned the almost sainted and equally compelling Rocket Richard from the Stanley Cup playoffs for striking a linesman in the middle of his inordinately violent fight with Boston defenceman Hal Laycoe near the end of the regular season. The Richard Riot – perhaps the Quiet Revolution itself – and Montreal's game seven Stanley Cup final defeat at the hands of the Detroit Red Wings followed. What isn't as well known is that at the end of World War II, Campbell "was appointed [one of] the prosecution lawyer[s] for the Canadian War Crimes Commission" and participated in the postwar prosecutions at Nuremberg ("Clarence Campbell: Biography"). To be fair, there is some debate on this point. Campbell's Wikipedia entry affirms his postwar legal role, but also notes that regarding his "widely reported" participation in the Nuremberg Trials themselves, "he said that was untrue in a *Sports Illustrated* article published in the late 1960s." Regardless of his exact proximity to them, Campbell was part of the historical moment when the charisma-worshipping Nazi elite, brought low, were brought to trial. Time and again Campbell was part of a team that prosecuted men for the monstrosities that are born when some people think that they are above the laws and rules that govern the rest. It is there that I believe that Campbell, like Agamemnon, learned to fear the chaos in the hearts of others and resolved to be a force of law against it. In the deepest sense, when I want to find sympathy for Agamemnon in *The Iliad*, I see him as Campbell, and I see Campbell as a man doing what he sees as both right and continuous with every noble action in his life.

I think of Bobby Clarke as Odysseus: "the slash" is one of the, if not *the*, most controversial moments in the series. Game six, in the Soviet Union, Bobby Clarke fractures Valery Kharlamov's ankle and hobbles the Russians' best player. And even though Kharlamov returns to the ice before the series ends, the tide turns in Russia. In the end, Canada, with its Pandarus, sniper Paul Henderson, its Greater Ajax, Phil Esposito – both men deserving Homer's description as "that bulwark of the Achaeans" (7.242) – and its Lesser Ajax, Phil's younger brother, Tony, standing firmly in the gap, and so on, take the battle. Later,

Canadian commentators, and some players, most notably the pious Henderson, question the morality of "the slash" (Fisher). But as someone from the Greek army would have pointed out, if we have to question the ethics of what's done on the battlefield, better to do so from the winning side.

According to the story – and, again, esteemed hockey writer Red Fisher – it's John Ferguson, Team Canada's Nestor, the old king who you know could still lace 'em up and go at it with men half his age, who says of Kharlamov in his warrior code, "I think he needs a tap on the ankle." It is Clarke, the wily Odysseus for whom winning is the only end for the story, who both understands what needs to be done and has the guts and skill to do it.

But "the slash" is more than what some call a foul. It is, I say, Canada's Trojan Horse – an artifact (also made of wood) both sacred and something other than a weapon, used instead to break a battlefield stalemate. Consider the Horse. It was a symbol of Athena, goddess of wisdom and war, protector goddess of Troy whom the Greeks, who also worshipped her, had offended during one of their raids on the city. Odysseus arranges for the Horse to be made, filled with soldiers and left as a peace offering on the shore to mark not only Greek defeat but also Greek honour. It symbolizes not just the conflict's conclusion but also a commitment to that conflict's nonviolent end. It assures the Trojans that the rules of war and peace are being followed. Odysseus's genius – and his blatant disrespect of the morality of his actions – lies in using the Horse to get the Trojans to let down their guard. It is an old tactic for an outnumbered and outfought army – turning a ploughshare into a sword. It still works. And for all the violence that we associate with hockey, even at our lustiest for blood, we shrink at the thought of the stick-swinging duel that cost Teddy Green his on-ice career and part of his skull. Even today, old-school and pro-fighting hockey people continue to use the prevention of stickwork as one of the main reasons for allowing hockey players to punch each other bare-knuckled. Or, as Lawrence Scanlan quotes a junior coach's succinct interpretation of the Don Cherry argument for fighting in *Grace Under Fire,* his extended treatment of the question of hockey violence, "This is how it is, and until we come up with a better system, we have to protect our best players" (167).

The stick is an instrument of skill and power in hockey, of leverage and authority, but it is not, for all the times it has been used to injure, a chosen symbol of the game's honourable violence – for that, we have the bodycheck and the fist, tools of violence that also risk the health of the ones who use them. The stick as a weapon is one of those things that hockey fighting is designed to protect "the best players" from. Yet Clarke deliberately used the stick against another player who, trusting the sacredness of the wood, had his back turned. Canada came home victorious. So did the Greeks. And as Odysseus might have said if he'd been asked, looking at the broken shell of the Horse that won his side the war, "Well, if I hadn't learned how to deliver a two-hander, I never would have made it out of Ithaca."

The symmetry can be made fuller: the prophetic Harry Sinden, bearing black-and-white game film to warn that the Soviets were better than everyone thought, as Cassandra met with a room full of players having "a hard time containing their laughter" (2). Team Sweden providing Canada with a vital tune-up battle between the four-game sets the Soviets played against Canada, the way the river Xander rises up between the resurgent Greeks and the Trojans and gives Achilles something to tune up with before the battle with Hector; Tretiak as Hector, holding back the invaders until he's laid out flat on his back and all is lost. There's even a pun: one king of the series (and its chief architect) was Alan Eagleson; Agamemnon, chief among the Greeks, belonged to the royal house known as "The Sons of the Eagle." But I want to turn to the connection between the social meanings of the Summit Series and the Greek epic, for there is more to say than just that one can be read through the other.

Why was 1972's victory so important to Canada? Because it didn't play out the way it was supposed to. We thought we'd win handily, the way the Greeks thought, the way the British thought they'd have World War I done by the Christmas of its opening year, the way, in 1812, Thomas Jefferson wrote that taking Canada itself was "just a matter of marching" (Munroe). History and story are riddled with such reversals. You'd think that we'd have heard them so often that we'd stop being surprised. Yet while mythology and story are built on unlikely victories, and every David downs a giant with a stone, in most real-world conflicts, Goliath wins, so it's both more reasonable and less interesting to think that he will. A conflict like the Trojan War or the Summit Series is a double story: the story of a group that sees itself as Goliath but finds out that it is more David than it thought and must find a way to win not just for the sake of victory but also in order to survive. It is in this sort of story where we see a people at the height, then the depths, then a new height of their powers, that we – and they – best perceive their character and their worth. They are tested not just against the strengths of others but against the weaknesses within themselves.

The Summit Series and the Trojan War are key events in the shaping of the cultures that participated in them. And beyond what I've pointed out as symmetry between the two as stories, the *narratives* of the Summit Series and the Trojan War, as valued creations of their respective societies, each represent choices about what their respective cultures desire to show or not show in their national story. Both Summit Series and *Iliad* are told in the language of a clear opposition between the home side and the foreigner. Each makes a clear distinction between "us" and "them." And even though there are those on the "them" side who are worthy adversaries and admirable people, the upshot of the story is to reinforce the sense of national selfhood found within the "us." I'd like to question that by reopening the Summit Series narrative through its connection to *The Iliad* in terms of the great poem's relationship to the history that surrounds it.

Exact dates for the events that lead up to the Trojan War, the Trojan War and its possible consequences, even the writing of *The Iliad*, are still subject to debate. The most definitive that Louise Schofield, a former curator in the British Museum, is willing to be on the matter is to say that the poem as a single work can be attributed to Homer "in the late 8th century BC" (10). That appears about right to everyone. Classics scholar Steven Cavan, to whom I'll refer several times, pegs it more precisely at 750 BCE, and notes that the poem was widely quoted by 720 BCE in Sparta, the proudest warrior city in Greece (pers. comm.).

In his chapter in *The Cambridge Companion to Homer*, "Homer: The History of an Idea," James Porter traces the complex and centuries-long debate about who, or what, Homer was: everything from "a complete fiction" to "a case of mistaken identity" to "a historical person as presented," and it engaged some of the world's most significant thinkers in philosophy, literature and archaeology. At this point, the prevailing view among modern scholars is that *The Iliad* is a collection of orally told poems about various aspects of the war itself (or related battles), written down, cut, edited and shaped into a single narrative, attributed to one poet, but more likely the work of several. In the method of the oral tradition, the work of many became personified under the name of one – perhaps a real person, perhaps the name given to the guiding spirit of the work.

That spirit did its work several hundred years after the Trojan War was over. Again, dating that event precisely is controversial: arguments from various thinkers using different premises place it anywhere from 1260 (Blegen, 163) to 1184 BCE (Eratosthenes of Alexandria in the third century, quoted in Blegen, 162). Caroline Alexander calls it "cautiously" at 1250 (1). Cavan and Schofield say 1180 (Cavan, pers. comm.; Schofield, 194). All of these dates put the war far enough in the past for the Greeks who wrote about it to write about it gloriously, and close enough to their present to be a bitter part of the fate of the Greeks who waged it. *The Iliad* and its companion, *The Odyssey*, were desired by eighth-century BCE Greeks as their national poem because in the period between the Fall of Troy and Greece's reassertion as a Mediterranean power, Greek society suffered a calamitous collapse. Many, if not most, of its proudest cities were destroyed, and the civilization they created fell into a four-hundred-year-long Dark Age during which the Greek people were scattered to small colonies around the Mediterranean, or left clinging to the remains of their great cities. Their culture was so thoroughly obliterated that, as Schofield says, a great portion of the population forgot how to write (185). In its Dark Age, for all intents and purposes, Greek ceased to be a language in any form other than oral use and memory; it was an age without record and thus without history (185). What *The Iliad* and *The Odyssey* did (along with their companion pieces in the Epic Cycle), four centuries later, was fill in that illiterate blank with written declarations of the long-standing glory and character of a society taking its place in the world and feeling its pride and power in doing so. *We are Greeks*, it declares both to itself and to outsiders: *look upon us now and know us in our greatest story*. Rather than being an account of the past, then, *The Iliad* was at the core of the texts by with the resurgent Greeks made themselves into what, those same texts argued, they had always been.

The Summit Series may or may not be Canadian hockey's finest moment, but it is Canadian hockey's greatest story; its narrative begins after years of Canadians being left on the periphery (and hence outside the history) of the international game, fielding team after team that met defeat after defeat, belying the true quality of Canadian hockey. The Summit Series' story, like *The Iliad*, stands as the declaration that Canadian hockey – its power no longer restrained by outside forces – is ready to take its rightful place in world. Like the Trojan War, it is not the story of a power simply rolling over its adversaries. That could be the result of weak opponents and impress no one. It is the story of a power that found the world as strong as the world could be (*Pay attention; we fought the best!*), and which dug down deep to touch the eternal character of its people to earn the victory that came less from what we did than from who we were (*We did it once; we can do it again*). In the same sense that *The Iliad* is, the Summit Series story is the beginning (again) of the history of Canadian hockey on the world rink. Canada's win in '72 is the country's (re)introduction as a hockey great power precisely because not only do all the Canadian victories in international play thereafter confirm it, but Canadian defeats (though harsh measured against the expectations it established) are also answered by its mythic moral lesson: when down, Canadians are the kind of people who come from behind to win in the end.

But the myths *as stories* choose to omit the surrounding history that makes them both possible and needed. As I've said, much about this period in Greek history is open to interpretation and argument. In fact, calling it "Greek history" is to distort it. It is, in fact, the history of several peoples and regions whose lives and paths diverged, came together, and split apart again before a culture we could call "Greek" emerged. We can say that events fell side by side; how closely connected they were in time, or what causal relationship existed between them, will probably always be open to debate. But I offer here, given favourable interpretations among the agreed-upon dates, a thought experiment with history in order to get at a truth (I hope) of both myth itself in general and the Summit Series in particular.

Think of The Trojan War not as triumph but as disaster for the Greeks. By the time it had run its ten-year course, the wealth of Troy that the Greeks had hoped to take was gone. Gone, too, were the major trading partners who had made Troy worth attacking at all: they'd set up shop in cities not under siege. And the Greek kingdoms that had banded together to fight a foreign war with all that fighting a foreign war entails – young men recruited as overseas soldiers, extended supply lines, exhaustion of the ability to barter or borrow, diversion of labour at home from farming, fishing, trade, all the things that had brought them their wealth in the first place – had left themselves deeply financially depleted if not effectively bankrupt. No army comes home unwounded. The Greeks who returned after the Trojan War were a spent force; the home they came to was a severely depleted one.

What we know from the archaeological record, according to Schofield (though I make no claim about her opinion of this interpretation) and Cavan, is that the Greeks who remained at home during this period spent their time fortifying their cities against the attacks that would ultimately destroy their civilization. Scholars cite several reasons for the Greek decline (Schofield, 170–85). Some say it was Doric invaders from the north, others "Sea People" from the south and east; some cite earthquakes, others ruptures of the political kind – slave revolts brought on by the collapse of the monarchic economies. Most commentators agree that the decline set in around 1180 BCE (the latest arguable date for the end of the Trojan War), and the downfall was finished around 1100. Knowing what centuries of war have taught us about war's real costs, I want to argue that the victory at Troy was the beginning of that end. Whatever it was from the *outside* that the Greeks fell to, it was their society's inner exhaustion that made it possible for other peoples, whoever they were, to defeat them in battle, absorb their society into its own, and set about, from the poverty, disease and weakness of the Dark Age, to rebuild. Whom I have called "the Greeks" of the Trojan War in this essay, and who are hailed in *The Iliad* and *The Odyssey* as winning Greece's greatest triumph, are known by archaeologists as the Mycenaeans; in *The Iliad*, despite all their varied clan names, they are "the Achaeans." And it was the Achaeans that, effectively, the Trojan War consumed.

If history is written by the winners, *The Iliad* is a paradox: it is a story that eighth-century Greeks wrote and their descendants revered even though it is about the victories won by those whom the writing culture replaced – as if the later Greeks who replaced the Achaeans had actually defeated the Trojans themselves as well. *The Iliad* is what happens when, along with everything else, the winners take possession of the loser's history, preferring it as they do to their own.

The pattern is rich, even more complicated than I cast it here. In a complex and politically charged modern parallel, look at the way that pro sports teams in North America wear the names and colours of groups that North American history has displaced, assimilated or pushed to near extinction: Chicago Blackhawks (changed from Black Hawks in 1986), Kansas City Chiefs, Washington Redskins. These dominant-culture names for its worthy "others" are set side by side with the names of groups representing its worthy "self": New York Rangers, Columbus Blue Jackets, New England Patriots. But then there's an *Iliad*-like mixing of name and iconography: The Minnesota Vikings, for example, are proudly named after the Europeans who settled in the coldest prairies of North America in the eighteenth and nineteenth centuries. But even this Viking heritage is, I would argue, a reconfigured one, blending the conquered with their conquerors as if the result represented a single group. Anyone familiar with the history of the Danish seafarers of the Middle Ages will tell you that, contrary to popular opinion, the Vikings did not wear horns in their helmets. Or spikes. Or eagles' wings. These, I suggest, are the warrior symbols of Cree and Sioux, Blackfoot and Apache, lifted from their heads, which are "other" to us, and (re)placed on the heads of the people who are "self" to us because we claim to be their descendants by culture if not by blood.

How does this pattern affect the narrative of the Summit Series? It is now commonly understood that the Summit Series was Canadian hockey as *Canadian* hockey at both its best and its last. Search "effect of the Summit Series" online, and after the talk of politics, both of nations and Team Canada's makeup, almost all the entries, including those endorsed by the NHL whose corporate politics interfered with the national nature of the team, remark on how the series changed the game itself. Kent Russell quotes Tarasov who, writing in 1995, two years before his death, said,

> The appearance of the pros on the international scene and their games against the Russian hockey players in particular demanded that they change their game's style. It sure didn't happen all at once. In the series of games against our players, the Canadians played "their" hockey. But having sensed the power of Russian hockey, they quit their "we'll win easily" attitude, which is harmful, not only in sport, but in all aspects of life as well, and, having compared their style of

> play with ours, decided to reorganize a lot of things in their performances.... Both hockey schools, the Canadian and Russian, are the best in the world. Each of them strives to come out on top. So be it.

In the four years that followed 1972, the all-and-only Canadian-born B Team from the WHA lost its series with the Russians, but Team Canada 1976 (a combined NHL and WHA all-Canadian squad) won the Canada Cup (in two one-goal games against the Czechs); the Russians didn't play in that final, but lost their sole game against the Canadians 3–1. Overall, that gives Canada an impressive two trophies out of the three on offer. But its record against the Russians over the three tournaments was six wins, seven losses, and four ties: Canada remained dominant in the game, but (in a beautifully Canadian way) only because the distribution of tournament games in which they were not defeated let them outrank the games they didn't win. And as some Russians will tell you to this day, they, not the Canadians, scored more goals in that legendary first series in 1972. So be it, indeed.

But whether the Russians or the Canadians represented the better teams then is no longer the point. The series opened up the game itself, and Canadian hockey was, quite literally, invaded from the North. Not by Russian and European players – they came later. At first, confined at home and resisted here, their immigration to North American rinks was only a trickle. But their ideas – about year-round conditioning, attack techniques, puck possession, the rink as a field of lateral play, of a team coached by a staff rather than a solitary mind – came the way the Soviets played: in waves. And, to round out the metaphor, Canadian hockey has also been invaded from a "sea" – the United States, itself affected, of course, by the Russian and European games. Eventually, the composition of all North American teams was internationalized. The last all-Canadian team to win the Stanley Cup was Bobby Clarke's Philadelphia Flyers in 1974. The last Canadian-based city to win the Cup was Montreal in 1993. The proportion of Canadian players in the NHL has dropped to just above fifty per cent (Mirtle). And though nine of the top ten all-time goal-scorers and all-time points-getters in NHL history are Canadian (Jaromir Jagr being eighth in points and tenth in goals) ("All-Time Points Getters"; "All Time Goals"), of the last ten players to score their five hundredth NHL goal (through 2012), only three – Pierre Turgeon, Mark Recchi and Jarome Iginla – are from Canada (of the rest, Jaromir Jagr, Teemu Selanne, Peter Bondra and Mats Sundin are from Europe; Keith Tkachuk, Jeremy Roenick and Mike Modano are American) ("List of Players with 500 Goals"; "Jarome Iginla Scores 500th Goal").

Despite the fact that we often call them "hard," numbers often describe what we cannot observe, so they are at best talking points. And though we could argue about the meaning of those particular numbers, they do suggest that Canadian players, representing a nationality, remain a force, but only one force among others, even in the league they once dominated. But Canadian hockey players weren't displaced first by demographics; everything in the game they were used to was changed first by the migration of philosophy, and unlike people, whose movements are often contained by political and economic boundaries, philosophies can expand to wherever they are considered. It's worth noting that even though the 1974 Flyers was all-Canadian by birth and, arguably, played the ultimate game of Canadian tough-guy hockey, it was at least partly Russian by training, long before Russian players earned places on NHL teams. Its coach, Hall of Famer Fred Shero, was one of the first and most all-in adopters of a Soviet-style system, bringing in a collection of techniques and philosophies strange to his rough-and-tumble team and expanding his reputation as "Freddy the Fog." Just as inscrutable to the kings of *The Iliad* would have been the Greeks who celebrated them while also contriving the forms of democratic government that rendered their kind obsolete.

We might have characterized Canadian hockey in the 1970s as hockey by platoon, where dump-and-chase individualism allowed for the spontaneous formation of small-group plays around the most prominent and talented skaters, and Russian hockey as hockey by battalion, in which whole on-ice groups worked as a unit, sharing puck control by distributing its possession. We could have noted the differences between them in that where Canadians were coached supplementing overall team strategy with in-the-moment line matching and changes, the Russians emphasized a relentless consistency of play in waves and a refusal to match lines. We might have said that if Russian hockey was soccer on ice, the Canadian game was rugby. But increasingly, in hockey's blended universe, it is becoming less and less clear whether the differences among players and teams from Canada, Sweden, the United States,

Russia, the Czech Republic, or even Switzerland or Germany are differences in national styles or personal approach.

Clearly, among all these, Canada has consistently been a dominant force since 1972, or if you want to put it this way: we have. But the game played in the Summit Series is not the hockey that Canadians play now. We've changed, and in the eyes of many, changed for the better. To take only one voice in the chorus of approving observers quoted on the NHL's own website, Rod Gilbert says, "Look at hockey today – they're playing like the Russians in the old days. They're all changing wings and forechecking differently. It really improved hockey, that series" (quoted in Kreiser). The best of Canada's players now could skate in Russia and blend right in – and do; Russians come here, and some stand among our biggest stars. And players, like Flames defenceman Mark Giordano (to take a local example for me), have taken to playing in Russia (or Europe) and returning to assume much more important roles on their teams than they would have had they stayed in the fourth-line roles they left behind to go overseas. In their movement across the ice, their puck handling, their expectations of the game, any Team Canada today could just as easily play the role of Team USSR in a reenactment of the Summit Series as they could of Team Canada '72. When we say it is *our* game – and thus a representation of the "us" that won in 1972 – and our *game* now, we aren't talking about the same game. In terms of play, the game long ago gave up the distinction between *us* and *them*. It absorbed it, kept the same name, and played on, growing as it did.

And yet the Summit Series has not faded away, one could argue, the way even the 1976 or other Canada Cups have. It has persisted, grown, taken root in Russia itself where the Canadian players in the series, particularly the once-hated Phil Esposito, are "rock stars" now (Kreiser), and continues to underscore the value of hockey as played by Canadians. Even Canada's most recent hockey triumphs in the Vancouver Olympics are measured beside '72. Why? I think the answer is this: As the game played by Canadian professionals became increasingly indistinguishable from the game that defined their opponents in 1972, what became foregrounded in the story of the Summit Series was the *way* that Team Canada was *seen to have played it*. What won that game, the story tells us, wasn't tactics or style, but heart. The Summit Series isn't the story so much of hockey strategy; it's the story of how a team *refused* to lose. Famously,

Henderson scored three game-winning goals *after* being taken from the ice on a stretcher in game five. According to the IIHF website, Henderson suffered a concussion that game when his head hit the boards, and, "Luckily, he was wearing a helmet, and both he and team doctors acknowledged the injury might have been fatal without the headgear" ("Paul Henderson," *IIHF Hall of Fame*). Tony Esposito said, "I was never the same after that. Never. I never reached the pinnacle that I reached in that series" (quoted in White). Phil Esposito put it in its strongest terms. In his interview with Charles Wilkins for *After the Applause*, he said, "I've said this before, and I'm not very proud of it because I've never even killed an animal…but there's no doubt in my mind that I'd have killed to win that series. It scares me, but it's true" (89). The Summit Series may have begun in Phil's laughter at Sinden's unheeded prophecies, but in the end, in Phil's words, "it was war" (88).

Consider *The Iliad* one last time. Poring over its pages, I am struck over and over by how difficult the Greeks were to deal with. The disaster that befalls the Greeks begins with the quarrel between Agamemnon and Achilles, both extraordinarily stubborn men who refuse to put aside their pride, even when begged to by all who depend on them for their lives. Jealousies abound in the Greek camps, and the kings among them are keenly aware of their place in the pecking order and how to change it. A lot of the poem is spent placating rivals – not just human ones, but also those among the gods, whose personal foibles are remarkably like those of their worshippers. In Book 10 of *The Republic*, Plato (in the voice of Socrates) quite rightly criticized the claim that *The Iliad* was a great military book on the grounds that Homer was only imitating the language of people who directed the fighting, or making things up. But *The Iliad* isn't a book about fighting a war with antiquated weapons; it's a book about how a group of talented, headstrong, charismatic and powerful people can be made to work together in a crisis. Even fighting the almost hopeless Trojan War called up the best and the worst traits in every one of whom the epic speaks. The most compelling characters are the most difficult – weaknesses, failings, triumphs and all. It was not an Achaean *event* that the later Greeks wanted to preserve; it was the Achaean character with which they identified. And that identification still crosses national or ethnic lines. You don't have to be Greek to see the Greek in us all, or want to know about the Achaeans as an extinct people in order to learn from their trials as described in Homeric detail.

Similarly, not just Canadian hockey, but Canada can be seen to have gained as well as lost in its relationship to the story of the Summit Series. If the implications of the series were felt only in hockey, then the last heroic surge of Canadian play that opened up the game to a new, hybrid style of international play isn't so great a price to pay. We still love our game. European stars in the jerseys of North American teams still brighten the eyes of the children they visit in North American hospitals; I heard Montreal arenas resound as fully with Saku Koivu's name as I have with Patrick Roy's.

In being destroyed and recreated, Greek culture was able to rewrite its past to suit its present; *The Iliad*, like all myths, is a pick-and-choose assemblage of stories. In the narrative of the Summit Series, too, there are things left out, most likely because their omission preserves something we have accepted or decided to preserve. If the communist-organized team lost the Summit Series (and, as John Soares demonstrates in his essay "Boycotts, Brotherhood and More," the Summit Series was a theatre within the Cold War itself) and "team NHL" won, then, despite Canadians' *national* pride in the result, it was *capitalism* that won. That outcome, ultimately the happy one for Canadian players and fans, allowed the weaknesses of professionalized sport and the country that loves it to remain unchallenged. So we are left with owners and teams having to work out how, when, where and by whom the game is played in the fighting words of management and labour. We have a commissioner whose position in the game is defined first through the needs of the team owners who pay him. We have players who have to look after themselves through their own contracts supported by a collective bargaining agreement. And we have a large number of people who depend on hockey for not only a living, but also all the things that fans of a sport, who cannot directly affect the relationship between players and owners, get from its play. We have national teams whose makeup is still dependent on the needs of team owners, and we hope (sometimes with reward, sometimes in vain) that, in their love of the game and their loyalty to it, they put the needs of the game first. All of this is a mirror, perhaps, of the distributions of power and wealth currently posing such difficulties in North American economic and political life across the board, but that would only be saying that for all the shocks it has taken, the way of life that gave us Team Canada 1972 is still here.

And however you criticize it, the fact remains, under the conditions in which it entered the contest, and in terms that make sense today, Team Canada 1972 was victorious. In the end, too, Agamemnon's troops, minus Achilles, won on the road and sacked Troy. The way that the Canadians played is an example of hockey fortitude acknowledged by all involved, regardless of the nationality of the players. The Greeks had to write *The Iliad* anew because both the poem and their civilization had been scattered to the winds. Greek culture had to be reinvented in order to survive, so the Greeks fashioned at least part of themselves around the qualities they found in an epic poem they saw as their inheritance. But as Caroline Alexander points out, as much as the Greeks saw their own greatness in the greatness of their predecessors proved in war, *The Iliad* is a war story that ends "in funerals, inconsolable lamentations, and shattered lives" (225). Homer is a poet, not a propagandist: even as it serves its national purpose, *The Iliad* reminds all who read it of the losses that come with even the greatest of gains. Canadian victory parts company here with the Achaean one: despite the failings that led to the near debacle the series became for us, because of the way the story turned out, Canadians had to change only the game on the ice, not the social terms and conditions under which it was played in response to it. So perhaps the Summit Series remains troubling as well as fulfilling: it represents great things accomplished, and it can still show us things that might have been – and that still remain unfinished.

---

[1] With Bobby Hull, nothing, it seems, is simple. At the time of this writing, the Chidlovski website, the most thorough and detailed online source on the 1974 series, accounts for only six Hull goals in its Game Summaries of that series, while its own Series' Statistics section claims he scored seven, the number listed in HockeyReference.com, NHL.com, the Hockey Hall of Fame site and Gare Joyce's biography of Hull. The *Globe and Mail* Game Summaries at the time (Sept. 18, 20, 23, 24; Oct 2, 4 and 7, 1974) confirm the seven and correct the notation for Canada's first goal in game eight: Hull from Backstrom and Tremblay. However, as Chidlovski's site confirms, and the news articles of the day complain about, in a gesture some saw as contemptuous, the USSR put Sidelnikov, their backup goalie, in net rather than Tretiak in the final game of

a series they'd already won. Hull scored on him. But there is one more twist of the sort that keeps pulling Hull to the centre of the drama. The Russians won the series in its game seven, but only then because of the disallowance of a pivotal goal that most commentators agree that Hull scored on Tretiak in the last second of play – a game-winner that was improperly ruled to have been scored after time expired. With it uncounted, the WHA team lost the chance to tie a series they couldn't by then have won (Joyce, 144–47). Clearly, having had him score six goals in four games against their best goaltender, the Russians keyed in on Hull in the second half of the series, keeping him from scoring, and restricting Canada to the great but aging stars of the WHA for their goals. But this is the nature of events that create stories as well as accounts: they give us a might-have-been, as well as a what-was: Hull able to shake his tormentors at last, tallying a last-second goal, and setting up a final game to stave off defeat.

Works Cited

"1976 Canada Cup." Wikipedia. Last modified March 23, 2014. http://en.wikipedia.org/wiki/1976_Canada_Cup (accessed April 2014).

Alexander, Caroline. *The War That Killed Achilles: The True Story of Homer's* Iliad *and the Trojan War*. New York: Viking, 2009.

"All-Time Goals." StatsHockey.net. Last modified February 1, 2014. http://statshockey.homestead.com/alltimegoals.html.

"All-Time Points Leaders." StatsHockey.net. Last modified February 1, 2014. http://statshockey.homestead.com/alltimepoints.html.

Anderson, H. J. *The Canada Cup of Hockey Fact and Stat Book*. Victoria, BC: Trafford, 2005.

Blegen, Carl W. *Troy and the Trojans*. New York: Barnes & Noble, 1995.

"Bobby Hull." Hockey Reference.com. http://www.hockey-reference.com/players/h/hullbo01.html (accessed April 2014).

"Bobby Hull." NHL.com. http://www.nhl.com/ice/player.htm?id=8448108 (accessed April 2014).

Chidlovski, Arthur. "Game Summaries." The Summit in 1974: Team USSR vs. Team Canada. 2013. http://www.chidlovski.com/personal/1974/game00.htm (accessed July 2013).

———. "Summit Statistics 1974." The Summit in 1974: Team USSR vs. Team Canada. 2014. http://www.chidlovski.net/1974/74_statsform.asp (accessed April 2014).

"Clarence Campbell: Biography." Hockey Hall of Fame. http://www.legendsofhockey.net (accessed March 2013).

"Clarence Campbell." Wikipedia. Last modified July 15, 2013. http://en.wikipedia.org/wiki/Clarence_Campbell (accessed March 2014).

"Dave Keon: Biography." Legends of Hockey. Hockey Hall of Fame. http://www.legendsofhockey.net/LegendsOfHockey/jsp/LegendsMember.jsp?mem=p198602&type=Player&page=bio&list= (accessed July 2013).

Dryden, Ken, and Roy MacGregor. *Home Game*. Toronto: McClelland & Stewart, 1989.

Esposito, Phil, and Peter Golenbock. *Thunder and Lightning*. Toronto: McClelland & Stewart, 2004.

Fisher, Red. "Summit Series 40th Anniversary: Clarke's Game 6 Slash on Kharlmov Was Turning Point for the Series." *Gazette* (Montreal), September 24, 2012.

"Game Summaries." *Globe and Mail*, September 18, 20, 23 and 24, 1974; October 2, 4, and 7, 1974.

Harpur, Tom. *The Pagan Christ*. Toronto: Thomas Allen, 2004.

Homer. *The Iliad*. Translated by Robert Fagles. Deluxe edition. New York: Penguin, 1998.

"Jarome Iginla Scores 500th Goal." *Red Mile, The Calgary Flames Blog*, January 7, 2012. http://redmileblog.com/2012/01/jarome-iginla-scores-500th-nhl-goal.

Joyce, Gare. *The Devil and Bobby Hull*. Mississauga, ON: Wiley, 2011.

Kreiser, John. "Summit Series Changed Hockey Forever." *Summit Series 40th Anniversary* (blog), NHL.com, September 29, 2012. http://www.nhl.com/ice/news.htm?id=642109.

"List of NHL Players with 500 Goals." Ice Hockey Wiki. http://icehockey.wikia.com/wiki/List_of_NHL_players_with_500_goals (accessed January 2014).

Marion, Michael-Allan. "Espo Charms Builders with 90-Minute Talk." *Brantford Expositor*, March 30, 2012. http://www.brantfordexpositor.ca/2012/03/30/espo-charms-builders-with-90-minute-talk.

Mirtle, James. "The NHL by Nationality: 52 Per cent Canadian Content." *From the Rink* (blog), SB Nation, November 26, 2008. http://www.fromtherink.sbnprivate.com/2008/11/26/673622/the-nhl-by-nationality-52.

Munroe, Susan. "9 US Presidents' Quotes about Canada." Canada Online. http://canadaonline.about.com/od/canadausrelations/a/uspresquotescan.htm (accessed April 2014).

"Paul Henderson." Hockey Reference.com. http://www.hockey-reference.com/players/h/hendepa01.html (accessed April 2014).

"Paul Henderson." International Ice Hockey Federation. http://www.iihf.com /competition/352/home/hall-of-fame/paul-henderson.html (accessed July 9, 2013).

"Phil Esposito." Hockey Reference.com. http://www.hockey-reference.com /players/e/esposph01.html (accessed April 2014).

Porter, James I. "Homer: The History of an Idea." In *The Cambridge Companion to Homer,* edited by Robert Lewis Fowler, 324–43. Cambridge, UK: Cambridge University Press, 2004.

Proteau, Adam. "The Summit Series at 40, Extended Version." *The Hockey News,* August 29, 2012. http://www.thehockeynews.com/articles/48309-Summit-Series-at-40-extended-version.html.

Russell, Kent. "Sid/Ovie (Part Two)." *n+1,* March 18, 2011. http://nplusonemag .com/sid-ovie-part-two.

Scanlan, Lawrence. *Grace Under Fire: The State of Our Sweet and Savage Game.* Toronto: Penguin, 2002.

Schofield, Louise. *The Mycenaeans.* Los Angeles: The J. Paul Getty Museum, 2007.

Sinden, Harry. *Hockey Showdown: The Canada-Russia Hockey Series, the Inside Story.* Toronto: Doubleday, 1972.

Soares, John. "Boycotts, Brotherhood, and More." In *Now Is the Winter: Thinking about Hockey,* edited by Jamie Dopp and Richard Harrison, 97–112. Hamilton, ON: Wolsak and Wynn, 2009.

"Summit Series Goalies All-Time Goals-Against-Average Leaders." QuantHockey.com. http://www.quanthockey.com/summit-series/en/records /summit-series-goalies-all-time-goals-against-average-leaders.html (accessed April 2014).

Tretiak, Vladislav. "When It Is Hot on the Ice: Vladislav Tretiak's Diaries 1974." The Summit in 1974: Team USSR vs. Team Canada, Arthur Chidlovski. http:// www.chidlovski.com/personal/1974/recaps/rec01tr.htm (accessed April 2014).

"WHA vs USSR Statistical Leaders." Hockey Hall of Fame.com. http:// www.hhof.com/htmltimecapsule/StatLeadersWHA1974.shtml (accessed April 2014).

White, Patrick. "The Story of the Summit Series, as It's Never Been Told Before." *Globe and Mail*, September 16, 2012. http://www.theglobeandmail.com /sports/hockey/the-story-of-the-summit-series-as-its-never-been-told-before/article4546471.

Wilkins, Charles. "In the Capital of the World: Interview with Phil and Donna Esposito." In *After the Applause: Ten NHL Greats and Their Lives after Hockey*, by Colleen Howe, Gordie Howe, and Charles Wilkins, 76–96. Toronto: McClelland & Stewart, 1989.

Watching *Weekend*: The Summit Series as Discourse on Modernity

♦

J. ANDREW ROSS

Two Countries, Two Systems

For Canadians, the eight games of the Canada-USSR Summit Series were a long-awaited chance for their professionals to reassert Canadian dominance over the sport by humbling the Soviet pseudo-amateurs. But what started as an exercise in humiliation quickly became a thrilling test of equals and brought the series a cultural significance that transcended the sport arena. Contemporary observers began to see it through the lens of the Cold War as yet another episode of confrontation between the Communist East and Capitalist West. By the time the series reached Moscow for the last four games, Soviet player Boris Mikhailov was quoted as saying that "it feels like war on ice. But I see now, it's like a real war: two countries, two systems fighting to show the world who is most powerful" (McKinley, 223).

This sense of a battle over two ways of life – democratic and communist – has also become the dominant view of the series in social memory, and of both historians and the participants themselves.[1] Yet an analysis of at least one cultural text of the time – a documentary segment produced right after game eight for CBC television – suggests that the nature of the belligerence, and the identity of the belligerents, was not so straightforward to contemporary observers. The series was a (literally) cold battle of the Cold War, but there were some reorientations. First of all, there was a role substitution: unlike recent similar events, such as the Fischer-Spassky World Chess Championship in the summer of 1972, this time it was Canadians representing the West and Americans cheering from the sidelines. Second, it wasn't just about Canadians and Soviets. Scholars like Brian Kennedy have argued that the series was about the production of Canadian national identity and that the Soviets provided "a visible other" through which Canadians "could create a sense of self-identity and a set of cultural symbols that would come to bind them together as a group" (Kennedy, 47). However, it was usually the Americans to whom Canadians saw themselves in opposition, and anti-American themes are very evident in the discourse. So how did the Americans fit in as "third term introduced into the… binary of us-versus-them" (Kennedy, 52)? The words of those interviewed after the catharsis of game eight offers an insight: Canadians saw the conflict not in binary (or ternary) geopolitical terms, but rather as a more fundamental conflict over their own place in the modern world.

Weekend Watching

The Summit Series took place in September 1972 before the start of the National Hockey League (NHL) season. Team Canada lost unexpectedly 7–3 in the first game, and won only one of the next three, so that by the time the teams flew to Europe mid-month to play the final four games in Moscow, all of Canada was watching as the reputation of Canadian hockey was put on the line. In Moscow, Team Canada turned the tide and won two of the first three games, tying the series at three wins apiece (with one tie) and setting the stage for a decisive game eight. The final game was broadcast across Canada on both major networks (CBC and CTV) and drew an estimated broadcast audience of sixteen million, almost three-quarters of the population. The whole country cheered when Canada tied the game late in the third period, and when Paul Henderson scored the winner to put Canada up 6–5 with thirty-four seconds remaining in the game, and as Team Canada held on for victory.

The producers of CBC's flagship information program, *Weekend*, evidently recognized history in the making and arranged to film public reactions to the final moments of the game, and afterwards conducted apparently spontaneous interviews. The resulting nine-minute segment, "1972: 'Henderson has scored for Canada,'" has been preserved on the CBC archives website and offers a fascinating glimpse into the meanings contemporaries immediately ascribed the series.[2] In the segment not all the watched groups can be identified, but they include the staff of the Soviet embassy in Ottawa; former prime minister John Diefenbaker and his wife, Olive; Premier Dave Barrett of British Columbia (who predicts Henderson will score the final goal); a group of NHL players; Canadian heavyweight boxing champion George Chuvalo; and ordinary Canadians watching from their living rooms and a local diner. Afterwards, the program hosts, primarily Charlotte Gobeil, interviewed several spectators to obtain their reactions to the event, including novelist Morley Callaghan; artists Dennis Burton and Gerry Gladstone; athlete and professional hockey critic Bruce Kidd; and Minister of National Health and Welfare, and Minister of Amateur Sport, John Munro.[3] (The complete transcript of the interviews appears in sections following.)

> **Morley Callaghan, novelist**: "You know I jumped up and screamed?"
> **Charlotte Gobeil:** "What did you scream?"
> **Callaghan:** "I don't know what the hell I screamed, but I... This has been a... I don't know... I watch sports all the time, and I don't know when I've been so excited and when the thing has been so personal to me. Do you see?"
> **Gobeil:** "Why personal...is it, is it linked with nationalism?"
> **Callaghan:** "No, I hate super patriots. They're a pain in the neck. And I think it's just because they're the boys from home."

> **Bearded man:** "When they scored the sixth goal, I felt I was a Canadian."

> **Gerry Gladstone:** "Finally, we put together a bunch of guys who represent us, and they won. That's what you're supposed to do – you're supposed to win – it's about time Canada started realizing that."

What strikes the viewer right away is that even in these unprepared comments, the words and themes are not just about patriotism. The bearded man, who spoke with a French accent and was presumably a French-Canadian or Québécois, felt he "was a Canadian" when they scored the sixth goal, suggesting that the series might have a binding effect. For his part, Morley Callaghan dismisses the idea that nationalism is the central emotion; rather, in his case, it is his simple affection for the "boys from home." Gerry Gladstone sees the team as "a bunch of guys" that had learned to win, and implies that Canadians have been too comfortable with losing. This was a common sentiment in Canadian cultural discourse, and noted critic Northrop Frye had even identified an inferiority complex as "one of the essential Canadian moods" – a sense that Canada was second-rate and that the world outside was a better or more authentic society (MacLennan, 75). After a decade in which Canada lost its dominance in the world championships of the country's national sport – hockey – there was no more acute symbol of being second-rate in the modern world than losing at hockey.

> **Bruce Kidd:** "Too often we've been telling ourselves that what happens in this country doesn't count – we really don't amount to that much – it makes more sense to sell our resources to the United States for a few cheap dollars instead of developing them ourselves…"
>
> **Gobeil:** "Including human resources?"
>
> **Kidd:** "Including human resources. Our best athletes – our Canadian heroes – are taught every day that if they want to make their living they have to go to another country because we can't do it for them here. Now, you know, the players in that way personify a lot of what, what's unfortunate, what's bad, what's wrong with Canada, but they also personify what's good – that we do believe that we do have a gut faith in ourselves and we can, when we want to, respond. And they certainly responded in a magnificent way and that gives me a great deal of courage. What I'd like to see is us develop a league in this country – a professional league, but not a professional league that has been commercialized – with teams in just about every major city in the country. So we can have this kind of hockey in our own country where we can go and see it."

Bruce Kidd, proponent of Canadian economic nationalism, interviewed on CBC's *Weekend*, September 28, 1972. ©CBC

Bruce Kidd translates the theme of national failure to the wider capitalist system and Canada's languishing in the shadow of the world's largest economy. His comments were in tune with an angst that had grown in the 1960s, when Canadian nationalism emerged as a potent force, fuelled by concerns about American geopolitical interests and dominance over the domestic economy.[4] The integration of markets (globalization) was continuing apace, and the question being asked was whether Canadians could compete in the global marketplace, or would take what others were willing to give. Kidd argues a popular line of criticism in Canadian economic nationalist discourse of the 1960s and 1970s – that Canadians preferred to sell resources "for a few cheap dollars instead of developing them." In this case, the resources are human capital, and he shows himself to be an opponent of the integration of labour markets, believing that Canadian athletes should personify Canadian "gut faith" and "make their living" back home by individually resisting continentalizing (globalizing) forces and returning to play in a non-commercialized professional league with clubs in every major Canadian city.[5]

John Munro, minister of national health and welfare [and minister of amateur sport]: "Canada cannot really say to our artists – and hockey players are artists in a very real sense, too – that they cannot pursue their careers in other countries. We don't control and own them. And if we want to have rigidities built into our system so that we can more appropriately charter a given course [and] achieve a given objective – such as they can in a totalitarian state where the communists control, government in a sense controls, almost everything, well, that's one thing, but I don't… I don't think the Canadian people want that."

Red-headed fan: "Well, I think they did pretty well considering [NHL President] Clarence Campbell almost screwed it up for them. [I] think Bobby Hull and Derek Sanderson and J. C. Tremblay should have played for Canada.…"

John Munro, Canadian minister of amateur sport, interviewed on CBC's *Weekend*, September 28, 1972. ©CBC

The minister of amateur sport, John Munro, seems to be responding directly to the idea that the state should exert control over markets. He expounds the common liberal free-market line that individuals should be free to pursue their economic careers without state interference. He suggests that Canadians would refuse to emulate totalitarian states "where the communists control...almost everything." Yet, as the red-haired fan points out, capitalism is also a system of control, especially over labour. Like many other Canadians, he held Clarence Campbell, the president of the NHL, responsible for preventing non-NHL players like Bobby Hull, Derek Sanderson and J. C. Tremblay of the World Hockey Association from playing on Team Canada.[6] We can infer that the fan's ire was directed in particular at American owners, who formed a majority in the NHL, and this was even voiced by Harry Sinden, the coach of Team Canada – and also general manager of the Boston Bruins – who later wrote that Canadians were "hogtied" by the American owners over Hull (Sinden, 56).[7]

Fear of the usurpation of Canadian hockey by American capital had a long history dating from the 1920s, and had been brought to a zenith during the 1967 expansion of the league, which saw six American – but no Canadian – teams added to the NHL (Ross, "Hockey Capital," 184–86, 526–27). But the fear was not just about hockey: it was coeval with wider Canadian concerns about American economic dominance in those eras, and both were expressed in anti-American sentiment. While Canadian criticism of the United States had waxed and waned back to the origins of the two countries,[8] the root of the discomfort went beyond the bilateral relationship itself. Canadian anti-Americanism was not merely a parochial response to a strong neighbour, but could be seen in the context of a more global resistance to the modern industrial world (Ross, "Hockey Capital," 580). Nor was this a unique Canadian perspective. Tony Judt has argued that anti-Americanism in the twentieth century was often "a convenient shorthand for expressing cultural insecurity," and that the American way of modernity "threatens local interest and identities" (Judt, 11, 13, 19). Paul Hollander states it more directly: anti-Americanization expresses "a protest against modernity" (444). Thus the Canadian criticism of the American influence in hockey represented a much wider cultural discomfort, which was especially evident in the vibrant Canadian cultural and economic nationalism of the 1960s. The greater project was resistance to modern capitalism, which was seen to be pulling hockey away from its traditional and natural place (Canada) to serve the interests of modern industrial society (the United States).[9]

Robots and Romantics

> **Red-headed fan:** "And that's the only point, but they [the Canadians] played wonderful hockey, they really, they played from down here – and the thing with the communists – from their heart. That's something the Russians forget about – they don't have a heart – they're robots. And that's what they did – they just played mechanized hockey but the Canadians played from deep down inside."

> **Callaghan:** "What fascinated me about it, the whole business, was that our pros were really the beloved amateurs, emotionally, in every way. You know they got uptight, they blew their tops – they behaved like Romantic figures all the way down the line. And Russia, the land of Slavic Romanticism, they behaved, their players, their coaches, if you watched the bench, if you watched the players, they behaved with a kind of mechanical exactitude. Did you notice this? And, you know, when a Russian player got a penalty, if you looked at him, he sat on the bench utterly impassively. Sometimes his coach spoke to him, and the coach was just impassive. When a Canadian player got on the bench, he became a Romantic figure. He sat there and literally he was bleeding. You know all his emotions were stirred up and so on."

In these statements, both the red-haired fan and Callaghan propose a fundamental gulf between Canadians and Soviets – that their bodies and souls are different. The Canadians "played down here...from their heart"; and it was not rational play directed by the mind, but rather passionate play "from deep down inside." In contrast, the Soviets were heartless "robots" who played "mechanized hockey." These comments echoed contemporary analysis that saw the Russian advantage as lying in their "system." This in turn can be read on two levels. One is the Soviet on-ice tactical strategy that featured sophisticated passing and emphasized team over individual success, but the other is the wider Marxist-Leninist political, economic and ideological system that subordinated the individual to the collective. The two were often conflated. Paul Henderson later wrote that the Soviet coaches were "dictators" (56) and that the "players were essentially a decent group of people trying to survive in a brutal system" (74). He did not dispute that hockey was also a collective endeavour for

Canadians, but this was from collective personal choice: having "started out as individuals...[Henderson and his teammates] came together as a team to win the series" (81–82).

Morley Callaghan, Canadian novelist, interviewed on CBC's *Weekend*, September 28, 1972. ©CBC

Morley Callaghan draws a further distinction between the professional and amateur spirits. A traditional narrative of Canadian sport held that amateurs had created sport for the love of the game, but that the once-pure activity had been industrialized and commercialized by capitalists, who engaged professional players who replaced passion for pay. There is a sense that the series regressed the players to the amateur state, and that the Canadians had to shake off their modern identity (as professionals/workers) and rediscover and rekindle their amateur passion. The transitional moment might have been Phil Esposito's famous comments at the end of game four, when he bookended his "rant" against booing with a defence of the pros' efforts ("We really tried," etc.).[10] By playing outside the confines of the NHL (and without their NHL salaries) as part of Team Canada, the professionals were able to return to the amateur Garden of Eden, before the original sin of commercialization, and in so doing had become "beloved amateurs...in every way." For Callaghan, and perhaps others, the non-industrial premodern player was more authentic and more representative of Canadian values.

The amateur-professional narrative was part of an even larger cultural narrative with relevance beyond Canada – a Romantic reaction against the triumph of reason brought by the Enlightenment. The Canadian players were not only amateurs but also men who "blew their tops…[and] behaved like Romantic figures all the way down the line." And the price they had to pay was not rational, but corporeal: the Canadian players were "literally…bleeding." Alienated from their own Romantic heritage, the Soviet players were forced to remain "impassive" and to behave "with a kind of mechanical exactitude," devoid of emotion and imprisoned in the spiritual void of the modern industrial system.

Artists of the Antimodern

Therein lay a paradox: how could the representatives of the capitalist West, the inheritors of the Enlightenment – the triumph of reason over passion – have symbolically replaced men from Russia, "the land of Slavic Romanticism"? The answer was: by revolution. Nineteenth-century Russia, the progenitor of the Soviet Union, had long been a symbol of a failed transition to modern society, a state mired in cultural and economic backwardness. A radical modernization project came with the Russian Revolution of 1917, which came to be dominated by the Bolsheviks and saw the application of Marxian analytical philosophy and technocracy. For some scholars, the Soviet Union was not a modern state because it rejected central Western tenets such as individualism and Western liberalism, and also because it ultimately failed.[11] Canadian observers of game eight appeared to disagree. Those interviewed by *Weekend* clearly viewed the Soviet Union as the apogee of the machine-driven modern state enterprise, and Team Canada as a force of resistance to it. We can see this resistance as antimodernism, which Arthur Versluis defines as "an instinctive reaction against the mechanization and bureaucratization of life, against the destruction of the natural world, against the destruction of traditional cultures, and against the destruction of the quality of human life" (122).

In this regard it is telling that the Team Canada players are not seen as workers, the products of modern industry, but as either amateurs or, in the words of John Munro, "artists in a very real sense." The amateur versus professional dichotomy has been discussed earlier, but the reference to art is also an important metaphor. It tapped into a powerful current of Canadian cultural nationalism that feared the subsuming of Canadian cultural identity – its art, among other things – into the American mass market. In this context, then, playing hockey was a celebration of the individuality of the artisan in a world of homogenizing mass production. By winning the series, the Canadian antimodern "artists" achieved a symbolic victory over modern industry.

White Magic, Man

> **Dennis Burton, artist:** "Well, I believe the Russian players, excellent as they were, marvellous hockey players, and the whole thing that was like that part of the world is still, like, hung up in black magic, whereas Canada and Canadian players represent white magic. And it, like, never hit me all the way through the series – and I watched every game avidly, except for the double images I got on the other channel – and, and I suddenly started to yell in the last part of the third period: "Use white magic! Use white magic!" And I got to believe strongly in white magic, which I've never tried or used for anything before. It's positive magic, you know, like Jesus, Moses, you know…Western tradition…."
> **Gobeil:** "You're not drunk now, are you?"
> **Burton:** "Of course not, no, no. Uh, that I really believe that, that if I, you know, prayed, if you…"
> **Gobeil:** "I still don't understand. What is white magic?"
> **Burton:** "Well, it's opposite to black magic!"
>
> **Red-headed fan:** "I mean God was on our side, let's face it. God is…God is Canadian!"

Though he is hard to take seriously, even Dennis Burton's enthusiasm about magic resonates with the tensions of modernity. The Soviets are the purported practitioners of "black magic," and Burton exhorts the Canadian players to counter it with positive "white magic," which he identifies with the Judeo-Christian tradition – "like Jesus, Moses." On the face of it, religion seems one of the easiest ways to frame the conflict in an era when reference to "godless Russians" was commonplace. The red-haired fan makes this connection with his conclusion that "God was on our side, let's face it…God is Canadian." But religion had an awkward place in Western society: it was a core cultural institution and yet, by being based on faith and not reason, was also a challenge to the rational drive of the Enlightenment. In rejecting it entirely, the Soviet Union – an explicitly atheistic state – was the more modern in this perspective. Yet the specific brand of religion Burton cites is telling. He pays lip service to Judeo-Christian tradition, and yet speaks in terms of the repurposed folk religion of a premodern era. The practices were used as an antimodern tool. Scholars have noted that the practice of "mystical arts" is a means of expressing discontent with modernity and dealing with its deformities (Comaroff and Comaroff, 244). In North America, the adoption of Neo-Pagan and witchcraft (Wicca) traditions, which Burton appears to be influenced by (or perhaps under the influence of), dates from the 1960s and has been seen as a direct response to modernity and the rational world brought forth by the Enlightenment (Berger, 123–24).

Silent Violence

Seeing the meaning of the series as a discourse on modernity also helps resolve some inconsistencies that have troubled scholars about the Summit Series, and Canadian hockey in general. Fitting in the Americans is one, as discussed earlier. Another might be Canadian worry about the prominence of violence in the national game.[12] It is curious that the rough play by Team Canada in the series does not rate mention in the interviews (although it might be implied through the evident valorization of the Canadian player body). Perhaps in this moment of national elation Canadians were loath to criticize, but it may also be that the violence was literally unremarkable because it conformed to an expression of antimodern sentiment. There are two dimensions. First, the violent play itself was a pure expression of the primal, premodern and anti-rational. Second, violence could also be seen as a tool to combat modernity. Versluis notes that "hard" antimodernism could be expressed through "direct attack" (105). By this, he means ecological and ideological terrorism, and while the Canada-Russia series did not engage this level of active resistance, in the hockey arena the players could symbolically express physical resistance to the system, and slash at the ankle of modernity as the opportunity arose.

"Victory"

> **Crowd [chanting]:** "We're number one! We're number one!…"

Watching the *Weekend* interviews about this cathartic moment in Canadian cultural history supports the idea that an important dimension of cultural discourse was being given voice. Above all, it shows the conflict to be about more than East versus West, or democracy versus communism, and as much about an event that tapped into a deep passion in Canadians that they expressed in terms of the process of accommodation to modernity. It seems evident that Canadians were anxious about their place in the world, and while the United States was the usual *bête noire*, the Summit Series gave opportunity for Canadians to test their most treasured cultural product, hockey, against a new villain – and the era's biggest – the Soviet Union. Even with the change in target, the analysis of this brief television text, while not necessarily representative, shows that some fundamental Canadian preoccupations remained constant: the Canadian sense of being challenged culturally and economically, and the fear of being found inferior on both fronts. For Canadians, the discussion was really about themselves, and the Soviet Union and the United States were mere stand-ins for the same thing – modernity. The Summit Series gave Canadians a symbolic victory over all of them ("We're number one!"), but there was ultimately a paradox in this triumph of antimodern sentiment: it was professional hockey players (workers), products of modern training techniques and specialization, who had been needed to "defeat" the foes.[13]

---

[1] For examples, see McKinley; MacSkimming; Jokisipilä; Ludwig; Mahovlich, 151; Henderson, 51.

[2] The interviews begin at about 3:30. The piece was formerly titled "God is Canadian!" and the change in title reflects the twenty-first-century mythologizing of Paul Henderson's role and the centrality of "the goal" to the narrative. The CBC site notes

that "the clip was edited for copyright reasons." For more on *Weekend*, see http://www.tvarchive.ca/database/19335/cbc_weekend/details/ (accessed June 8, 2013).

3   Morley Callaghan's son Barry was a former host of *Weekend*.

4   For an overview of the sixties in Canada with reference to Americans as the "other," see Anastakis, as well as Edwardson.

5   Kidd had just co-written a book amplifying his ideas; see Kidd and Macfarlane.

6   Campbell and his bosses, the NHL owners, would allow only NHL players to be eligible for the series, and the exclusion of Hull in particular had caused public uproar.

7   Ten American clubs were American-owned, and so was Vancouver. The Los Angeles team was owned by Jack Kent Cooke, who was a Canadian-born dual citizen.

8   On Canada's long history of anti-Americanism, see Granatstein.

9   See also Ross, "The National Hockey League."

10   "Home Fans Boo, Espo Lets Them Have It," interview by Frank Herbert and Bruce Rogers, *Sunday Magazine*, CBC, September 10, 1972. http://www.cbc.ca/archives/categories/sports/hockey/canada-soviet-hockey-series-1972/home-fans-boo-espo-lets-them-have-it.html (accessed June 10, 2013).

11   Johann Arnason argues that using a theoretical framework that considers multiple, often regional, variations on modernization allows us to see the Soviet Union as clearly modern. See Arnason.

12   For an example, see Robidoux.

13   On this antimodern paradox, see Lears.

Works Cited

Anastakis, Dimitry. "Introduction." *In The Sixties: Passion, Politics, and Style*, edited by Dimitry Anastakis, 3–23. Montreal: McGill-Queen's University Press, 2011.

Arnason, Johann P. "Communism and Modernity." *Daedalus* 129, no. 1 (Winter 2000): 61– 90.

Berger, Helen A. *A Community of Witches: Contemporary Neo-Paganism and Witchcraft in the United States*. Columbia, SC: University of South Carolina Press, 1999.

Comaroff, J., and J. L. Comaroff. "Occult Economies and the Violence of Abstraction: Notes from the South African Postcolony." *American Ethnologist* 26, no. 2 (1999): 279–301.

Edwardson, Ryan. "'Kicking Uncle Sam Out of the Peaceable Kingdom': English-Canadian 'New Nationalism' and Americanization." *Journal of Canadian Studies* 37, no. 4 (Winter 2003): 131–50.

Granatstein, Jack. *Yankee Go Home? Canadians and Anti-Americanism*. Toronto: HarperCollins, 1996.

Henderson, Paul. *Shooting for Glory*. Toronto: Stoddart, 1992.

Hollander, Paul. *Anti-Americanism: Critiques at Home and Abroad, 1965–1990*. New York: Oxford University Press, 1992.

Jokisipilä, Markku. "Waging the Cold War on Ice: International Ice Hockey Tournaments as Arenas of Ideological Confrontation between East and West." Paper presented at "Canada's Game? Critical Perspectives on Ice Hockey and Identity," Plymouth, MA, 2005.

Judt, Tony. "A New Master Narrative? Reflections on Contemporary Anti-Americanism." In *With Us or Against Us: Studies in Global Anti-Americanism*, edited by Tony Judt and Denis Lacorne, 11–31. London: Palgrave MacMillan, 2007.

Kennedy, Brian. "Confronting a Compelling Other: The Summit Series and the Nostalgic (Trans)Formation of Canadian Identity." In *Canada's Game: Hockey and Identity*, edited by Andrew C. Holman, 44–62. Montreal: McGill-Queen's University Press, 2009.

Kidd, Bruce, and John Macfarlane. *The Death of Hockey*. Toronto: New Press, 1972.

Lears, T. J. Jackson. *No Place of Grace: Antimodernism and the Transformation of American Culture, 1880–1920*. Chicago: University of Chicago Press, 1981.

Ludwig, Jack. "Team Canada in War and Peace." In *Canada On Ice: 50 Years of Great Hockey*, edited by Michael Benedict and D'Arcy Jenish, 231–45. Toronto: Viking, 1998. First published 1972 by Maclean's.

MacLennan, Jennifer. "Dancing with Our Neighbours: English Canadians and the Discourse of Anti-Americanism." In *Transnationalism: Canada–United States History into the Twentieth Century*, edited by Michael D. Behiels and Reginald C. Stuart, 69–85. Montreal: McGill-Queen's University Press, 2010.

MacSkimming, Roy. *Cold War: The Amazing Canada-Soviet Hockey Series of 1972*. Vancouver, BC: Greystone, 1996.

Mahovlich, Ted. *The Big M: The Frank Mahovlich Story*. Toronto: HarperCollins, 1999.

McKinley, Michael. *Hockey: A People's History*. Toronto: McClelland & Stewart, 2006.

"1972: 'Henderson has scored for Canada.'" *Weekend*. TV. Hosted by Jim Eayrs and Charlotte Gobeil. Toronto: CBC, September 28, 1972. http://www.cbc.ca/archives/categories/sports/hockey/canada-soviet-hockey-series-1972/henderson-has-scored-for-canada.html (accessed June 8, 2013).

Robidoux, Michael A. "Imagining a Canadian Identity through Sport: A Historical Interpretation of Lacrosse and Hockey." *Journal of American Folklore* 115, no. 456 (Spring 2002): 209–25.

Ross, J. Andrew. "The National Hockey League as Agent of Globalization." Paper presented at the Sport & Globalization conference, Toronto, ON, June 4, 2011.

———. "Hockey Capital: Commerce Culture and the National Hockey League, 1917–1967." Ph.D. diss., University of Western Ontario, 2008.

Sinden, Harry. *Hockey Showdown: The Canada-Russia Hockey Series*. Toronto: Doubleday Canada, 1972.

Versluis, Arthur. "Antimodernism." *Telos* (Winter 2006): 96–130.

The
Series
in the
World

Les Russes et Nous: The 1972 Summit Series and the Birth of Hockey Sovereignty in Quebec

♦

ANDREW C. HOLMAN

"It is easy, sitting in a comfortable chair in front of a colour television screen, drink in hand, to say that the Russians are 'more fit,' more numerous and therefore beneficiaries of a better choice of players, or…that they are 'robots,'" letter writer Dominike Brunelle wrote to the Montreal newspaper *La Presse* on September 10, 1972, two days after Team Canada was beaten handily by the Soviet Union 5–3 in Vancouver's game four. That game had completed the Canadian leg of the Summit Series and a shocking reversal of Canadian expectations. Even before Team Canada stepped on Moscow ice, they trailed the USSR in games 2–1–1. Brunelle's missive was one among the many mid-series attempts by Canadians to make sense of the unfathomable. Her assessment was searching, blunt and uncommon. Don't look at the Soviet team, or the individual Canadian players for answers: we are to blame.

> The system in which we evolve here is destitute of discipline.… We have no tradition – a young and proud country, we want to excel at a game or a series, but we do very little between these meetings. We can't believe that a violent effort and a will to win will be enough to gain victory. Good, steady work, over a long period, will be the key.… Our system is flawed because it does not encourage young people to acquire the necessary skills to achieve strength in any area whatsoever, but our state of mind is most responsible. Very proud, like a rooster, we peck the feathers that we are losing or have lost.[1] (Brunelle)

For Brunelle, the simple apologia to which both the anglophone and francophone media were resorting were naïve. Team Canada was failing for reasons larger than a deficit of physical fitness, poor coaching decisions, professional hubris or the Americanization of Canada's game.[2] Team Canada, with all its flaws, was Canada writ *sport*, and the adversity the team faced in the Summit Series posed a unique opportunity to equate hockey with the challenge of national identity. What is more, for her, the lesson was just as important for Quebecers, whose Quiet Revolution had since 1960 spawned a passionate debate about the future of the Québécois nation and the prospects for Quebec as a sovereign state. Team Canada's woes were Quebec's woes, too. "Separate us, we the Québécois? From whom?... And what would we do with our freedom, we who have so much already and who don't know how to use it well? It is easy to always find a reason for our weakness, to blame others. But who are we to never be able to accept responsibility for our failures?" (Brunelle)

The 1972 Summit Series has long been lauded in English Canada as a moment when Canadians' sense of themselves became crystallized in positive fellow feeling. The dramatic come-from-behind finish in Moscow to that eight-game series confirmed for much of the country that national unity was possible and that, in *their* sport, Canada was still best. But in Quebec, where the Quiet Revolution had achieved full momentum, the meaning of the series was (and is) more complex. The *Série du siècle* took place in a charged political environment, happening, as it did, on the heels of the formation of the separatist Parti Québécois (PQ) in 1968, the October Crisis of 1970, the failed constitutional process involving the Victoria Charter (1971) and a provincial election (1970) that saw the PQ established as a permanent force. Moreover, the series happened in the heat and midst of a federal election campaign in which incumbent Liberal Prime Minister Pierre Elliott Trudeau was pushed in Quebec to paint his multicultural vision of federalism against the backdrop of national alternatives: the *deux nations* concept of federalism and outright separatism. Across Canada, Team Canada's fortunes on the ice spurred larger questions about Canadian character. But in Quebec it drew into high relief ongoing discussions about Québécois identities and the national future.

The Quebec aspect of the Summit Series offers an important and missing chapter to this national sport story, one that arguably is still taking shape. This

chapter traces the historical context of the Série du siècle and examines its resonance in Quebec during September 1972. Most important, it speculates about
the effects that the Summit Series had on hockey as national expression in that
province. The Série du siècle in Quebec is an event best assessed in the *longue
durée*. The 1972 Summit Series helped grow the seed of sport sovereignty and
the ongoing pursuit of a Quebec national team.

Hockey and French-Canadian Identities before the Summit Series

Until recently, there was precious little scholarly research on hockey
and its importance in Quebec's history, though a great deal of popular discourse (in journalism, fiction and film) has flourished. Much of it, including
Roch Carrier's long-lauded short story *The Hockey Sweater* maintains a common theme: hockey was a source of strength and unity for French-speaking
Québécois. For much of the twentieth century, the game was also a salvation,
a place where members of a francophone underclass could express their identity as a distinct nation within a nation. If they couldn't "win" in their daily
material struggles in the anglophone-dominated economic world, they could
win (symbolically, at least) on the ice. French-Canadian teams (and especially the Maurice Richard–led Montreal Canadiens of the 1940s and '50s, and
Jean Béliveau's "firewagon" Canadiens teams of the 1960s) were the standard
bearers of the embattled Québécois nation, and hockey a lightning rod for
national expression (Melançon, 189–97). This narrative has become orthodoxy.
It continues to ring true today, though, as Quebec sport scholar Jean Harvey
and others have argued correctly, less loudly since the 1980s, when globalization, a decline in francophone players and coaches, competition from a second
National Hockey League franchise in the province (Quebec Nordiques) and,
for a spell, an American owner conspired to make the Canadiens seem less
iconic than ever (Harvey, "Whose Sweater Is This?," 39–49 ; see also Gitersos
69–81; Laurin-Lamothe and Moreau 7–12).

But this monolithic view papers over a more complex reality. Hockey
in Quebec has always been contested terrain *within* Quebec, among French
Canadians for whom the sport meant different things. Hockey was always
politicized. Even during the hegemonic mid-century heyday of the Canadiens,

the game's real worth was pointedly challenged. In the 1950s and '60s, the popular reverence of the game concerned an increasingly vocal francophone intelligentsia who saw the popular enthusiasm for hockey as an embarrassing parochialism, an impediment to modernization in a province seemingly slow to enter the twentieth century. This emergent, self-conscious middle class, many of whom were educated in Europe in the 1930s and '40s, saw themselves, as intellectual Claude Ryan wrote in 1951, as the "spiritual guardian" of Quebec's distinctive national culture (quoted in Gauvreau, 70). They were willing a modern Quebec into existence and despaired of their countrymen's rusticity, their lowbrowism. In progressive journals such as *L'Action nationale* and *Cité Libre*, Quebec's intellectuals cast hockey as a reflection of the society's political infantilism and a faulty vessel for carrying a new, elevated, modern national spirit. "A society that finds the food of its national pride in the exploits of a hockey player," Jean-Marc Léger argued in *L'Action nationale* in 1956, "is a society governed by a mentality of abdication" (70–71).[3] In a 1962 *Cité Libre* editorial, renowned essayist Jacques Godbout despaired of his countrymen who "satisfy their pride...with parish bingos [and] hockey heroes" (22). And just as troubling for these elites was the lexicon of hockey: an anything-goes repository where proper French terms were routinely anglicized and *joual* passed unchecked (Poisson). To some Quebec intellectuals before the Quiet Revolution, hockey embodied much of what was objectionable in their own national culture.

But even more hotly debated among Quebecers was the question of power: who controlled the game of hockey. In much of Quebec until the 1940s, hockey was rejected by francophone Catholic clergy, the powerful arbiters of traditional French-Canadian culture. They saw in a sport created by anglo-elite Protestant Montrealers and wildly embraced by English Canadians, a danger for the assimilation and contamination of francophone youth, as well as risk to Catholic morality and proper attitudes toward bodily modesty (Harvey, "Sport and the Quebec Clergy," 73–75). By the end of World War II, leading Quebec clergymen began to reverse their stance on the matter and champion the playing of hockey (and other sports) by the French-Canadian masses as an antidote to sloth and a way to both develop useful skills and honour God. Church-run *oeuvres des terrains de jeux* (playground works) were the places where generations of francophone children first learned sports such as hockey (Harvey, "Sport and the Quebec Clergy," 81–82). In the shadow of the Church, administered by parish priests, hockey for mid-twentieth-century francophone youths had become a performance of national culture. And yet, that construction was short-lived. After 1960, when the election of the Jean Lesage Liberals ushered into power new, modern values of statism and secularization, the organization of hockey in the province was affected, too. In time, youth sport became secularized. Recreational and minor hockey, first rejected then embraced by the Church, was now co-opted by laymen who wrested control of it away from church organizations and reorganized it new civic organizations, most notably the Association de Hockey Mineur du Québec (AHMQ). Founded in Trois-Rivières in 1968, the AHMQ used the collective power of its membership to relocate youth hockey organization from church affiliation to town and neighbourhood communities.

By the late 1960s, the identity politics in Quebec hockey had taken a new direction. No longer was it a question of whether the sport was a useful vessel for the expression of Québécois identity; that debate had been won. Now, the question was how to cement control of it for the benefit of the province's majority francophones. In the years immediately prior to the Série du siècle, that debate focused on the Quebec Amateur Hockey Association (QAHA), the governing body of the province's elite, adult amateur hockey organizations (senior, intermediate and junior levels). Founded in 1919 by Westmount elites and McGill old boys at the Montreal Amateur Athletic Association, the QAHA suffered from the image that it served first the interests of Quebec's anglophones. It was, after all, a regional branch of the Canadian Amateur Hockey Association and, though it had had several French-Canadian presidents in its long history, the Montreal-heavy QAHA board and membership had always overrepresented the province's English-speaking community. "The QAHA," one 1972 report to the federal commission on bilingualism and biculturalism noted bluntly, "was an anglophone agency in which francophones had no power" (quoted in Harvey, "Sport and the Quebec Clergy," 85). Relenting to popular pressure, it translated its name in 1969, becoming the Association du Hockey Amateur du Québec (AHAQ) (Prince, "Sur la route," 5). Soon after the AHMQ began operations in 1968, it began to butt heads with the

QAHA/AHAQ over jurisdiction and, especially, player transfers. Eventually, a mediator recommended the fusion of the organizations to create one governing council and dissolve constituent interests. Though the first attempt at fusion (1973–74) failed, a second one in 1976, encouraged by the Quebec state, succeeded. On June 2, 1976, representatives from the AHMQ, the old AHAQ and the Quebec ministry of Youth, Leisure and Sport brought into being the Fédération québécoise de hockey sur glace (FQHG) (Prince, "La naissance," 1).[4] In all of this transaction, one fact was plain: by the mid 1970s, French had become the language of hockey administration in the province, and the FQHG (and its immediate antecedents) a symbol of Québécois control. Even by the time the Summit Series arrived in September 1972, hockey had served, in many ways, as a proxy for a much larger discussion in Quebec: who we are and how to become *maîtres chez nous*.

The Série du siècle in Quebec

The Summit Series commanded the attention of Quebecers in September 1972, much as it did in the rest of Canada. As Simon Richard observes in his 2002 chronicle *La Série du siècle*, a study based largely on francophone media coverage of the series, Quebecers were enthralled. All eight games were broadcast on television in French, on Radio-Canada, through the "magnificent voice and judicious commentary" of respected veteran *Soirée du hockey* play-by-play announcer René Lecavalier (Richard, 32). The French station Radiomutuel carried the radio broadcast of each of the series' games to francophone homes in Quebec, featuring the voice of broadcaster Jacques Moreau (Richard, 80). Newspaper coverage of the series in Quebec was impressively extensive. Part of this had to with the fact that the series opened in Montreal, which hosted the pre-series social activities and much of the pre-game-one hype. Coverage of the Montreal leg of the series was front-page and multi-page news in many Quebec newspapers. However, Quebec newspapers sustained their interest in the Canada-Russia games throughout the series. Montreal's *Le Devoir*, Trois-Rivières's *Le Bien Public* and Quebec City's *Le Soleil*, for example, each combined Canadian Press wire stories with local commentaries as the series progressed. Several Quebec organs, such as *Montréal-Matin*, sent their own reporters to all eight games. At home, newspapers featured editorials railing about Team Canada's weaknesses as well as individual spotlights on francophone stars such Serge Savard, Yvan Cournoyer, Guy Lapointe and Jean Ratelle. Moreover, adding to the attention that this "sport-spectacle" had already drawn were voices and views of hockey greats Maurice Richard, whose reactions were sought throughout the Series, and Jean Béliveau, who travelled with Team Canada across Canada and to Moscow. All this coverage, it seems, fed Quebecers' attention to and curiosity about this novel sports engagement, a following that didn't wane even after Team Canada fared unexpectedly poorly in the first four games. As writer Jack Ludwig recalled, among the most vocal and enthusiastic of Canadian fans who accompanied Team Canada to Moscow was a contingent of French Canadians (Ludwig, 91, 121).

Quebecers were four-square behind their Team Canada. "I remember well the Summit Series," former NHLer and francophone rights advocate Bob Sirois recalled recently. "To my knowledge, all the Quebec nation supported Team Canada, the same as I did."[5] Naturally so, perhaps. As in English Canada, the Quebec press framed the series as a consequential event with Cold War meaning. The Russians were the unknowable others, symbols of a loathsome enemy regime. The Quebec press "scrutinized them as if they were Martians," Richard writes, noting every detail of difference (Richard, 67; Thibault, "Des Russes"; Boivin-Chouinard, 230). Before the series began, Quebec sportswriters were wholly in agreement with the members of the English-Canadian press who predicted Team Canada's domination in the series. After seeing the Russians practise, Pierre Gobeil of *Montréal-Matin* revised his initial prediction of six wins for Canada to seven in an article headlined, "They came here to learn, they'll learn" (Richard, 82). Moreover, French-Canadian players had prominent positions on this team, making it French Canada's team as well. Nine of the thirty-five Team Canada players (about twenty-six per cent) were francophone Quebecers: Jocelyn Guèvremont, Guy Lapointe, Serge Savard, Yvan Cournoyer, Marcel Dionne, Rod Gilbert, Richard Martin, Gilbert Perreault and Jean Ratelle.[6]

The support of Team Canada among the francophone press wavered only briefly during the series, caused (as it was in English Canada) most sharply by the discomfort that resulted from Canadian players' use of violence and intimidation tactics. In the wake of the team's violent mid-series exhibition games in Sweden, Pierre Gobeil declared, "I was ashamed to be Canadian," a statement that was echoed almost word for word by Michel Blanchard in *La Presse* and Red Fisher in the *Montreal Star* (Richard, 167–68).[7] Predictably, perhaps, defenders of Team Canada's play quickly responded in the francophone press. In Montreal's *La Patrie*, *joualiste* Tit-clin replied: "Me, I'm ashamed of the journalists" (Tit-clin, "Moe, j'ai honte"). Moreover, when four of the team's members returned to Canada from Europe at the start of the Russian leg of the series complaining of a lack of playing time and desiring to start training with their respective NHL teams for the coming season, Quebec newspapers had little sympathy for them. *La Patrie* called them *"nos quatres bébés"* ["our four babies"] (Tit-clin, "Nos"). Significantly, three of the four returnees – Guèvremont, Martin and Perreault – were francophone Québécois.[8] Beating the Soviets seemed to make everyone feel Canadian, even, one mischievous *La Presse* cartoon held, PQ Leader Lévesque, whom it depicted jumping for joy in front of a television set, cigarette in mouth , shouting *"Vive les Canadiens!"* (Richard, 262). Team Canada's violent and tumultuous march to victory, winning three games and losing one on Moscow ice and narrowly capturing the Series 4–3–1, seemed a vindication for Quebec sportswriters and hockey fans who had placed their faith in the team. A triumphalism, not wholly warranted, coloured the end-of-series summaries in several Quebec newspapers. "The Russians wanted to learn," wrote *La Patrie*'s Maurice Brodeur, "and they learned!" (Brodeur).

Toward a *Série du siècle québécoise*

Gauging precisely the effects of the Série du siècle on Quebecers is a difficult task. Much as in English Canada, the media in Quebec referred variously to the lessons that the confrontation with the Russians offered. In many ways, their purported lessons echoed those of their English-Canadian counterparts. Francophone sportswriters harped upon the need for better fitness for elite players, and the need to rethink the way Canadians conceive and play the game. They engaged, too, post-series, in what seems in hindsight to be unseemly reveling: Team Canada had won after all, and Quebec sportswriters could not help but interpret the victory as confirmation of the worth of capitalism, "freedom" and the Canadian way of life. "We say that if the players of Hockey Canada learned anything," journalist Maurice Huot wrote in Trois-Rivières's *Le Bien Public*, "the Russians also learned it; they learned that in America, individual liberty counts for something and the people can express themselves without always fearing repression" (Huot, "Ne sautons pas"). Views (such as those of Dominike Brunelle) that called for reflection on Quebecers' own *mode de vivre* were rare and were lost in the immediate busyness of the beginning of a new professional hockey season and the continued politics of the 1972 election.

One other effect was obvious. The experience of the series whetted Canadians' (and Quebecers') appetite for more international play. "[I]n the immediate aftermath of the monumental Summit Series," Todd Denault writes in *The Greatest Game*, "there was an overwhelming clamour from Canadian hockey fans for more clashes featuring NHL professionals on the international stage" (173). Their wishes came true. In the short term, it wasn't NHL professionals who took centre stage, but their professional rivals, a Team Canada made up of World Hockey Association all-stars. In that 1974 series, the eight-game format was replicated featuring WHA all-stars, with game one played in Quebec City. Outcome notwithstanding (the Soviets dominated the WHA-version Team Canada by 4–1–3), the international spectacle captivated Canadian fans through national television broadcasts of each game. Following up on their popularity, selected NHL clubs staged a "Super Series" in December and January 1975–76, hosting top Soviet club teams the Central Red Army and the Soviet Wings. The series included a memorable New Years' Eve contest in Montreal between the Canadiens and the Red Army, a 3–3 tie that demonstrated the very best talents of Canadian and Russian styles of play (Denault, 233–60). The shadow of the 1972 series had grown long and wide.

In Quebec, imperceptibly at first, the Summit Series accelerated another train already in motion. The Série du siècle had shaped a new context, a new arena and new possibilities for those in Quebec who implicated hockey in the search for Québécois national affirmation. The Summit Series opened international hockey's potential as a "sport-spectacle" (Genest, 182), a vehicle for the expression of an international personality for Quebecers. The effect could not have been lost on ordinary Quebecers, who were experiencing a convergence of influences that pointed in a common direction. First, by the mid 1970s, the nationalization (that is, secularization and *francisation*) of youth and amateur hockey in the province was complete. At the same time, the traditional mantle (*"portée politique"*) of the Montreal Canadiens as a national vessel of Quebecers had become compromised, challenged by the rise of the WHA's Quebec Nordiques (1972–79), whose colours, logo and discourse openly carried a separatist message, and haunted by the popular impression that the Canadiens' establishment was firmly federalist. In short, the political terrain in Quebec had become too fractured by the mid 1970s for the Canadiens alone to capture that symbolism. Underlying all of this change was the unsubtle push by the Quebec government to promote and expand an international personality of its own, one separate and distinct from that of Canada. Acting upon a doctrine first asserted in 1965 by Education Minister Paul Gérin-Lajoie, by the mid 1970s Quebec had signed international education and cultural agreements (that is, within the province's constitutionally assigned areas of jurisdiction) with foreign nations and had established its own delegations in several foreign capitals and commercially important cities (Meren, 145–63). By the mid 1970s, a new confidence had emerged among Québécois. A new system for governing hockey in the province, a sharpened sensibility to the need for a better, less subordinate relationship with Canada (and a willingness to advocate for it), and an already growing paradiplomatic presence for Quebec beyond Canada flowed logically together. The idea of a national hockey team for Quebec, eligible and engaged in international play, sprang logically from the circumstances and events – the moment – of the 1972 Summit Series.

In June 1976, Quebec City lawyer and founding member of the Parti Québécois, Guy Bertrand, openly posed this novel idea: *une équipe nationale québécoise*. To advocate for it, he created the Comité Équipe-Québec, for which he was spokesman. No stranger to sport (he was a varsity basketballer at McGill and served as agent for a handful of Québécois pro hockey players in the 1970s), Bertrand was well connected politically. When René Lévesque's separatist PQ government took office after its surprise November 1976 electoral victory, the new government's minister for sport, Lucien Lessard, approved Bertrand's project and mandated him to meet with international sport federations on the matter. In 1977, Bertrand presented a memorandum to the Government of

Canada's Parliamentary Committee on International Hockey, formally proposing the formal creation of a Team Quebec for elite international tournaments, much as Scotland, England or Wales, separate nations within the United Kingdom, had competed abroad in their own rights (in soccer and rugby) internationally for decades (Bertrand). But Parliament demurred, influenced perhaps by the intransigence of Hockey Canada (successor to the CAHA as amateur hockey's governing body in Canada), raw feelings in English Canada, and the daunting task of seeking International Ice Hockey Federation (IIHF) approval. Moreover, few outside of Quebec could separate the hockey proposal from the push for political independence in Quebec.[9]

But the Lévesque Government's referendum on political sovereignty in 1980 failed. Quebecers weren't ready for out-and-out independence. In 1981, Bertrand floated the national team concept once again, buoyed, ironically, by the logic that followed the failed referendum. Perhaps, some believed, outright sovereignty isn't required for national affirmation among Québécois; they could find that elusive feeling in measures short of independence, such as a national hockey team. In 1981, Bertrand resurrected the Comité, recruited sports celebrities (including Guy Lafleur) to the cause, secured the support of the FQHG and the provincial government, and published a manifesto in *La Presse* (Béliveau; "Équipe-Québec"; "Le FQHG"; "Guy Lafleur"; Tremblay). The concept of a Quebec national team garnered significant media attention in the summer and fall. However, this campaign, well-conceived and better organized than the first iteration in 1976, also fizzled. But it hasn't died, and periodically since then new life has been breathed into the idea. When NHL teams were accused of discrimination against francophone players in 1986, and when Canada's World Junior team selection was alleged to have slighted French-Canadian talent in the 2000s, an independent Équipe-Québec was proposed as the only satisfactory solution to the problem (Robillard; Sirois, 206, 208).

In 2006, prompted by Canadian Prime Minister Stephen Harper's statement in Parliament that Quebec forms "a nation within a united Canada," Bertrand revived the Équipe-Québec campaign once more. With the 2008 IIHF World Tournament in Quebec City approaching, Bertrand addressed the prime minister in an op-ed piece in *Le Devoir*: "Here is a great occasion for you to put into practice what you believe" ("Une nation"). In Fall 2006, Bertrand hired a Quebec polling firm – Léger Marketing – to plumb Quebecers' views on the matter, and the results were impressive: seventy-two per cent of those polled supported the idea of a Team Quebec in the 2008 World Tournament. But as with earlier attempts, the notion of a Team Quebec separate from (and potentially competing against) Team Canada in IIHF competitions continues to rankle and confuse. Does Quebec, like every other entry in the IIHF tournament, have to work its way up the ranks into the elite division? Does it need the consent of Hockey Canada? Would elite Quebec hockey players, given the chance, choose to play for Quebec and not for Canada? In the end, there was no Team Quebec entered into the 2008 World Tournament in Quebec City, an outcome that did not sit well with many hockey-mad Quebecers. Today, the issue remains alive and unresolved, but its prospects are good. In August 2010, Hockey Canada authorized the creation of a Team Quebec to host and play in a tournament against national teams from France, Italy and Switzerland in August 2011. In the end, the vaunted 2011 Coupe Québec hockey tournament never came to pass; plans foundered when the Swiss national team declined the invitation (Hamilton). But the idea won't die. In summer 2013, Parti Québecois Premier Pauline Marois declared her interest seeing the Équipe-Québec project come to fruition, and appointed a two-person commission (one of whom is Bob Sirois) to prepare a feasibility study (King).[10]

Whatever its outcome and whatever its merits, the quest for a Quebec national hockey team, formed to play in international tournaments, is not a capricious endeavour. It is, rather, the product of a long train of events, motored and steered by many influences, among them the complex politics of Québécois national affirmation, the cult of personalities and the desire to control the administration of hockey within the province of Quebec. What is more, the thumbprint of the Summit Series, the series that first staged and gave trajectory to international hockey in North America as a meaningful "sport-spectacle," is discernible. "A Team Quebec would bring about a strong collective sense of identity...part of a concrete national affirmation," CEGEP Vieux-Montréal philosopher Tony Patoine wrote in 2009. "It would symbolize by its 20 players a...Québécois 'us,' who, on a given night, could cross swords with the Canadian 'us' in a duel that would stir at least as many passions as the clashes with the U.S.S.R. in 1972" (23).

That hockey is a part of the national fibre in Canada, one of many cords that tie together a country in search of unity, is a truism that requires little in the way of evidentiary exploration. It *feels* true. Canadians believe that hockey has the potential to heal its fissures, those that have dominated Canadian identity politics since before Confederation. Hockey, we are told, was and is the crucible for nation and the vehicle for reconciliation. In recent months, the fortieth anniversary of the Summit Series has again pushed this myth, reinforcing the notion that, for one month, in September 1972, Canadians dissolved their political differences and channelled their aspirations into a common cause. The myth of the Summit Series is evidence, for many, of the potential for a promising, unified future for Canada. That may explain why Canadians return to it, again and again, to revere a seminal national moment and reengage an unshakeable collective memory.

There is some irony, then, in what this essay suggests. In Quebec, the Summit Series, a powerful vehicle for national unity, contained, too, the seeds of dissent, a contradiction and potential food for the contest of two nationalisms that prevailed (and prevail) in Canada. The Série du siècle succeeded, and perhaps too well. The Summit Series informed unanticipated versions of national feeling in Quebec and affirmed the use of sport as means for national identity building at home and an international personality abroad. That is a legacy worth considering, and one that is still playing out before us.

---

[1] All quotations from French-language sources have been translated into English by the author.

[2] These avenues of explanation are explored in LaPlante; Ludwig, 84–85; Dryden; and Richard.

[3] The player who Léger had in mind, undoubtedly, was Richard, a reluctant working-class hero – a "busher" in mid-century parlance – whose unpolished demeanour was hardly the sort of exemplary character, intellectuals held, that was needed for a modernizing Quebec. Richard is "not...exactly what one can call a 'prototype' of French civilization, delicacy and subtlety," one *Cité Libre* columnist offered in 1958 (Cléobule, 44).

[4] The FQHG changed its name to Hockey Québec in 1996. In the 1973 attempt at fusion, the united body became known as the Fédération de hockey sur glace du Québec (FHGQ). When it split, in 1974, the half of the organization constituted by old AHAQ members retained the name FHGQ – section majeure (Prince, "Sur la route," 5).

[5] Personal communication with the author, August 22, 2013. Author's translation. At the end of the series, Quebec Premier Robert Bourassa telegrammed Team Canada: "[y]our teamwork and your determination to win has earned you the admiration of Quebeckers and all Canadians" (Quoted in Earle, 123).

[6] Three others, Ken Dryden, Frank Mahovlich and Peter Mahovlich, wore the Montreal Canadiens uniforms. Jean-Paul Parise was a Franco-Ontarian. The francophone press echoed the criticism offered in English-Canadian papers that only NHL players were selected for Team Canada. The exclusion of World Hockey Association (WHA) players meant that not only would superstar Bobby Hull not appear for their national team but also neither would Quebec Junior and NHL star Jean-Claude Tremblay, who had recently contracted to play with the WHA's Quebec Nordiques (Richard, 54–55).

[7] The widely repeated condemnation even reached the ears of a depressed Ken Dryden; see Dryden, 108.

[8] The fourth was Anglo-Canadian and New York Ranger Vic Hadfield.

[9] Bertrand openly and ardently campaigned for the yes side in the referendum vote, organizing sixty prominent athletes and sportsmen into a *Comité des athlètes pour le "Oui"* as requested by Premier Lévesque (Bertrand).

[10] The other co-author is André Matteau. The study (formally titled the *Rapport Sirois-Matteau*) is being financed by the Quebec government's Ministère de l'Éducation, du Loisir et du Sport and has been submitted to the non-profit separatist advocacy body the Conseil de la Souveraineté du Québec. At the time of writing, the full report has not yet been published.

Works Cited

Béliveau, François. "Le ministre Lessard s'intéresse à une Équipe-Québec." *La Presse*, September 25, 1981.

Bertrand, Guy. "Implications dans le Sport." Guy Bertrand Avocats. http://www.guybertrandavocats.com/implication-dans-le-sport (accessed August 27, 2013).

Boivin-Chouinard, Mathieu. *Chaïbou! Histoire du Hockey Russe 1. Des origins à la série du siècle*. Longueuil, QC: Les éditions Kéruss, 2011.

Brodeur, Maurice. "Les Russes voulaient apprendre et…ils ont appris!" *La Patrie*, September 28, 1972.

Brunelle, Dominike. "Les fautes aux russes." *Le Devoir*, September 10, 1972.

Cléobule. "Le dangereux tricolore." *Cité Libre* 19 (January 1958): 44.

Denault, Todd. *The Greatest Game: The Montreal Canadiens, the Red Army, and the Night that Saved Hockey*. Toronto: McClelland & Stewart, 2011.

Dryden, Ken. *Face-Off at the Summit*. With Mark Mulvoy. Boston: Little, Brown, 1973.

Earle, Neil. "Hockey as Canadian Popular Culture: Team Canada, 1972, Television and the Canadian Identity." *Journal of Canadian Studies* 30, no. 2 (1995): 107–23.

"Équipe-Qucbec est lancée!" *La Presse*, August 19, 1981.

"Le FQHG endosse Équipe-Québec" *La Presse*, October 2, 1981.

Gauvreau, Michael. *The Catholic Origins of Quebec's Quiet Revolution, 1931–1970*. Montreal: McGill-Queen's University Press, 2005.

Genest, Simon. "Le Canada et l'internationalisation du hockey sur glace." In *La Culture du Sport au Québec*, edited by J-P Augustin and C. Sorbets, 179–86. Talence, France: Éditions de la maison des Sciences de l'Homme d'Aquitaine, 1996.

Gitersos, Terry Vaios. "'Les frogs sont menacés': Media Representations of the Nordiques and Canadiens, 1979–1981." *Sport History Review* 40 (2009): 69–81.

Godbout, Jacques. "Pour se Déniaiser." *Cité Libre* 41 (November 1961): 22–23.

"Guy Lafleur donne un coup de pouce." *La Presse*, July 30, 1981.

Hamilton, Graeme. "Others Nations Pass on Challenge from Quebec-Only Hockey Team." *National Post*, March 9, 2011.

Harvey, Jean. "Sport and the Quebec Clergy, 1930–1960." In *Not Just a Game: Essays in Canadian Sport Sociology*, edited by Jean Harvey and Hart Cantelon, 69–87. Ottawa: University of Ottawa Press, 1988.

———. "Whose Sweater Is This? The Changing Meanings of Hockey in Quebec." In *Artificial Ice: Hockey, Culture, and Commerce*, edited by D. Whitson and R. Gruneau, 29–52. Scarborough, ON: Broadview/Garamond, 2006.

Huot, Maurice. "Ne sautons pas trop vite aux conclusions." *Le Bien Public* (Trois-Rivières, QC), October 6, 1972.

King, Ronald. "Équipe Québec: l'idée fait son chemin." *La Presse*, June 20, 2013.

LaPlante, Laurent. "Le crépuscule des idoles." *Le Devoir*, September 11, 1972.

Laurin-Lamothe, Audrey, and Nicolas Moreau, eds. *Le Canadien de Montréal: Une légende repensée*. Montreal: Les presses de l'Université de Montréal, 2011.

Léger, Jean-Marc. "Pour sortir des chemins de la résignation et de la servitude." *L'Action nationale* 46, no. 1 (September 1956): 70–71.

Ludwig, Jack. *Hockey Night in Moscow*. Toronto: McClelland & Stewart, 1972.

Melançon, Benoît. *The Rocket: A Cultural History of Maurice Richard*. Vancouver, BC: Greystone, 2009.

Meren, David. *With Friends Like These: Entangled Nationalism and the Canada-Quebec-France Triangle, 1944–1970*. Vancouver, BC: University of British Columbia Press, 2012.

Patoine, Tony. "'On est Canayen ou ben on l'est pas': Hockey, nationalism et identités au Québec et au Canada." In *La Vraie Dureté du Mental: Hockey et philosophie*, edited by Normand Baillargeon and Christian Boissinot, 9–25. Quebec, QC: Les Presses de l'Université Laval.

Poisson, Jacques. "La soirée du Hockey." *L'Action nationale* 51, no. 8. (April 1962): 721–24.

Prince, Raymond. "Prologue. Sur la route de la Fédération québécoise de hockey sur glace." Unpublished articles on Hockey Québec provided to author by Sylvain B. Lalonde, directeur général, Hockey Québec, October 2011. Microsoft Word file.

————. "La naissance." Unpublished articles on Hockey Québec provided to author by Sylvain B. Lalonde, directeur général, Hockey Québec, October 2011. Microsoft Word file.

Richard, Simon. *La série du siècle: Septembre 1972.* Montreal: Les Éditions Hurtubise, 2002.

Robillard, Guy. "La LNH néglige les talents francophones. L'idée d'une équipe québécoise internationale refait surface." *La Presse*, August 8, 1986.

Sirois, Bob. *Discrimination in the NHL: Quebec Hockey Players Sidelined.* Montreal: Baraka, 2010.

Thibault, Marc. "Des Russes qui, avant de chausser leurs patins, jouent à la souris." *Le Devoir*, September 1, 1972.

Tit-clin. "Moe, j'ai honte des journalisses [*sic*]." *La Patrie*, September 21, 1972.

Tit-clin. "Nos quatres bébés." *La Patrie*, September 28, 1972.

Tremblay, Réjean. "Le projet d'Équipe-Québec: Bertrand s'est bien repris." *La Presse*, August 10, 1981.

"Une nation, un club de hockey, dit Guy Bertrand." *Le Devoir*, November 28, 2006. http://www.ledevoir.com/politique/canada/123736/une-nation-un-club-de-hockey-dit-guy-bertrand.

Lions in Winter:
The Summit Series, Professionalism and the Renewal of Hockey in 1970s Britain

♦

DARYL LEEWORTHY

> When Paul Henderson scored the winning goal with thirty-four seconds left in the final game, thus propelling Canada to victory, the result was an outpouring of national feeling that reminded us what hockey meant to us Canadians.... From that time on, professional hockey was on the ascendancy, not just at home but around the world. (Howell, 77)

These words, by the historian Colin Howell, encapsulate the drama and subsequent outpouring of victorious emotion that accompanied the challenge series of September 1972. It was a defining "Where were you when...?" moment for an entire generation of hockey fans – matched, perhaps, for those in their teens and twenties, by Sidney Crosby's remarkable overtime goal in the 2010 Winter Olympics in Vancouver. In both instances, the glory of victory came to be seen as a restoration of Canadian dominance over the world of hockey and a return to the natural order of things. And like most where-were-you-when moments, it's easy to imagine that ripples thundered across the globe, even in countries where ignorance rather than jubilation reigned. In Britain, for example, most people were unaware of what was going on in September 1972. Aside from some perfunctory records of the final scores printed in the national daily newspapers such as the *Times*, the *Daily Mirror* and the *Guardian*, the series passed by unnoticed. Ironically, the series might not have been visible to Canadians but for British technicians, whose role in converting and relaying the notoriously unreliable signal from the arena in Moscow to Halifax was essential in ensuring that events were able to be beamed, by the CBC, to expectant hockey fans across Canada.

The absence of British interest in the Summit Series – or the "Eight-Match Series," as it was known in the dry tones used by domestic journalists – might be expected. After all, Britain was not widely considered a hockey-playing nation. Yet, just a few months before, Britons could settle down in front of their television sets and watch the Stanley Cup final featuring the Boston Bruins and the New York Rangers; they could see, too, the World Championships from Prague and the Olympic hockey tournament from Sapporo in Japan at the beginning of 1972. Indeed, just a year after the Summit Series, the editor of the BBC's flagship Saturday afternoon sports program, *Grandstand*, was able to remark in an interview with the *Guardian* that "we decided to treat ice hockey as a major sport and it paid off" ("Paving Way"). Over the course of the 1970s, as a result, television audiences in Britain were treated to the Stanley Cup, the Winter Olympics, regular NHL matches and the World Championships – notably the Canada versus USSR game on April 24, 1977, that marked both Canada's return to international competition and the inaugural use of professionals in international competition. Only the Summit Series, it seems, escaped the schedules.

It would, however, be wrong to suggest that the consequences of the Summit Series did not register in Britain. Indeed, the immediate aftermath of Canada's Pyrrhic victory in Moscow in September 1972 can be read as a turning point, with British hockey drawn increasingly into the shifting dimensions of the international game. Alongside professionalism and big-time capital came questions about new styles of play, violence, the emergence of powerful, non-North American (particularly non-Canadian) alternatives in the sport, and a materialist-consumerist attitude amongst hockey fans themselves. They were all to weigh heavily on the fortunes of the London Lions, Britain's first NHL-style franchise hockey club, which was formed in 1973 by the owner of the Detroit Red Wings, Bruce Norris. Norris, together with his allies, envisaged a professional European League affiliated to the NHL with clubs established in each of the major capitals and the prospect of a Europe versus North America summit match at the end of each season ("Big Bruce"). Whilst this dream floundered, the London Lions skated their way across much of Europe, playing seventy-two games against teams from Austria, Czechoslovakia, Finland, the Netherlands, Sweden and, of course, the Soviet Union. They won fifty-two of them.

This chapter seeks to recover something of the forgotten history of British hockey in the 1970s and to follow the themes of the Summit Series as they impacted the sport's development in what was, at that time, an amateur backwater. Given the absence of scholarship on British hockey, this chapter is equally an attempt to contextualize the sport by setting it alongside international events with the goal of understanding why hockey took off again in the 1970s and 1980s and why the gaze of British television cameras came to be fixed on the NHL, Team Canada and their great rivals, the USSR. It begins with a brief overview of British hockey's development prior to the Summit Series, since what occurred in the early 1970s was not divorced from an earlier "golden age" of British hockey, with its Olympic triumphs, national leagues and loyal fan base, and then moves to consider what happened to the game after the showdown of September 1972. What follows argues, in essence, that the Summit Series, which encouraged – forced, even – greater engagement with the hockey-playing cultures of Britain and Europe, eventually enabled those living on a rainy island in the Atlantic to see and to understand the great spectacle of pro hockey in their own backyard.

Building the Game

Hockey has a long history in the British Isles. From the halcyon days of hockey and bandy played on frozen lakes and ponds to the artificial ice of the interwar hockey arenas at Wembley, Earl's Court, Richmond, Harringay, Brighton and Oxford, the sport has been a part of the British way of life for almost as long as that of their Canadian cousins. In the 1890s, for example, newspapers across Britain reported how "ice hockey is very popular amongst us just now" and that frozen ponds in (often newly laid out) public parks were being cordoned off to create pay-per-use skating rinks ("Our London Correspondence"). What we recognize as hockey, today, was brought to Britain by Canadian students at the beginning of the twentieth century, and clubs were formed at Oxford, Cambridge, Manchester and Leeds and in London (Erhardt, 9). Its popularity was encouraged by the establishment of large public rinks such as the Ice Palace in Manchester, which opened in 1910. By the outbreak of the First World War, British hockey was at the forefront of the amateur game in Europe: British clubs were successfully competing on the international stage, and enthusiasts had formed the British Ice Hockey Association and affiliated to the Ligue Internationale de Hockey sur Glace (the international governing body).

It was not until the 1930s that hockey, after undergoing a commercial revolution, was able to compete with more traditional mass spectator sports and was being played in arenas that actively evoked the atmosphere and experience of Maple Leaf Gardens or Madison Square Garden. With their bright lights and booming public address systems, these arenas stood alongside jazz clubs in offering a break from the more sober pastimes of old and a singular release from the routine rhythms of work, study or unemployment. Large crowds were clearly attracted to what was an appealing spectator sport. Spectators became consumers of statistics and a vast array of memorabilia, including matchday programs, cigarette cards, dedicated newspapers and team photographs printed on postcards. These mass-market consumables were soon traded and hoarded with the same passion as the ones featuring famous soccer players or cricketers. Such was the scale of hockey's ambitions in 1930s Britain that historians have estimated that £1 million was invested in its development over the course of the decade, with some newspaper accounts suggesting that it may even have been as much as £2 million (Jones, 45; "For 'Tough Guys' Only"). In the words of a local politician from Edinburgh, hockey made money ("Ice Hockey Proposal").

Such sums, in the midst of the Great Depression, reflect the contemporary importance of hockey both to British society and to the Canadians who looked across at the "old country" and saw a way out of the strict amateur regulations at home and a means of making money from playing their favourite game. And make money they did: the average player was earning around sixty dollars a week by playing for hockey teams across London (MacPherson, 10). The arrangements were barely within the bounds of amateurism and regularly deplored by the Canadian Amateur Hockey Association; in fact, even the NHL considered the British National League to be "a professional organization akin to itself"

("C.A.H.A. Boss Insists"). The players themselves, however, saw it as a bit of an adventure that took them from tough, Depression-era lives in Winnipeg or the Maritimes to the bright lights and television cameras of the British capital. Nor were they alone in finding work in the burgeoning British hockey industry of the 1930s: Canadian radio commentators, coaching staff, referees and newspaper journalists all took advantage of the public's appetite for the sport and the money that it generated.

Towards the outbreak of the Second World War, hockey organizers in Britain began to formulate a new, £5 million master plan that would have seen the end of clubs' reliance upon imported labour from Canada and a nineteen-rink expansion into the Midlands, Northern England and Wales. The *Daily Express*'s sports correspondent John Macadam outlined the plan in his column on November 2, 1938. The aim, he wrote, was "to attach junior sides to the existing British rinks, give expert coaching to the youngsters and gradually eliminate the necessity for importing Canadian players in droves." In an interview to accompany the article, Bunny Ahearne, secretary of the British Ice Hockey Association, remarked that "inside five years I visualize Britain as a real self-supporting hockey country" ("Three-year Plan"). Similar efforts were taking place in Scotland, which had an independent governing structure, with a decree from the Scottish Ice Hockey Association in April 1938 stating that member clubs could have only six imported players. Despite this momentum, when war was declared in September 1939 there were nearly one hundred and fifty players registered for transfer from Canada to play with British clubs, and some, such as Streatham (which had only one native player on its roster), were completely reliant upon them ("Winnipeg Seeks"; "Hockey Head"; "Canadian Players").

Ahearne's hoped-for reduction in the Canadian dominance of British hockey did not happen until the declaration of war in September 1939, which prompted most of the Canadian players to return home and left rink managers and clubs with the choice of postponing activities or turning to their under-developed British juniors. Although a drop in playing standard was registered by long-term fans, this newly "independent" form of hockey with a somewhat different style of play (less violent and more focused on the key skills of hockey) reached new audiences and was found to have "a beneficial effect on the game in this country" ("Searchlight on Sport"). Even the Canadian press, which had little taste for the more restricted nature of wartime sport, considered that these new circumstances had the potential to save the British game:

> To anyone liking his hockey neat, the wartime English brand, blacked out and tied up with restrictions, leaves much to be desired. But there is a growing belief the war may prove the salvation of the game which has cost millions of pounds to introduce. It has been argued that hockey started here the wrong way – promoters transplanting shiploads of Canadian experts in an effort to consolidate patronage overnight...so hockey never got the chance to develop the natural British way. ("War May Save")

Yet, despite such a belief, the overall feel of hockey during the war became even more Canadian. After a successful season in 1939–40, the sport fell into abeyance and was not revived again until 1946. The only matches that the public could access were those played by the numerous Canadian Forces clubs that were set up by the stationed personnel. Many towns were exposed to the game first-hand for the first time, as they were introduced to baseball by American troops. In addition, the broadcast of the final period of the traditional Saturday *Hockey Night in Canada* game on the BBC Forces Programme radio station every Sunday night brought the finest professional hockey in the world to British audiences. Although the Forces Programme was designed specifically to serve the military, the BBC hoped it would cater to general interests and tastes as well. As a consequence, it accelerated demand for the British game to provide a similar form of spectacle at war's end, and when hockey returned after the war, the brief experiment with independence and open professionalism was set aside, not to be revived until the early 1970s.

Reaching the Summit

From the point of view of international observers, the meeting of Canada and the Soviet Union in September 1972 was intended to settle, once and for all, the question of which style of hockey was better: professional, violent North American hockey with its well-paid players and franchises or "amateur," graceful European hockey with its focus on skilful stickwork and locally rooted clubs. Every facet of divergence was on show, and, viewed critically, the Summit Series exposed just how far the European game had developed despite its amateur status. For Canadians, though, the series was supposed to show the dominance of their country over their game. Thus when Canada lost the opening game in Montreal, it prompted widespread comment, domestically and internationally. Bunny Ahearne, the British Ice Hockey Association and International Ice Hockey Federation president, was particularly ebullient. "Good God, I'm delighted," he declared. "I've always said the Russians were better skaters, shooters and passers but all I've ever heard from Canada is wait until they meet the professionals.... I've never had much faith in all-star teams in any sport. I much prefer a club team than an all-star team" ("Ahearne Chuckles"). Ahearne was certainly no fan of Team Canada: as he joked with a journalist from the Montreal *Gazette*, "one of [the] Toronto papers has practically said I'm on the payroll of Russia" ("Transatlantic").

From that moment on, the series was defined as a battle for the future of hockey. As the *New York Times* reflected, "Behind the headlines there is a remarkable study in cultural contrasts that points up the vastly different treatment of sports in East and West" ("Russian and Canadian"). The dividing line lay between a European hockey-playing culture that winced at bodychecks and a Canadian one that cheered. Today, of course, the relationship between violence and hockey is well documented and still accepted by some fans and commentators as a natural part of the sport (Gruneau and Whitson, 175). Whereas the game was hardly genteel in Europe, particularly in Britain with its imported North American stars, it was certainly less focused on violence in comparison to skills. Fights were, after all, alien both to the community-centred club structure and the family ethos that promoters were seeking to build in their arenas. The following words, from *Ice Hockey World*, a long-running British hockey newspaper, give a sense of the foreignness of the European form of hockey for Canadians in particular. It tells the tale of a small-town Canadian editor who visits the Empire Pool to watch the Wembley Lions versus Streatham in 1951.

> The game is fast. There is not a slouch on the ice.
> Three sticks are broken in the first period.
> The quality of the hockey is finer, and the speed of the game
>   faster than that, say, of the Northern Ontario League.

> Dinner is served! A few rows below the press box is a long wide opening where dinner tables are set, overlooking the ice.

> Only the English are of such serene temper as to enable them to dine while watching the fastest, most exciting game in the world. ("You've Got to See," 7)

This cultural difference found expression at various moments of confrontation between Canadian hockey promoters and their European counterparts.

In the 1930s, for instance, amateur players such as Carl Erhardt, captain of the victorious British team at the 1936 Winter Olympics in Germany, viewed the impact of semi-professionalism and imported players with dismay, believing traditional British hockey was being stripped away from them. Erhardt wrote openly that the violence that plagued this new form of hockey was "imported from the other side of the Atlantic" (30). Likewise, in the 1960s, hockey's rise and fall led some British commentators to question whether it was because of the violence. In the view of the left-leaning *Guardian* newspaper, "the British spectator has some ethical judgment when he watches a game" ("The Ice Man," 7). Such views on hockey violence found themselves echoed in the columns of the Russian press in the aftermath of the Summit Series. "The Canadians," wrote one journalist in the popular *Sovietskii Sport* newspaper on September 29, "demonstrated some unpleasing sides of professional hockey. It wasn't nice to see how some players behaved on the ice.… Being the centre of attention, creating publicity, this is one of the hooks frequently used by NHL players.… But, of course, what they do at home is none of our business" (quoted in "Newspapers in U.S.S.R."). It could have been easily written by British journalists in earlier times.

For Europeans, then, before, during, and after the Summit Series, the essential foreignness of hockey violence was allied to its professionalism in North America. The Swiss newspaper *L'Express*, for example, observed that "it is well known that professional hockey, in Canada, is rough" concluding that, unlike in Europe, "teams (professionals, let's not forget!) compensate for their poverty of skill by the pure and simple nastiness of 'players' they hire to eliminate the opposition's stars." In West Germany, too, there was a focus on the "rough professionals," with one newspaper pointing out that the differences between the NHL and Europe's amateur players were "inconceivably large." The East Germans were even more damning, with the *Berliner Zeitung* complaining of the "brutal cruelty" of Canada's professionals and their style of play ("L'escalade"; "Kämpfe"; "Bilanz"). This dispute over the consequences of professionalism was at its most bitter in the 1970s because of Canada's withdrawal from international competition for much of the decade. Without it, the debate would likely not have taken place.

What lay underneath the argument, however, was not simply disgust at violence, although that was certainly a factor; it was also an easy target and provided commentators with ready rhetoric. Instead, there was deep frustration at Canada's continued belief in its "divine right" of ownership over the game and its unwillingness to recognize the impressive skills and dedication of European players. Bunny Ahearne, speaking for many European officials, considered the amateur-professional crisis to be part of the growing-up process as Canada adjusted to no longer being the sole major hockey-playing nation. "They must get it out of their system that they're the creators," he explained to the Montreal *Gazette* in January 1972, "England created soccer and cricket and Scotland golf and tennis. Where are they today in these sports?" ("Transatlantic"). The Summit Series, to an extent, did begin the process of realization that hockey was no longer solely Canada's game. NHL expansion in 1967 had brought to an end the "Original Six" era, reducing the ratio of Canadian to American teams from one in three to one in six, and the World Hockey Association (formed in 1971) had shown that European players could become stars in their own right in North America.

The trauma of the opening night loss and the fact that a series win was scraped through bloody attrition shook an expectant, complacent Canadian nation and forced a reassessment that was particularly difficult to contemplate. For a small group within the NHL, spearheaded by Bruce Norris of the Detroit Red Wings, one of the many lessons of the Summit Series and the WHA was the need to look beyond North America to inculcate their brand of hockey and to take the fight (and the fighting) to the hockey-going public in Europe. They needed an environment conducive to NHL-style hockey, with all its violent idiosyncrasies, that would prove the viability of the Canadian game and wipe away the debacle of the Summit Series. Their gaze turned to London, where they found hockey in a deep crisis of its own following the collapse of the domestic league a decade earlier. Facing little competition and believing in a healthy appetite for professional hockey, Norris gambled, with the full backing of Bunny Ahearne, who hoped for a great European championship to rival soccer's European Cup, on an outfit he christened the London Lions ("Bunny").

Lions in Winter

It was, felt the *Calgary Herald*, a "baffling revival" ("Baffling"). Wearing red jerseys with a logo that merged a lion and the red wing of Detroit's hockey team, the London Lions seemed, to the Canadian commentators that were aware of it, like something pulled back to the future. For Britons, though, it was exciting and new, and the club even enjoyed a slot on *Blue Peter*, the BBC's leading children's television show. Norris set out his vision in September 1972 with the story breaking into the British press in the midst of the Summit Series. "What they [the fans] like in Detroit," he said, "they could also like in London. It's a family sport. We have as many women fans as men. But to attract the women you've got to give them comfort. So our long-term plan is to build an 18,000- to 20,000-seater stadium with every comfort. Then people will be prepared to pay top prices." When professional hockey collapsed a decade earlier, fans were paying an average of twenty pence (or four shillings) to enter the arena; to watch the London Lions at Wembley, they had to find between one and four pounds in the midst of a growing economic crisis ("Big Bruce"; "Lions Revived"). The old entrance fee covered only the cost of the match program.

Norris's gambit was that there was an appetite for the NHL present in Britain and Europe in this period and that financial rewards were there for the taking, eventually. In fact, he spent around £430,000 ($1 million) to establish the Lions and suffered personal losses of £100,000 over the 1973–74 season. For the British Ice Hockey Association, though, which levied professional fees, the arrival of the Lions was a bonanza providing over £3,000 in revenue and doubling the Association's annual income (British Ice Hockey Association, 1973–74). That would prove vital in the latter half of the decade, when a grassroots revival of hockey took place in Britain. The players too enjoyed a windfall break with the past, earning an average salary of around £5,000 over the season – a significant advance on the £600 a season that had prevailed in the 1950s when a maximum wage was in force ("The Lions in Winter"). To those continental European teams, such as IFK Helsinki or the Swedish team Djurgårdens, whose players earned tiny salaries and often had to work part-time elsewhere to support their playing career, the contrasts between their model and that of the NHL were stark.

On the ice, the team performed very much like an NHL farm team – the roster was composed principally of Canadians, with a small number of Swedes and Americans as bolster – and played in a physically dominant style. Upon seeing the team for the first time, Bunny Ahearne observed caustically that "they play the man and not the puck" ("The London Lions Are Coming"). Games against Soviet teams, of course, were accompanied by "fiery tempers" and were instinctively understood as further test of the Canadian and Soviet systems. When the Lions played Spartak Moscow in London in March 1974, for instance, one Swiss journalist wrote baldy that this "game of the season" pitted a perfectly formed Soviet hockey-playing machine against a less skillful but (as a form of compensation) more physically aggressive Canadian outfit ("Tournoi"). It ended, to his obvious amusement, in a tie. This vigorous presence often threatened to spill over into violence and resulted in players being sent off, regardless of the opposition. In a particularly stormy match played against West Germany in Oberstdorf, on the Austrian border, the Lions lost their captain, Rick McCann, after a punch-up on the ice. For much of the second period of that match, the team played with four men until a second fight, two minutes before the period break, prompted the referees to halt proceedings.

Ironically, given Britons' earlier qualms about hockey violence, the Lions' style of play was considered attractive and, on the whole, an improvement on the British hockey from earlier times. Colin Maitland, for example, writing in the *Guardian*, considered that "from the first match it was obvious that the Lions' playing standard was not only better…it was also very much more physical." Similarly, Ron Beagley, writing in the *Daily Mirror*, enjoyed the "storm" of goals as the Lions scored sixteen against the Dutch Internationals in November 1973. It is for this reason that audiences at the 10,000-seater Wembley Arena rose considerably over the season from largely empty houses of between 1,500 and 2,000 spectators in October 1973 to upwards of 7,000 by the time the last game was played in March 1974. Amongst them were some of the leading celebrities in Britain, including Bobby Moore, the World Cup–winning England soccer captain, Bob Wilson, the then-goalkeeper of Arsenal Football Club, and the comedian Eric Morecambe ("Paving Way"; London Lions Ice Hockey Club, 3).

To a large extent, of course, the Lions were sustained at the grassroots level by the enthusiasm of a dedicated group of fans, who formed themselves into a supporters' club early in 1974. Supporters clubs had long been a feature of British professional sport and a vital lifeline for sides that otherwise struggled. They provided a vital link to the community and underpinned those clubs they served through fundraising, trips to away matches and the organization of junior clubs and district cup competitions. Not all of this was applicable to the Lions, but, as the notes in their March 31 program reveal, the traditional role of a supporters club was foremost in members' minds:

> We were all pleased, and not a little surprised, when one of the new committee volunteered to be the club's cheerleader. Surprised because the volunteer was an attractive young *lady*…you may well have seen her at Lions' matches, dressed in white jumper and red skirt and yelling like crazy. [She] is inseparable from her toy red and white lion and the Club has decided to adopt it as their mascot.… Many excellent ideas were aired at the meeting. One was for a sportsman's bowl to be presented to the Lions' most valuable player; another for a Junior Supporter's Club especially for members under 16 years of age. (12)

Besides a mascot and membership badges, the supporters club offered special discounted tickets as a means of driving up public support and building a community around the Lions.

Despite a growing sense of popular enthusiasm, the club failed to re-form in the autumn of 1974. Lack of agreement over the establishment of a European super league and the financial implications for the Lions gave the impression that the venture had not been a success. The baffling revival, in short, remained just that. In reality, however, the Lions increased hockey's exposure in the press and on television, and gave succour to the grassroots revival that was beginning to take place ("The Lions in Winter"). Above all, the Lions proved that professionalism was the way forward for British hockey, thereby fulfilling the promise of the 1930s. Likewise, the Lions proved that there was a popular appetite for NHL-style hockey, violence and all, in Europe and that it could be successful on the ice. Except, perhaps ironically, against the Soviets, where the Lions' record stood at one victory (vitally, in Moscow itself), two losses and a draw. In December 1973, the Lions' managing director, Joseph Besch, confidently declared that "ice hockey will be a paying proposition in Britain in the future" ("Paving Way"). He was right, though it took over a decade to get there.

On a visit to the United States in 1977, BBC journalist John Humphrys attended a hockey game in an effort to escape the all-powerful Super Bowl. Reflecting on what he saw for the radio program *From Our Own Correspondent*, Humphrys noted that "for years, it's been like a religion in Canada, and it's getting that way south of the border too – and I can see why. Ice hockey is, in a word, magnificent" ("They Shoot Horses"). Many of those who visited Wembley Arena to watch the London Lions shared this sense of curiosity and enthrall; when the Lions failed in the summer of 1974, fans set about forming and supporting new clubs across Britain to ensure a domestic future for hockey, professional or amateur. In the 1980s, a fully professional league was created similar in form, if not in ambition, to the NHL. Skill, though not subsumed by physicality, was a much less fundamental facet of clubs' style of play, and those, such as the Cardiff Devils, that readily adopted NHL-Canadian physicality proved more successful than those that did not. Bruce Norris's belief in Britons' appetite for professional hockey was belatedly vindicated.

Britons, of course, never heard the chants – *Da, da, Canada!* or *Nyet, nyet, Soviet!* – nor did they ever see or hear the events in Toronto, Montreal, Winnipeg and Vancouver, nor Moscow, on television or radio. For that reason, the Summit Series has little place in the annals of British sport. Yet, the early 1970s were a period of significant transformation bringing new opportunities for hockey in Britain and elsewhere. It was the Summit Series that unleashed that change, and without it ventures such as the London Lions and the British revival could not have happened. The great themes of the Summit Series – the triumph of professionalism, the battle between skill and physicality, and the ending of Canada's automatic status as the world's leading hockey nation – all impacted, heavily, on Britain and the British style of hockey. Spectators, in short, came to demand their hockey played in the Canadian way. That, in the end, was the great legacy of the Summit Series in the old country, amongst the lions in winter. Nothing would ever be the same again.

Works Cited

"Ahearne Chuckles after Loss." *Gazette* (Montreal), September 5, 1972.

"A Baffling Revival." *Calgary Herald,* October 20, 1973.

"Big Bruce Has Plans." *Daily Express* (London), September 15, 1972.

"Bilanz nach dem Treffen der Asse." *Berliner Zeitung,* October 2, 1972.

British Ice Hockey Association Ltd. Annual Reports and Accounts, 1970–80. Companies House, Cardiff: Microfilm Company Records, Company No. 306186.

"Bunny Wants New League." *Leader-Post* (Regina, SK), April 13, 1974.

"C.A.H.A. Boss Insists Pros Must Not Approach Amateurs." *Winnipeg Free Press*, February 24, 1938.

"Canadian Players in Scottish Sides Position to be Reviewed." *The Scotsman* (Edinburgh), January 13, 1939.

Erhardt, Carl. *Ice Hockey*. London: Foulsham, 1937.

"For 'Tough Guys' Only." *The Argus* (Melbourne), May 8, 1937.

Gruneau, Richard, and David Whitson. *Hockey Night in Canada: Sport, Identities and Cultural Politics*. Toronto: Garamond, 1994.

"Hockey Head Airs Pro-amateur Tangle." *Winnipeg Free Press,* November 6, 1939.

Howell, Colin D. *Blood, Sweat and Cheers: Sport and the Making of Modern Canada*. Toronto: University of Toronto Press, 2001.

"Ice Hockey Proposal for Portobello." *Glasgow Herald,* March 1, 1939.

"The Ice Man Goeth." *The Guardian*, January 31, 1961.

Jones, Stephen G. *Sport, Politics and the Working Class: Organised Labour in Inter-War Britain*. Manchester: Manchester University Press, 1988.

"L'escalade de la violence inquiète fort les Canadiens." *L'Express* (Neuchâtel), August 5, 1976.

"The Lions in Winter." *The Guardian*, March 30, 1974.

"Lions Revived by Big Dollar Gamble." *Daily Express,* September 7, 1973.

"The London Lions Are Coming to Town." *Daily Mirror,* October 9, 1973.

London Lions Ice Hockey Club. *Program No. 9: Djurg*årdens *I. F.* March 31, 1974. London: London Lions Ice Hockey Club.

MacPherson, Stewart. *The Mike and I.* London: Von Thal, 1948.

"Newspapers in U.S.S.R. had different take on 1972 Summit Series." *Toronto Star,* September 22, 2012.

"100 Kämpfe für rauhe Eishockey-Profis." *Passauer Neue Presse,* December 27, 1965.

"Our London Correspondence." *Manchester Guardian,* January 6, 1893.

"Paving Way for a British Foothold on the Ice." *The Guardian* (London), December 1, 1973.

"Russian and Canadian Hockey Players Offer Vivid Contrasts." *New York Times,* September 30, 1972, Sports Section.

"Searchlight on Sport: Ice Hockey, February 24, 1940." BBC Written Archive Centre, Caversham Park, Reading: Draft Scripts Microfilm.

"They Shoot Horses." *The Listener* (London), February 10, 1977.

"Three-Year Plan to Spend £5,000,000 on Ice Hockey." *Daily Express,* November 2, 1938.

"Tournoi du Salon." *24 Heures* (Lausanne), March 20, 1974.

"Transatlantic Shouting Match Develops." *Montreal Gazette,* January 7, 1972.

"War May Save Ice Game for Old County Moguls." *Saskatoon Star-Phoenix,* January 9, 1940.

"Winnipeg Seeks." *Winnipeg Free Press,* September 4, 1939.

"You've Got to See to Believe." *Ice Hockey World,* May 12, 1951.

Boom or Bust?
The Impact of the 1972 Summit Series on the Development of Women's Hockey in Canada

♦

JULIE STEVENS AND ANNA H. LATHROP

One of most often cited events in the history of Canadian hockey is Paul Henderson's game-winning goal during the 1972 Summit Series. For many, this event was iconic – a story subsequently told and retold with nostalgic fondness in affirmation of the national identity that all Canadians shared. Indeed, the fortieth anniversary of this event was recently heralded in the *Globe and Mail* as the time when "Canada went to war." The article goes on to describe the Canadian men's team as "national heroes" (Dryden). Following the Summit Series, men's hockey continued to rise in prominence and gain popularity. Professional men's hockey grew to include high-profile commercial events such as the Canada Cup, the Super Series and the World Cup. Within the amateur game, the Canadian Amateur Hockey Association (CAHA) created an elite men's hockey initiative called the "Program of Excellence."

Four decades later, one wonders whether the series truly captured the minds and hearts of *all* Canadians. Did the event spark an increase in access, participation and visibility for women who enjoyed and identified with the sport? Did the series inspire women to effect change in the game? Did feminist activists take up the call for greater access to the game? Did the event ignite a groundswell of support for women's hockey?

In response to these questions, we examine the impact of the series on the development of women's hockey in Canada. Amid the backdrop of the foundational women's rights activism during the 1970s and the steady and dramatic progress in women's rights during the 1980s and 1990s, this commentary poses the question, Was the Summit Series a transformative event for women's hockey that ignited a boom in participation and access – or was it a bust? We reveal our hand at the outset and present our answer to the question as a resounding "bust." We argue that it was not until 1998, when Canada's women's hockey team competed at the Olympic Winter Games, that a real case could be made that women had, truly, made inroads into what Kidd referred to as one of the most definitive and distinctly nationalistic arenas of men's cultural activity ("Men's Cultural Centre," 31). As such, we question the universal claim that the 1972 Summit Series inspired a hockey-loving nation for all Canadians – both men and women alike.

Despite the enthusiasm and activism of women's rights advocates in the post–Royal Commission on the Status of Women decade, why did the emergence of women's hockey take over two decades to mature to a level of participation and competition to garner national visibility? Given the firestorm of nationalism ignited by the Summit Series, we explain why it took so long for any evidence of this allegedly nation-inspiring event to impact women's hockey. Indeed, the extensive delay actually raises the question of whether the series had an impact upon the women's game at all. First, we examine the evolution of women's hockey with attention to participation, competition, access and governance, both before and after the series. Second, we analyze the impact of the Summit Series within the context of the second wave of feminism in Canada and note how social and political reform did not translate into significant gains for women in the arena of Canada's national sport.

Uneven Development: The Evolution of Female Hockey in Canada (1910–2012)

In order to discuss the impact of the 1972 Summit Series on women's hockey in Canada, it is important to first understand the state of women's hockey development both before and after the series. Figure 1 contrasts women's and men's hockey development before and after the series. The first documented women's hockey game occurred in 1891, where a group of women, including Lady Isobel Stanley, daughter of former governor general Lord Stanley (who donated the Stanley Cup), played on the frozen water of the Rideau Canal, near Ottawa, Ontario (McFarlane, 20). Early beginnings of the game reflected outings where women of privilege participated in the sport, albeit rarely, as a winter pastime. Organized women's hockey did not take hold in urban areas of the country until the early 1900s. Spearheaded by women who formed teams at universities, the sport gradually expanded into communities where teams from different towns and cities competed in various challenge games (Avery and Stevens, 59). By the 1920s, women's hockey was managed in some regions of the country by a provincial women's hockey association, and competition occurred within university and community leagues. The Ladies Ontario Hockey Association (LOHA) was the first provincial association for the sport in Canada and established a women's hockey structure based a great deal upon the existing men's system managed by the Ontario Hockey Association (Adams, 4).

The 1930s was a prolific decade for women's hockey. The Dominion Women's Hockey Association, formed in 1933, established regulations for a Dominion Championship with the Preston Rivulettes winning the first title the same year (Adams, 7). The championship involved a contest between top teams from Eastern and Western Canada, which spawned more expansive club competition in both regions of the country. However, the activity came to an abrupt halt due to the Second World War and postwar attitudes that were far less supportive of women in masculine domains, such as sport, than previously existed (Etue and Williams, 43). Rosenberg and Stevens (37) claim the decline was due to a rise in professional men's hockey, a lack of media attention and government support, and a return to more traditional roles for women in the postwar era. Regardless of the cause, the outcome, an absence of women from all levels of hockey in Canada, lasted well into the 1960s and early 1970s.

By 1972, when the Summit Series was held, women's hockey had not regained its prewar status, and efforts to reignite interest and participation were sporadic. The series profiled a team composed of professional Canadian male hockey players, but a commercial women's version of the sport was irrelevant. Individuals supporting the female game struggled to simply reestablish an amateur presence. This period reflected tension in the sport as women and girls staged legal battles to challenge overt discrimination that prevented their access to hockey. Opportunities for women in hockey were created through the use of the courts to start legal challenges to the obstacles raised by the male-dominated Canadian hockey establishment (Stevens, "Development of the Canadian Hockey System," 58).

The late 1970s and 1980s involved slow progress for the female game. Etue and Williams argue that during this time women's hockey "inched along," largely at the senior level, and that minor girls' hockey was nonexistent outside of Ontario (47). Ontario's pivotal role in women's hockey advocacy was formalized with the creation of the Ontario Women's Hockey Association (OWHA) in 1975. Similar to previous women's hockey associations in the 1920s and 1930s, the OWHA was an independent association that managed female hockey within the male-dominated hockey system. No other province established a similar separate governance structure, although three provinces, Alberta, Prince Edward Island and British Columbia, created governance bodies for female hockey within the provincial male hockey association (Etue and Williams, 48). However, it took significant time for these entities to have impact at the national level, as the CAHA (later called Canadian Hockey Association, and then simplified to Hockey Canada) did not establish a Women`s Hockey Council and reinstate the Senior Women's National Championship until 1982, ten years after the Summit Series.

From the 1990s to the present time, female hockey growth has reflected an expansion of elite provincial, national and international high-performance programs and events (Stevens, "Women's Hockey in Canada," 90). For example, new domestic female hockey included the Ontario Winter Games in 1985 and the Canada Summer Games in 1991. The Under-18 National Championship, Canadian Interuniversity Sport (CIS) championship and Midget Girls' National Championship were first staged in 1993, 1998 and 2009, respectively. The National Women's Under-22 Team (U-22 NWT) and National Women's Under-18 Team (U-18 NWT) programs were created in 2000 and 2007, respectively. International activities included the first Women's World Hockey Championship (WWHC) in 1990, and the initiation of a National Women's Team (NWT) program led to other high-performance events such as the Pacific Rim in 1995, the Three Nations Cup (now the Four Nations Cup) in 1996 and, ultimately, the Olympic Winter Games in 1998.

Overall, women's hockey development during the past 120 years reflects a cyclical pattern between near obscurity in the game to active periods. However, following the Summit Series in 1972, the expansion of women's hockey remained delayed for nearly two decades, and thereafter was still slow to develop – unlike the steady growth of the men's game. The reason for the absence of the Summit Series "halo effect" on the women's game may be attributed to the larger social and political agenda of the period. Feminist activists held other issues in their sights.

The "Lost" Agenda: Feminist Activism and Women's Hockey in Canada (1972–98)

The second wave of feminism in Canada took root during the 1960s and developed into a multi-layered tapestry of competing priorities during the 1970s. As Rebick (10) suggests, these competing priorities during the 1960s were distinctive by virtue of their national goals and regional interests. During this decade, national interests included peace activism, career access and women's health (Rebick, 13). In Quebec, feminism was linked to national identity and trade unionism. In 1966 the Committee for Equality of Women in Canada lobbied the Pearson government for a Royal Commission on the Status of Women – which was granted in 1967. Among the 167 recommendations identified by the Royal Commission, just two distinguished the importance of developing policies and practices to motivate and engage girls in athletics and sport activities.

Nevertheless, by 1970 only one woman sat in the House of Commons. Within this context, several currents of feminism surfaced in Canada. One current focused on the reform of the system – and the other on a more radical approach of transformation. Rebick notes, "Social feminism believed in women's liberation via anti capitalist transformation and radical feminists identified patriarchy as the problem. Much of the debate in the 1970s focused on difference in analysis, strategy and tactics" (21). Tong (1) also highlights these dual approaches and contrasts the strategies and goals that differentiate liberal and radical feminism. The feminists experienced various trials and tribulations as they sought to give traction to the women's movement during the 1960s and 1970s.

Research by Keyes ("Feminist Lobbying and Decision Making Power"), Kidd (*The Struggle for Canadian Sport*) and Hall (*The Girl and the Game*) in the field of women's sport in Canada also recognizes the challenges faced by women who carved out new possibilities for women in sport. Keyes (419) identifies this activism for women and sport in terms of five areas of advocacy. The areas include Canadian legislation related to women's rights, the women's movement, catalytic conferences related to women in Canadian society and sport, the influence of significant women sport leaders, and Fitness and Amateur Sport national policies, programs and services. Each of these will be briefly discussed and then related to the context of women's hockey in Canada following the Summit Series.

Keyes argues that in order "to understand the ideologies and the strategies employed by women in sport and fitness...it is essential to discuss the women's liberation movement in Canada since the sixties because it was in this environment that sport and fitness leaders began to seek change" (420). Upon review, it is apparent that before and after the time of the series, the second wave of feminism within Canada struggled to gain recognition of women's issues from the federal government. Given this, a great deal of attention and action sought to establish formal women's movement entities and to mobilize for change. While it may be unfair to claim feminist activists were unconcerned with challenges women and girls faced in the male-dominated terrain of hockey during the 1970s, it is reasonable to say this issue was seen as a smaller component of a more central concern for universal women's rights and freedoms (Eaton, 122). In Canada, the feminist agenda at the time took up larger and more systemic issues such as peace, abortion and women's health. Women's hockey simply wasn't the priority at the time. Kidd suggests "'women's sports run by women' is so utopian an ideal that it cannot be imagined" (*Struggle for Canadian Sport*, 144), and this is true, at least for women's hockey during the 1970s.

Canadian legislation provided some building blocks to advance sport for women. The Canadian Charter of Rights and Freedoms was enshrined in 1982, the first Sport Canada Policy on Women in Sport was created in 1986, and the Commission of Inquiry into the Use of Drugs and Banned Practices

Intended to Increase Athletic Performance (the Dubin Inquiry), a federal government inquiry, was held in 1989. Keyes (426) argues each of these provided a basis upon which to initiate legislation and policy-based change for women in sport in Canada. Although the general women's movement was divided over the use of human rights strategies to effect social change, this tactic was important within the context of the women's sport movement during the 1970s and 1980s (Clément, 108). In terms of a post-series boost to female hockey, the latter two activities likely had little to no impact. The Sport Canada policy wasn't formulated until 1986, and any benefit from the Dubin Inquiry, which strongly recommended a more ethical and fair Canadian sport system, did not begin to reverberate until well into the 1990s. However, girls, and their parents, utilized the legislation to address the refusal of boys' minor hockey associations to allow girls to play on their teams. Etue and Williams claim one successful case that involved Justine Blainey, a twelve-year-old girl in Ontario who challenged the Ontario Hockey Association for access to a boys' team, "eliminated an exemption in the Ontario Human Rights Code that had permitted sports organizations in the province to discriminate against women" (162). Keep in mind, though – this occurred fifteen years after the series, and reflects one case, in one province.

A review of registration records offers further insight about the questionable impact of the Summit Series upon women's hockey. Registration for female hockey in Canada was approximately 975 in 1977.[1] From 1979 until 1989, the OWHA registration increased from 120 to 302 teams, which represents approximately 1,800 to 4,530 players (Etue and Williams, 73). Subsequent records reveal female registration was 11,341 in 1992 (Avery and Stevens, 129), 19,050 in 1995 (Etue and Williams, 40), 54,563 in 2002 and 86,675 in 2012 (CHA). Boys' hockey registration in Canada was 494,157 in 1995, 470,766 in 1999, 477,416 in 2002 and 530,432 in 2012. While female hockey has grown since 1972, its highest level in 2012 reflects no more than 13.9% of the total player registration in Canada.

The second factor related to the complex women's sport movement in Canada is the women's movement itself. Keyes (420) summarizes a chronology of the movement that began in the 1960s with the early Voice for Women organization, which focused broadly upon family well-being, but more important, included the 1967 Royal Commission on the Status of Women. Keyes argues that when the federal government failed to act on the commission's 167 recommendations, women's movement leaders continued to lobby, which led to the formation of a National Ad Hoc Committee on the Status of Women in 1971, which became the National Action Committee on the Status of Women in 1972, and the Advisory Council on the Status of Women in 1973. The timing of the formation of this national committee corresponds with the series and reveals the true nature of the challenges Canadian women faced at the time. As the series played out on the ice, women were fighting off the ice in a far more important national battle to simply gain official recognition from the federal government and challenge patriarchy through institutional change. Opportunities for women and girls in hockey, which normally played out at the grassroots level in communities across the country, were simply not the priority at the time, and did not become a priority until well after Paul Henderson scored his series-winning goal.

The third factor Keyes (423) identifies as a key influence upon Canadian women's sport was "catalytic conferences." In the general "women in sport" domain from 1961 until 1991, national conferences were important. Shortly after the series, national forums were held, including the 1974 National Conference on Women in Sport and the 1980 Female Athlete Conference, but the emphasis of these gatherings was to bring women's sport leaders together to meet and communicate. In the female hockey context, the closest example of a catalytic conference didn't occur until 1982, when the CAHA formed the Women's Hockey Council. The council provided a meeting place for female hockey representatives from each province and served as a springboard to advance female hockey programs at the national level, which then trickled down to the provincial level. In terms of the 1970s, the community level was where female hockey leaders most often met, if at all. The likely place was local tournaments, of which the Brampton Canadettes Hockey Tournament was the most prominent. The event began in 1967 with 22 teams, grew to 48 teams in 1972, the year of the series, and reached 137 and 179 teams in 1982 and 1992, respectively (Brampton Canadettes). The event provided a place for female hockey leaders to network, albeit on a smaller scale, and in the case of Ontario was a catalyst for the formation of the OWHA (Etue and Williams, 70).

The fourth factor involves the influence of women sport leaders. Keyes (424) identifies many influential women who played a role in the early stages of the women's movement in sport, including Abby Hoffman, the first female director general of Sport Canada, the federal government department responsible for fitness and amateur sport, and a former Olympian, and Dr. Ann Hall, an academic whose research on women's sport in Canada was instrumental in women's sport policy improvements. Key leaders also played a role in women's hockey during the post-series era. While director of Sport Canada, Hoffman provided the CAHA with funds to stage women's hockey workshops across the country, which, in turn, led to the formation of the CAHA Women's Hockey Council (Etue and Williams, 48). Rhonda Leeman and Karen Wallace served as chairs of the Women's Hockey Council at various times during the 1980s and represented female hockey on the male-dominated CAHA Board. Glynis Peters was hired in 1990 and served as the manager for female hockey within the CAHA for over a decade. Her tireless work was recognized in 2003 when she was awarded the Hockey Canada Female Breakthrough Award. In Ontario, Fran Rider, a former executive member of the Brampton Canadettes Girls' Hockey Association and one of the early founders of the OWHA, was influential in lobbying for a women's world championship and the inclusion of women's hockey in the Olympics (Etue and Williams, 249). Lastly, Susan Dalziel, a former player and volunteer in Prince Edward Island, was instrumental in advancing women's and girls' hockey in both the Maritime region and across the country through her service on provincial and national women's hockey councils.

Given that the female hockey governance structures that existed during the 1980s and 1990s were small in scale and power compared to male hockey governance structures, these women, and others, held dual roles as women's sport enablers. On one hand, they exemplified what Keyes refers to as institutional feminists who sought change through pressuring government, or in this case, the national sport governing body (CAHA). Campbell also refers to many women leaders as institutional feminists because they fought to reform the legal and institutional structures of Canadian society (54). On the other hand, they also worked within their own communities, both provincial and local, to effect change and in this way exemplified what Keyes terms grassroots feminists (421). In either case, the actions of women's hockey leaders, and the networks built through tournaments, were factors that had the most impact upon advancing women's hockey during the post–Summit Series era.

The final factor to influence the complex women's sport movement in Canada from 1961 until 1991 is the creation of Fitness and Amateur Sport policies, programs and services. The women's program within the Fitness and Amateur Sport branch of the federal government was created in 1980. In Canada public sector involvement in amateur sport is extensive, and as a result much of the women's sport advocacy was channelled through government (Hall, "Women's Sport Advocacy Organizations," 51). Keyes (424) indicates the program funding, initially set at $250,000, was earmarked for special projects. Another key development at the time was the formation of the Canadian Association for the Advancement of Women and Sport (CAAWS) in 1981, whose purpose was "to advance the position of women by defining, promoting, and supporting a feminist perspective on sport and to improve the status of women in sport" (Hall, *The Girl and the Game*, 425). With a designated organization and seed funding, the Canadian women's sport movement began to take hold in the 1980s. However, Comeau and Church (468) and Keyes (425) note CAAWS faced difficulty in its early years due to a small membership and internal dissension over strategies for change. These challenges slowed progress during the 1980s, which, in turn, meant progress within national sport organizations, such as the CAHA, was also delayed.

In the case of hockey, this final factor related to policies and programs provides the most vivid contrast of the post-series development within women's and men's hockey. On the men's side, the Summit Series set in motion a new era of lucrative commercial men's hockey spectacles (Kidd and Macfarlane, 19). The corporate-based agency called Hockey Canada gained control of managing international hockey events involving players from the National Hockey League (NHL). These unique, "first-of-their-kind" competitions became the staple of corporate hockey and led to several subsequent events, including the 1976 Canada Cup and the 1996 World Cup. For the men's game, the legacy of the series was the commercialization of international men's hockey. The model that emerged following the Canada-Russia Series experiment was an ad hoc approach to create and stage events for a "professional" men's Canadian national team. Given that women's hockey at the time was not represented in any formal structures within the CAHA and barely had a grassroots participation base, the corporate legacy generated by the series had scarce impact for women and girls interested in the sport. The hockey deals made in corporate boardrooms were far removed from the challenges faced by girls and women who just wanted to play the game.

The formation of Hockey Canada in 1970 usurped a great deal of control over men's international hockey from the CAHA (Stevens, "Development of the Canadian Hockey System," 57). However, the association remained the governing body for hockey in Canada, and the CAHA, not Hockey Canada, was recognized by the International Ice Hockey Federation (IIHF). In response to the growth of men's professional international competition and an increased appetite from the Canadian public for demonstrations of hockey supremacy, the CAHA created the Program of Excellence (POE) in 1981. The purpose of the POE was, and is, to "identify the most talented young hockey players and to provide these players with an opportunity to compete internationally at an early age" (Ontario Hockey Federation), and the primary objective of the POE was to "maintain Canada's position as a major force in international hockey" (Ontario Hockey Federation). The program focused on high-performance programs for male, not female, amateur hockey in Canada. After thirty years, Hockey Canada's POE now includes the men's national junior team (Under-20), the Under-18 and Under-17 programs and provincial POE programs for younger age categories.

Remnants of a women's POE did not emerge until the creation of the first WWHC in 1990, nearly two decades after the series. In order to field a competitive team, the CAHA established a selection process for the National Women's Team (NWT). Until 1999 the WWHC was held every second or third year, and this sporadic schedule meant a permanent NWT program wasn't established until 1997 in preparation for the 1998 Olympic Winter Games. Over time, the Under-22 NWT and the Under-18 NWT were added (in 2000 and 2007, respectively), and with this growth Hockey Canada added high-performance women's initiatives to the overall POE umbrella.

Thus while the series injected greater capacity into both amateur and professional men's hockey competition, any expectation for a similar boost for women's hockey was unrealistic. A lack of professional team sports for women is a major inequity for sporting women, a disparity that feminist sport scholars have failed to acknowledge (McCormack, 4). What is evident is that the women's game had no readiness for such complex, high-profile commercial programs and events, but that doesn't mean female athletes didn't, and don't, desire them.

Why did the 1972 Summit Series fail to empower women's hockey as it did men's hockey? Following the series feminist agendas were divided, and Keyes notes the "women's movement in sport followed the women's liberation movement by more than a decade" (428). Based upon the discussion developed here, it is fair to assert that the women's movement in hockey followed the women's movement in sport by ten to fifteen years. The series inspired a "hockey belongs to us" mentality among Canadians (Gruneau and Whitson, 252), but this proclamation falls short when it comes to women and girls. The 1972 Summit Series was not a catalyst for better women's hockey opportunities.

In his *Globe and Mail* commentary about the fortieth anniversary of the series, Ken Dryden, a member of '72 Team Canada, wrote that the series was "about performances for the ages and breakthrough achievements at breakthrough moments." The exemplary performance of the men who played in the series is forever held in collective Canadian memory. However, the breakthrough moments were far from collective. Breakthrough moments for whom? Shared memories of a hockey spectacle and shared experiences of hockey itself are not the same. Women may have united with fellow Canadians during the nation-building 1972 Summit Series victory celebration – but it didn't happen on the ice.

Women's Hockey Development		Men's Hockey Development
	1820	
		1828 – First documented men's game
	1860	
		1885 – Official rules game
First documented women's game – 1891		1886 – Amateur Hockey Association of Canada
	1900	
		1908 – Men's Senior Championship
		1917 – National Hockey League
		1919 – Junior Men's Championship
		1920 – Olympics
		1930 – World Championship
Dominion Women's Championship – 1933		
	1940	
		1963 – Men's National Team Program
		1967 – Canada Winter Games
	1970	
Summit Series – 1972		**1972 – Summit Series**
		1974 – Summit Series
OWHA formed – 1975		
		1976 – Canada Cup
		1976 – Super Series
		1978 – Super Series
		1981 – CAHA Men's POE
		1981 – Canada Cup
Women's National Championship – 1982		
		1987 – Canada Cup
World Championship – 1990	1990	
Canada Winter Games – 1991		
Under-18 Championship – 1993		
		1996 – World Cup of Hockey
Olympic Winter Games – 1998		
Women's POE – 2000s		

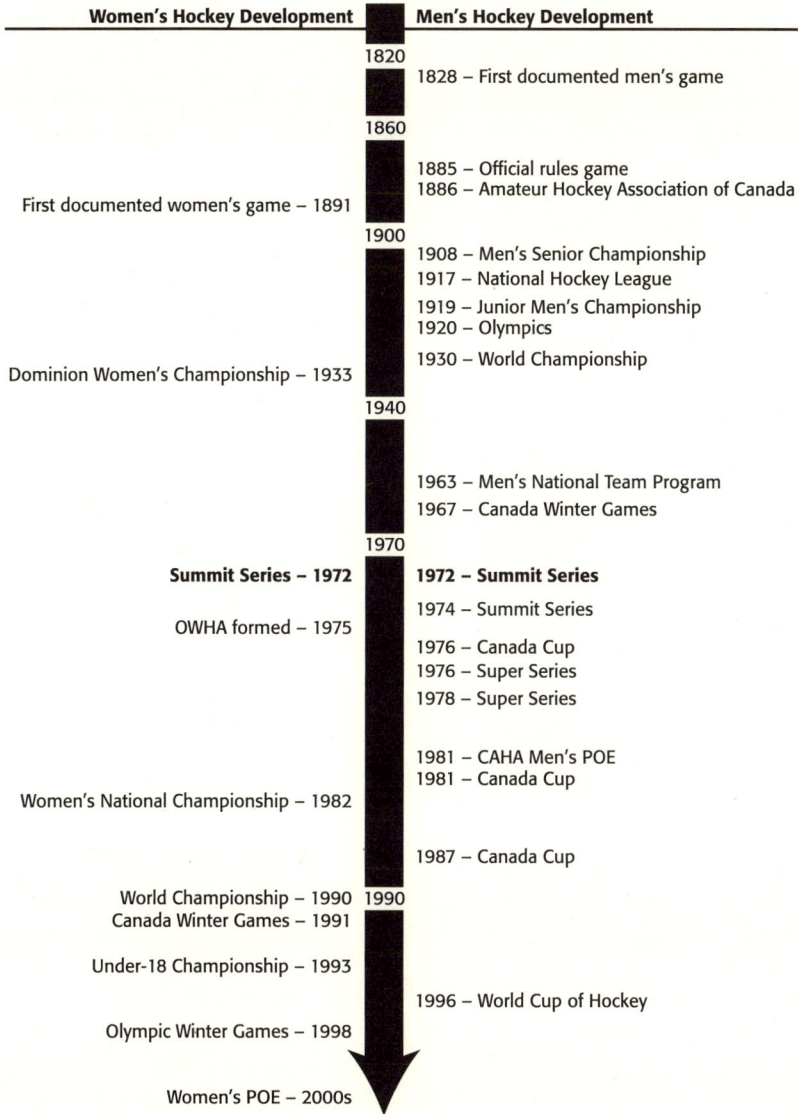

Figure 1: Pre- and Post-1972 Summit Series Development
Timeline for Women's and Men's Hockey in Canada

[1]   Etue and Williams (1996) reported the Ontario Women's Hockey Association registration was sixty-five teams in 1977. Based upon an estimate of fifteen players per team, this represents 975 registrants. No formal female hockey registrations were recorded in other provinces at the time and therefore, this number is the closest estimate available.

Works Cited

Adams, Carly. "'Queens of the Ice Lanes': The Preston Rivulettes and Women's Hockey in Canada: 1931–1940." *Sport History Review* 39 (2008): 1–29.

Avery, Joanne, and Julie Stevens. *Too Many Men on the Ice: Women's Hockey in North America*. Victoria, BC: Polestar, 1997.

Brampton Canadettes Girls' Hockey Association. "The Little Tournament That Grew." http://www.bramptoncanadettes.com/?page_id=472 (accessed August 13, 2013).

Campbell, Gail. "Are We Going to Do the Most Important Things? Senator Muriel McQueen Fergusson, Feminist Identities, and the Royal Commission on the Status of Women." *Acadiensis* 38, no. 2 (2009): 52–77.

Canadian Hockey Association. Registration Statistics. http://www.hockeycanada .ca/en-ca/Corporate/About/Basics/Registration.aspx (accessed August 13, 2013).

Clément, Dominique. "'I Believe in Human Rights, Not Women's Rights': Women and the Human Rights State, 1969–1984." *Radical History Review* 101 (2008): 107–29.

Comeau, Gina, and Anthony Church. "A Comparative Analysis of Women's Sports Advocacy Groups in Canada and the United States." *Journal of Sport and Social Issues* 34, no. 4 (2010): 457–74.

Dryden, Ken. "Alan Eagleson Always at Forefront." *Globe and Mail*, September 5, 2012. http://theglobeandmail.com/sports/hockey/alan-eagleson -alwats-at-forefront/article4522223.

Eaton, John. "Gender Equity in Canadian Ice Hockey: The Legal Struggle." *Legal Information Management* 12 (2012): 121–23.

Etue, Elizabeth, and Megan Williams. *On the Edge: Women Making Hockey History*. Toronto: Second Story, 1996.

Gruneau, Richard, and David Whitson. *Hockey Night in Canada: Sport, Identities and Cultural Politics*. Toronto: Garamond, 1993.

Hall, Ann. *The Girl and the Game: A History of Women's Sport in Canada*. Toronto: University of Toronto Press, 2002.

————. "Women's Sport Advocacy Organizations: Comparing Feminist Activism in Sport." *Journal of Comparative Physical Education and Sport* 16 (1994): 50–59.

Keyes, Mary. "Feminist Lobbying and Decision Making Power in Fitness and Amateur Sport National Policies, Programs and Services: The Case of Canada." In *Sport, The Third Millennium: Proceedings of the International Symposium*, edited by F. Landry, M. Landry, and M. Yerles, 419–30. Quebec City: Les Presses Université Laval, 1991.

Kidd, Bruce. *The Struggle for Canadian Sport*. Toronto: University of Toronto Press, 1996.

————. "The Men's Cultural Centre: Sports and the Dynamic of Women's Oppression/Men's Repression." In *Sport, Men and the Gender Order: Critical Feminist Perspectives*, edited by M. Messner and D. Sabo, 31–44. Champaign, IL: Human Kinetics, 1990.

Kidd, Bruce, and John Macfarlane. *The Death of Hockey*. Toronto: New Press, 1972.

McCormack, Shirley. *The Last Frontier: Women and Power in Professional Team Sports: The Gender Inequity in Canada Ignored by Feminists*. Lindsay, ON: GOH Press, 2002.

McFarlane, Brian. *Proud Past, Bright Future: One Hundred Years of Canadian Women's Hockey*. Peterborough, ON: Stoddart, 1994.

Ontario Hockey Federation. "Program of Excellence." Ontario Hockey Federation. http://www.ohf.on.ca/players-families/program-excellence (accessed on July 22, 2013).

Rebick, Judy. *Ten Thousand Roses: The Making of a Feminist Revolution*. Toronto: Penguin Canada, 2005.

Report of the Royal Commission on the Status of Women in Canada. Ottawa: Information Canada, 1970.

Rosenberg, Danny, and Julie Stevens. "The Ban on Bodychecking in Women's Hockey: An Ethical Appraisal." In *Putting It on Ice, Volume III: Women's Hockey – Gender Issues On and Off the Ice*, edited by C. Howell., 37–42. Halifax, NS: Gorsebrook Research Institute, 2005.

Stevens, Julie. "The Development of the Canadian Hockey System: A Process of Institutional Divergence and Convergence." In *Putting It on Ice*. Vol. 2,

Internationalizing 'Canada's Game', edited by C. Howell, 51–64. Halifax, NS: Gorsebrook Research Institute, 2002.

———. "Women's Hockey in Canada: After the Gold Rush." In *Artificial Ice: Hockey, Culture and Commerce*, edited by D. Whitson and R. Gruneau, 85–100. Peterborough, ON: Broadview, 2006.

Tong, Rosemarie. *Feminist Thought: A Comprehensive Introduction*. San Francisco: Westview, 1989.

From Sweden with Love:
The Summit Series and the Notion
of the Contemporary Canadian
Hockey Player in Sweden

♦

TOBIAS STARK

Faceoff

The 1972 Summit Series between Team Canada and Team USSR is generally recognized as a watershed in the history of hockey. The communications director of the International Ice Hockey Federation (IIHF), Szymon Szemberg, has even branded the tournament as the "eight games that changed the sport forever" (63). Much of the importance attributed to the event has to do with it being the first time the best European amateur players were allowed to square off with the top professionals of the fabled NHL. Besides, the series soon paved the way for the migration of generations of Europeans to North American professional hockey, as the NHL found out the hard way that the standout players in the Old World were truly world-class talent.

Given its notoriety amongst hockey fans and others alike, it is hardly surprising that the Summit Series has been the subject of considerable historical deliberation, ranging from several anniversary reunions and a flood of commemorative books to a series of TV documentaries and numerous academic treatises. In fact, the scrutiny of the outpourings on the Canadian national sentiments accompanying Team Canada's victory in the tournament has almost become a literary genre in its own right.

However, the impact of the Summit Series on the hockey world at large, and its influence on the international game, has yet to be thoroughly examined. In the following, I will analyze the implications of the Summit Series on the notion of the contemporary Canadian hockey player in Sweden, through an account of the Swedish reactions to the tournament at the time of the event. The aim is to build on the conventional historical narrative of the 1972 Canada-Soviet hockey series by situating it in the larger historical context of contemporary Sweden. I will argue that the Summit Series is not so much to be understood as "the birth of top level international hockey" as some commentators have contended (Pelletier and Houda, 7), but rather the beginning of the NHL's hegemony of the hockey world.

In order to consider the perception of Canadian hockey in Sweden, it is essential to note that since its "discovery" the American continent has served as a blank canvas in the Old World, upon which the Europeans have been able to project their innermost dreams and fears. Although the Swedish conception of "America" has been formed primarily with the USA in mind – while Canada has been more or less conceived of as being "the same but different" than its southern neighbour – the general Swedish understanding of the Canadian game of hockey is an excellent example of this logic. When hockey was introduced in Sweden at the beginning of the 1920s, it was not seen merely as a new sport, but rather as an expression of the coming of the modern age, as the notion of "America" was deeply interwoven with the concept of "modernity." For some this meant the promise of a better way of life, as openness, rationality and personal freedom were cherished features of the social fabric of the New World. Others dreaded the lure of "Americanization," as they equated North American customs with immorality, sensationalism, and alienation.

Thus, when hockey was introduced in Sweden in the interwar era, there were those who welcomed the game with open arms, as they envisioned it as an international sport perfectly suited for life in modern society. Still, others strove to thwart the launching of the new sport since they regarded it as a corrupting force, undermining endemic values and traditions. Gradually, however, most of the strong suspicion towards hockey gave way to a widespread appreciation of the game among the Swedes, prompted by, inter alia, a growing predilection for "American" commodities in general, as well as by Swedish triumphs in international competition and the great admiration Swedes held for visiting Canadian teams, such as the legendary Victoria Hockey Club (Montreal), whose players were publicly heralded as outstanding athletes and noble gentlemen of the greatest kind.

After 1945, the public interest in hockey exploded in Sweden, as the game was turned into a Cold War battleground. In the highly politicized culture of the time, the Swedish Nationals – or Tre Kronor (the "Three Crowns"), as they have been popularly known – came to function as a thermometer of how the so-called "Swedish model" (i.e., the blending of private and civic interests that has come to be seen as typically Swedish) stood up in comparison to the superpowers of the world. A central ingredient in the make-up of the Swedish self-image during the postwar era concerned Sweden as "a world conscience," working for peace and solidarity on the international level. This aspect of the national identity also came into play in sport, as the Swedish hockey community fought to put oil on the troubled waters of the international game. Simultaneously, however, the perception of the Canadian hockey players was transformed.

In the first half of the twentieth century, Canada ruled more or less supreme in international hockey competition. The quality of Canadian hockey was actually so high that second- and third-rated student and senior men's amateur teams could outplay the best European national squads on a regular basis; hence, the deep-felt adoration of the demeanour of the members of the Victoria Hockey Club and their countrymen in Sweden. However, the successful entrance of the Soviet Union on the international hockey scene in 1954 – beating the Canadian representatives, the East York Lyndhursts, by a whopping 7–2 on their way to capturing their first World Championship – marked the beginning of a new era in the game. Team USSR went on to dominate the international competition the following four decades, earning gold medal honours in a total of eighteen World Championships and five Olympic games, staged between 1954 and 1989. The Soviets' prowess, together with the steady improvement of the Czechs and the Swedes, meant that the college – and amateur – teams Canada sent to international tournaments could no longer count on placing high in the standings.

The sifting power balance in international hockey was hard to swallow in Canada. Canadian hockey representatives soon came to accuse the Soviets of cheating: the state-sponsored USSR players were not true amateurs but cloaked professionals, they maintained. Also, Canadian officials set out to persuade the IIHF to allow professionals to participate in the World Championships, subsequently withdrawing from international hockey in protest of IIHF President Johnny Francis "Bunny" Ahearne's opposition to the proposal. On the ice, the frustration manifested itself among Canadian players in a growing reliance on force – and intimidation – tactics (fighting, trash-talking, etc.) to overcome their opponents in international tournaments.

Concurrently, the notion of Canadian hockey was transformed in Europe, as the Canadian players went from being considered good sports to being characterized as violent goons. For the Swedes, the beginning of the 1960s seems to have been a particularly critical period in this regard, as the amateur senior men's team Trail Smoke Eaters toured Sweden in 1961 and 1963 and literally crushed their opponents. The result was a public outcry over the supposed brutality and unsportsmanlike conduct of the Canadians. Apparently, some Swedish parents even began invoking the Canadians ("If you don't behave yourself, the Trail Smoke Eaters will come and get you!") in order to "scare" their children "straight" (Mårtensson). Subsequently, while the notion of Canadian hockey was deteriorating in Sweden, the Swedes turned to Eastern Europe for influences and deliberately started to mimic the Soviets' game (i.e., their successful emphasis on team play).

Yet, the Swedes neither embraced the Soviets altogether nor spurned the Canadians completely. As Team USSR kept on dominating in the World Championships, it became increasingly evident that amateurs from Sweden and the rest of the hockey world could no longer compete with the "cloaked professionals" from Eastern Europe. In fact, in the absence of a viable Team Canada, the superiority of the Soviet players – and their Czech allies, who were state professionals as well – threatened to turn the World Championships into a farce, as all their opponents could aim for was to win the bronze medal. To breathe new life into the World Championships, and to have Canada return to the international hockey family for the sake of solidarity, Swedish officials began lobbying for the IIHF to allow Team Canada to use professionals in international competitions, even getting the IIHF delegates in 1970 to accept a "modernized" version of amateurism, meaning that an amateur was a player who got most of his income from his civic career (*Svenska ishockeyförbundets årsberättelse 1970/1971*, 5–6).

International hockey was at a crossroads: the only way forward was letting the best amateurs in Europe face the skilled North American professionals, it seemed.

The Fight of the Century

During the World Championships in Prague in April 1972, the news broke that the Soviet Union was to play a series of exhibition games later that year against an all-star team made up of Canadian NHL players. In Sweden, the report was met with mixed emotions. On the one hand, the hockey community greeted it with great jubilation, since it had been dying to see Canada return to the international hockey circuit – even more so because the event in question involved present-day NHL stars, rather than mere "re-amateurized" farmhands, as first might have been expected, as much of the debate on Canada taking part in international hockey since the 1960s had centred on how many reinstated former professionals Team Canada was allowed to dress. Hence, the forthcoming challenge series was widely acknowledged as "a dream tournament" and labelled "the fight of the century" since it was seen as the answer to a long-standing question: Which brand of hockey was the best – the European or the North American (Olsson, "Äntligen NHL"; Carlson, "…och en svensk"; Jansson, "Skandal")?

On the other hand, many Swedish commentators feared the Canadians took the task too lightly. The Swedes were truly flabbergasted the Canadians had agreed on facing Team USSR in September, a time of the year when the NHL players would not be in their best shape because of their summer holiday, while the Soviets were widely known for their tough year-long fitness regime. Albeit the general consensus in Sweden was that Team Canada would beat Team USSR, it was considered to be so much up for contest that neither side could afford to take any chances. Also, and more important, there was a nagging concern that the event beckoned the coming of a professional European hockey league that had been rumoured for some time, controlled by either the NHL or the newly founded World Hockey Association (WHA). Up until that point, only one European-trained player – the Swedish power forward, Ulf Sterner – had ever played in the NHL, but the growing numbers of professional scouts at international tournaments had the Swedish hockey establishment up in arms, as it feared losing its best players to North America.[1] Thus, it was not just the cloaked professionalism of the Soviets and the Czechs that haunted the Swedes in the beginning of the 1970s, but the fear of the North American hockey industry preying on the Swedish hockey program as well.

Amid all the initial hoopla about the Summit Series, it should be noted that when the puck finally dropped between Team Canada and Team USSR, the interest in the tournament seems to have been lukewarm at best among the Swedes, at least as far as the first games in Canada were concerned. Sure, all major Swedish media outlets had reporters on-site covering the tournament, but the all-overriding event in Europe in September 1972 was the Olympic Games in Munich, especially after the terrorist attack in the Olympic Village on September 5, which saw seventeen people killed. Unsurprisingly, this tragedy appears to have had a cooling effect on much of the general interest in sport in contemporary Sweden, even leading to a mounting criticism of the purported politicization, commercialization and elitism of modern sport ("OS ett hån"; "Politiken pressar idrotten"). Though only small portions of this criticism surfaced in the reporting on the Summit Series, the debate certainly worked to counter much of the initial excitement about the tournament among the Swedes.

Furthermore, the Swedish hockey community seems to have had much of their mind elsewhere. In fact, the president of the Swedish Ice Hockey Association (SIHA), Helge Berglund, was criticized in the press for leaving his post, having travelled to Canada to follow the first leg of the tournament on-site (Ericson, "Hockey-sekreteraren"). The status of Swedish hockey was questioned after a shaky performance by Tre Kronor in the World Championships earlier that year, and Berglund going abroad to witness the Summit Series first-hand was consequently not considered to be in the best interests of the national program. Unsurprisingly so, as the Tre Kronor coach in the aforesaid tournament was the former NHLer and Toronto native Billy Harris, who was much appreciated by the players but publicly challenged by vocal parts of the hockey community on the grounds of retaining a North American coaching style unfit for Swedish hockey culture.

Whereas the Swedes had taken the Canadian sport of hockey to their hearts decades before, and while the renowned NHL was universally celebrated as the best league in the world, the fear of the game being an instrument for distorting North American influences thus lingered on in Sweden. Actually, the end of the 1960s and the beginning of the 1970s saw the general notion of "America" take a turn for the worse in Sweden, by way of the Vietnam War and the flourishing environmental movement, which saw the US being criticized for its perceived bullish foreign policy and its supposedly cold and superficial consumer society. The fact that Canada was not part of the USA, but an independent nation, is an issue of mere academic interest in this context, as the two countries for most contemporary Swedes could be described as "same, same, but different."

In part, this revived anti-Americanization stance – or anti-Canadianization stance, to be more precise – also surfaced in the reporting on the Summit Series. Following the opening bout, the Soviets' 7–3 ousting of Team Canada in Montreal, all major Swedish newspapers ran quite spiteful stories on the so-called "death of the myth of the invincibility of the Canadian professionals" (Åslund, "En myt är avlivad"; Eklöw, "Otränade Kanadaproffs"; Norén, "Kanada chockat"). At great length, the authors discussed the supposed arrogance and hubris of the Canadians' icing such a badly conditioned team in "the fight of the century." At the same time, when reading the newspaper articles today, one is struck by the bliss the members of the contemporary Swedish hockey community must have felt, it having being proved that the European game was just as good as the North American game, if not even better. Yet, this contention appeared to be a double-edged sword, as it led to the bleak conclusion that the future would see a rising demand for Europeans in North American professional hockey. The news that the Detroit Red Wings' owner, Bruce Norris, was just about to launch a professional league in Europe, as announced a few days later, did nothing to ease that anxiety – quite the opposite.[2]

Still, it would be wrong to say that all the Swedish reporting on the Canadians was negative during the first leg of the tournament. For example,

Team Canada's victory in the second game against the Soviets (4–1) was hailed as a true test of character, where the players re-established Canada's tarnished reputation. Individual Canadian players, such as Phil and Tony Esposito, were also applauded for their splendid performance on the ice. Furthermore, the home crowds' sportsmanlike conduct – applauding the Soviets after they had outplayed Team Canada in games one and four – greatly impressed the Swedes, as patriotism did not get the better of the passionate Canadian hockey fans (Norén, "Kanada chockat" and "NHL-proffsens matcher").

Then again, neither the good nor the bad Swedish press on the Canadians regarding the first four games of the tournament could compare with the levels of deep adoration and severe aggravation directed at Team Canada while in Stockholm.

Team Canada in Stockholm

Though labelled "the fight of the century," the real treat of the Summit Series for the Swedes was not the Canadians' and the Soviets' battle for world hockey supremacy, but Team Canada's visit to Stockholm on its way to Moscow for the final leg of the tournament. The SIHA was celebrating its fiftieth anniversary, and the two exhibition games between Tre Kronor and the star-laden Team Canada, on September 16 and 17, were meant as the icing on the birthday cake. The Swedish National Stig-Göran Johansson captured the great excitement among the Swedes before the matchup well, when stating that facing the legendary NHLers "was something he had longed for since wearing knickerbockers" (Ericson, "Bara en match"). Besides, both games sold out in an instant, despite being aired live on national television while having ticket prices four to eight times more expensive (depending on where the seats were located in the arena) than during the Swedish Championships the same year.[3] Also, the organizers charged admission to Team Canada's practices, but that did not stop crowds of about five thousand people from following their workouts with great interest.

In fact, the fuss about the NHLers being in Stockholm was so great that Swedish reporters followed their every move. Upon arrival, all major Swedish media outlets were brimming with material on the "famous professionals" and the "super phenomena," as the Canadians were dubbed (Larsson; Norén, "Här är TV"). Among the players, the superstars Bobby Orr and Phil Esposito grabbed most of the attention, followed by the solid, but otherwise often overlooked, defender Gary Bergman. In the case of the former, it was the illustrious athletic abilities as well as the luxurious celebrity lifestyles of the idolized players that occupied the Swedes. In the later case, it was rather Bergman's Swedish heritage that fascinated the fans. Bergman talked with Swedish reporters in great detail about his parents leaving Sweden for Canada in the beginning of the twentieth century, his distant Swedish relatives and his dream of coaching in Sweden following his retirement from the NHL (Kvärre).

Swedish pundits also commented on Bergman's professed old age (thirty-two years old), his bald-headedness and the fact he had kept most of his own teeth, albeit being a seasoned NHL veteran. These remarks might strike a present-day reader as odd and offending, but they must be understood as expressions of the contemporary conception of sport in Sweden as a youthful undertaking, as well as a recurrent theme in the criticism of North American professional hockey in Europe during the Cold War: the terror of facial injuries. Actually, when Ulf Sterner left Sweden to join the New York Rangers in 1964, he was derided by the confounded SIHA – who were disappointed in him for ostensibly abandoning the national program – as an egoistic diva in great danger of having his teeth knocked out by the so-called North American hoodlums (*Ishockeyboken 1964/1965*, 90; Eklöw, "Första proffsfiaskot").

Apart from portraying individual players, Swedish reporters also took time explaining Team Canada's playing style to the fans, while underlining the North Americans' emphasis on shooting, forechecking and intimidation tactics. Before the first faceoff, all Swedish experts seem to have agreed that Tre Kronor was the underdog. Some believed Team Canada would win quite comfortably, but others maintained the Swedish Nationals could in fact beat the renowned professionals. After all, the Soviets had shown the world the fabled NHLers were mere humans, they argued (Åslund, "Ikväll bekänner"; Norén, "Så slår ni Kanada"). One to do so was the newly appointed Tre Kronor coach, Kjell Svensson, who had stepped in after the SIHA and Billy Harris had agreed on not extending the latter's contract. According to Svensson, the Swedes were more than able to beat their guests as long as they played their own game, putting emphasis on skating and puck possession, as well as if they held their own ground against the sturdy professionals. But, intimidated the Swedes were.

The Swedish National, and later Toronto Maple Leaf, Börje Salming has stated that the Swedish players were actually in awe of the Canadians just from reading their names in the paper. On the ice, the NHLers' abrasive and hard-hitting playing style startled the Swedes, who lost 4–1 in the first exhibition game on September 16. After the game, Svensson admitted to Tre Kronor of having had too much respect for the Canadians; some players were even said to have been downright scared of the North Americans. Nor were the players the only Swedes to be daunted by Team Canada's behaviour. The following day, all major Swedish media outlets ran stories on the contended upsetting actions of the Canadians. Headlines such as "Thrash, Canada" and "Team Ugly" were the order of the day. Overnight, the initial veneration of the prominent visitors was replaced by a belligerent criticism of Team Canada among the Swedes, in some cases bordering on real xenophobia. In fact, the disgust at the Canadians was so great that they received a bomb threat, meaning their hotel had to be searched by the police before they could go to sleep after the game (Jansson, "Skräp, Kanada"; Åslund, "Kanada"; Byström, "Team Canada"). Yet, the worst was to come.

Before the second game, Team Sweden talked about standing up to the Canadians. The result was a brawl-filled bout pigeonholed as the worst tussle the Swedish audience had ever seen (Åslund, "Blodet som bevisar"; Ericson, "Slagsmålen fortsatte I pauserna"). The game ended in a 4–4 draw, but the score must be characterized as a Pyrrhic victory for the involved parties, as the ice surface was literary covered in blood when the players left the rink after the final buzzer. The nastiest incident occurred near the end of the first period, when Ulf Sterner (accidentally as the Swedes saw it, but purposely according to the Canadians) cut Team Canada's Wayne Cashman quite badly in the mouth with his stick. Cashman left the game to get stitches but was soon back "in action" wearing street clothes while trying to get back at Sterner in the Tre Kronor dressing room, but he was hindered by the Swedish police, who wrestled him to the ground. Other notorious incidents included a fierce yelling match at centre ice – where Phil Esposito and Kjell Svensson exchanged unpleasantries, questioning each other's manliness – as well as Vic Hadfield's high-sticking of the later Winnipeg Jet Lars-Erik Sjöberg, breaking the Swedish captain's nose.

The next day, the Swedish press had a field day printing front page photographs of Sjöberg and his blood-spattered nose and calling the Canadian players "animals," "gangsters" and "perpetrators of violence." Some commentators even suggested the Canadians had better leave early for Moscow, as they were no longer welcome in Sweden. The aggravated situation actually had the Canadian ambassador, Margaret Meagher, going public to lament the excessive violence in the supposedly friendly games, something most Swedish onlookers must have taken as a formal apology and proof that Canada as a nation was officially disgraced. After the game, the members of Team Canada hung out in their hotel; those who wanted to step outside were instructed by coach Harry Sinden not to wear their team blazers, as the Canadians did not want to attract any more unwelcome attention before leaving for Moscow a couple of days later (Byström, "Kanadaglansen"; Åslund, "Blodet"; Sterner; MacSkimming, 137).

The notion of the Canadian hockey player was at an all-time low in Sweden. But things were about to change.

Curtain Fall

It is safe to say Team Canada's ill-fated stay in Stockholm put a strain on the Swedish-Canadian relationship, at least as far as hockey was concerned. In Sweden, for one thing, it meant the rejuvenation of the notion of the Canadian hockey player as a violent goon, an image that has been in circulation in one form or another since then. Also, Team Canada's visit stirred a spirited debate on what the future might hold for Swedish hockey, considering the NHL's and the WHA's rapidly growing interest in European talent. Some claimed allowing the semi-professionals in Tre Kronor to become full-time players was the best way to offset the coming wave of Swedes signing lucrative contracts with North American clubs (i.e., the draining of the national program). Others saw the realization of a professional European hockey league, such as the one Bruce Norris hoped to launch, as a way to keep the best players on home ice. However, according to SIHA President Helge Berglund, that line of reasoning did not add up, as most ice rinks in Sweden were aimed at recreational activities for the young, rather than being designed to suit the capitalistic exploits of the owners of professional hockey clubs. In the end, neither Norris's nor the WHA's rivalling attempt to launch a European professional hockey league materialized, because the Soviets and the Czechs bowed out of participation (Byström, "Proffshockey i Europa"; Lindberg; Olsson "Striden går vidare"). But the tide was turning.

In Sweden, there seems to have been a generation gap with respect to the issue of Sweden's position vis-à-vis the North American hockey industry. For one thing, the SIHA was divided into two camps, with old-timer Helge Berglund representing a fraction of the board that feared being subjugated by the NHL and the WHA, and the other – led by the younger Ove Rainer, who succeeded Berglund as the president of the organization the following year – maintaining it was better to work with the NHL and the WHA than being totally dominated by them. Besides, the Swedish players were keen on making hockey their full-time job. In fact, a number of the Swedish nationals later admitted that the exhibition games against Team Canada really got them thinking of playing in the NHL or the WHA for the first time, as they had proved to themselves and others they could compete with the best players in the world. At the time, Ulf Sterner was actually bold enough to reveal he saw the games as an opportunity to show his worth in order to get a lucrative WHA contract (Carlson, "Ulf Sterner spelar"?; Salming and Karlsson, 46).

Furthermore, while the Swedish interest in the Summit Series was lukewarm at first, the Canadians' stay in Stockholm turned the final leg of the tournament into a smoking hot affair, as the games were no longer perceived as a mere battle of world hockey supremacy but as a test proof of the future of the sport, per se. The major media outlets in Sweden reported the games and the undertakings of the NHLers unabatedly, in some cases even increasing the coverage. The fact that Swedish national television obtained the rights to a live broadcast of the last game of the series shortly before the event, and seemingly was the only European country to air the matchup, is a telling example of this (Jansson, "Nu skrattar"; Åslund, "Ingen drömhockey"; Kvärre and Sjögren).

Interestingly enough, most contemporary Swedish commentators agreed that the best team ultimately won the Summit Series. Sure, the Canadians were still considered to be brutish players, but their ability to rise to the occasion and come out on top after the poor start greatly impressed the Swedes. The Canadians might have been criminals on the ice, but they were proper gentlemen outside the rink; they only acted like villains in order to win, as they were so competitive they did whatever it took to triumph, it was argued (Ericson, "Dödstrött – men överlycklig"; "Trots allt bråk"). Apparently, the Swedes had an easier time digesting the Canadian's aggressive playing style when they thumped the Soviets than when Team Canada was facing Tre Kronor a week earlier.

At first glance, this seemingly abrupt leniency about the Canadians' ferociousness might appear strange. Yet, on closer examination, it appears to be a result of the tangible love-hate relationship the Swedes have had with Canadian hockey since the game was first introduced. It is a strong bond involving alternating emotions, ranging from sheer devotion to total disgust, though the pendulum has swung back and forth over time. Following the Summit Series, in Sweden the general notion of the Canadian hockey player seems to have slowly shifted in a positive direction. This is perhaps most evident in that aggressive-role players such as Bob Probert, Sean Avery and Dan Carcillo have become big fan favorites in Sweden, beside more traditional hockey heroes like the offensively skilled superstars Wayne Gretzky, Sidney Crosby and Steven Stamkos. This should come as no surprise, because the period in question has seen Sweden become all but completely incorporated into the North American hockey industry as the NHL has gained a hegemonic position in the hockey world at large.

The aforementioned Salming's stellar NHL career may actually be read as a barometer of the gradual Swedish adaptation to the NHL brand of hockey and the interrelated transformation of the notion of the Canadian player. When Salming signed with the Toronto Maple Leafs in 1973 after an impressive showing in the exhibition games against Team Canada in September 1972, he was considered a talented but somewhat unruly defender in Sweden. While most Swedes were happy for him, part of the Swedish hockey establishment seems initially to have lamented the move as a token of the dreaded draining of the national program. However, Salming's instant success in Toronto – as the first European superstar in the NHL – and the overwhelmingly warm welcome he received from the home crowd during the 1976 Canada Cup helped stir the interest in the NHL in Sweden tremendously while opening the door for the migration of generations of Swedish players to professional clubs in Canada and the USA.

When Salming, aged thirty-eight, returned to Sweden to play in the World Championships in Stockholm in 1989, he was treated as a "living legend," having played sixteen seasons in the "toughest league in the world." Before long, he was dubbed "the manliest" and "the sexiest" man in Sweden (*Treschow Andrén*; Israelson). This is particularly noteworthy because it was mainly his supposed sensual face and body – marked by numerous injuries sustained during his lengthy NHL career – on which the then middle-aged Salming's reputation as a genuine Swedish role model and potent sex symbol was grounded; that is, the same attributes (the old age and the tarnished body) that Gary Bergman and others were ridiculed for displaying before the mass movement of Swedish hockey players to the NHL began after the Summit Series.

Nowadays, the interest in the NHL seems as vibrant as ever in Sweden, and the ultimate dream for the players has more or less come to mean hoisting the Stanley Cup, rather than representing Tre Kronor in the World Championships. Thus, it can be argued that the Summit Series is not so much to be understood as the birth of top-level international hockey, but rather the beginning of the NHL's hegemony of the hockey world.

---

[1] Ulf Sterner made his NHL debut on January 27, 1965, for the New York Rangers in a game against the Boston Bruins. Sterner went on to play four games in the NHL before returning to Sweden the following season.

[2] On this, see Cruise and Griffiths.

[3] The ticket prices in the exhibition games ranged from forty to sixty Swedish kronor, compared to the five to fifteen Swedish kronor for tickets to the 1972 Swedish Championships.

Works Cited

Åslund, Nic. "Blodet som bevisar Kanadas svaghet." *Aftonbladet* (Stockholm), September 18, 1972.

————. "En myt är avlivad – Kanada chanslöst." *Aftonbladet*, September 3, 1972.

————. "Ikväll bekänner proffsen färg." *Aftonbladet*, September 16, 1972.

————. "Ingen drömhockey – men ett mycket gediget hantverk." *Aftonbladet*, September 23, 1972.

————. "Kanada, varför gjorde ni oss detta?" *Aftonbladet*, September 17, 1972.

Byström, Bobby. "Kanadaglansen bara bleknar." *Dagens Nyheter* (Stockholm), September 18, 1972.

————. "Team Canada en besvikelse." *Dagens Nyheter*, September 17, 1972.

Carlson, Thomas. "…och en svensk ordnade det." *Aftonbladet*, April 19, 1972.

Cruise, David, and Alison Griffiths. *Net Worth: Exploding the Myths of Pro Hockey*. Toronto: Penguin, 1992.

Eklöw, Rudolf (R:et). "Första proffsfiaskot för Kanada redan 59." *Dagens Nyheter*, September 20, 1972.

————. "Otränade Kanadaproffs hann inte med ryssarna." *Dagens Nyheter*, September 4, 1972.

Ericson, Singel. "Bara en match till Sverige." *Expressen* (Stockholm), April 19, 1972.

————. "Dödstrött – men överlycklig." *Expressen*, September 29, 1972.

————. "Hockey-sekreteraren har redan fått nog. Kan inte Samarbeta med Helge Berglund." *Expressen*, September 7, 1972.

————. "Slagsmålen fortsatte I pauserna." *Expressen*, September 18, 1972.

Ishockeyboken 1964/1965. Stockholm: Svenska ishockeyförbundet, 1964.

Israelson, Aaron. "Mat-Tina är svenska männens drömkvinna." *Nyheter24*, February 9, 2010. http://nyheter24.se/nyheter/inrikes /453929-mat-tina-ar-svenska-mannens-dromkvinna.

Jansson, Bertil. "Nu skrattar vi inte längre åt Kanada." *Expressen*, September 27, 1972.

————. "Skandal eller succé." *Expressen*, April 19, 1972.

————. "Skräp, Kaanda." *Expressen*, September 17, 1972.

Kvärre, Stellan. "Svenske Gunnar gläds att få möta 'svarta ögat' Sterner." *Dagens Nyheter*, September 16, 1972.

Kvärre, Stellan, and Per Sjögren. "Hockeyfinalen direkt i TV." *Dagens Nyheter*, September 28, 1972.

Larsson, Per-Gunnar. "Idag kommer NHL-hockeyns fenomen." *Aftonbladet*, September 13, 1972.

Lindberg, Helge. "Topplön i Tre Kronor." *Expressen*, September 19, 1972.

MacSkimming, Roy. *Cold War: The Amazing Canada-Soviet Hockey Series of 1972*. Vancouver, BC: Greystone, 1996.

Mårtensson, Per. "'Dirty Harry' är i stan." *Nya Wermlands-Tidningen* (Karlstad), February 14, 2009.

Norén, Helge. "Här är TV – stjärnorna i proffsens Europa – debut." *Expressen*, September 16, 1972.

————. "Kanada chockat. Sovjet har skjutit sönder NHL-myten." *Expressen*, September 3, 1972.

————. "NHL-proffsens matcher idrottshistoriens största felspekulation!?" *Expressen*, September 13, 1972.

————. "Så slår ni Kanada – proffsen." *Expressen*, September 13, 1972.

Olsson, Thorwald. "Äntligen NHL mot Sovjet." *Dagens Nyheter*, April 19, 1972.

————. "Striden går vidare. WHL vill bli först." *Dagens Nyheter*, September 19, 1972.

"OS ett hån mot idrottens idéer." *Aftonbladet*, September 7, 1972.

Pelletier, Joe, and Patrick Houda. *The World Cup of Hockey: A History of Hockey's Greatest Tournament*. Toronto: Warwick, 2003.

Podnieks, Andrew, and Szymon Szemberg, eds. *World of Hockey: Celebrating a Century of the IIHF.* Bolton, ON: Fenn, 2007.

"Politiken pressar idrotten." *Dagens Nyheter*, September 6, 1972.

Salming, Börje, and Gerhard Karlsson. *Blod, svett och hockey – 17 år i NHL.* Stockholm: Walhströms, 1995.

Stark, Tobias. *Folkhemmet på is: Ishockey, modernisering och nationell identitet i Sverige 1920–1972.* Malmö: Idrottsforum, 2010.

Sterner, Ulf. "Rena rama gangserttakterna!" *Expressen*, September 18, 1972.

Svenska ishockeyförbundets årsberättelse 1970/1971. Stockholm: Svenska ishockeyförbudnet, 1971.

Treschow Andrén, Adele. "I huvudet på Rafael Edholm." Nattstad (blog). http://www.nattstad.se/magazineread.aspx?id=464.

"Trots allt bråk – Kanada är bäst." *Aftonbladet*, September 29, 1972.

Hot Ice during Cold War:
Soviet Reflections on Summit Series 1972

♦

ALEXANDER KUBYSHKIN

In April 2012 a movie was released in Russia under the title *The Legend N 17*, about the life and sporting career of one of the most famous Soviet hockey players, Valery Kharlamov. The main character's role was performed by Russian movie star Daniil Kozlovsky, and the part of legendary Soviet coach Anatoly Tarasov was played by another star, Oleg Menshikov. It was exactly the time when all of Russia celebrated the fortieth anniversary of the Summit Series, which actually crushed the Cold War atmosphere in the very popular type of sporting exercises that hockey was for dozens of millions of Soviets.

As is well known, the Cold War reflected not only military and political controversy but ideological and socio-cultural competition as well. Sport in the Soviet Union, especially boxing, soccer, swimming, basketball and athletics, was an extremely important element for official propaganda to confirm and to advance the basic values and priorities of the Marxist-Leninist social and political system.

The Summit Series story has a large body of analytic and descriptive literature surrounding it, not only in the West but in contemporary Russia as well. It is interesting that a lot of publications directly connect these sporting events with the general situation of the Cold War competition. A recently published book by well-known Russian journalist Andrey Kolesnikov is named *The Cold War on the Ice*, which is very close to the title of a famous hockey book written by Roy MacSkimming, *Cold War* (1996).

The TV record of the first game between Team Canada and the USSR (September 2, 1972) on YouTube still gets thousands of watchers and has a lot of comments with not only sports context but also the inclusions of political and socio-cultural notes and reflections. But it is not enough to look at the Summit Series as representing Soviet hockey in the latter half of the twentieth century. Soviet hockey contexts are more complicated than such a view, perhaps held by those looking in from the outside, might represent.

Hockey's Genesis in the Soviet Union

Born in 1946, Soviet ice hockey entered a real boom that covered the period from 1963 to 1991. In 1991, the Soviet ice hockey national team won bronze at the World Championships and in two years more, under the leadership of Boris Mayorov, the new Russian team won the World Championship. After that, fifteen years of decline, disorder and uncertainty came.

The period from 1963 in Russian hockey is marked as the "Tarasov epoch." Like his colleague and opponent Vsevolod Bobrov, Anatoly Tarasov (1918–95) made a great effort to create in the Soviet Union a contemporary game of Western (Swedish and Canadian) style, combining high speed, well-organized tactics and the strong physical condition of the players. Carefully, Tarasov observed the games of the Swedish team and some Canadian amateur clubs and introduced into the training process of the Soviet players the elements of fighting and aggressive tactics (the so-called "cockfighting five minutes").

In the late 1950s in Moscow, a huge new arena, Luzhniki, was constructed. Tarasov was a great promoter of the creation of junior hockey clubs and associations; a lot of them were organized in dozens of Soviet cities and towns, not in the capitals (Moscow and Leningrad) only. Hundreds of hockey fields ("boxes") and arenas were built as well. The juniors had their own championship – called "A Golden Puck" – that prepared dozens of players for the national team. In 1964, the Central Club of the Soviet Army (CCSA) led by Tarasov got its new contemporary arena.

In the middle of the 1960s, ice hockey became a national game in the Soviet Union, sharing the popularity with soccer and boxing. The duels among leading clubs like CCSA and Dinamo or Spartacus attracted hundreds of thousands of viewers to the sporting halls or to TV transmissions. The first TV broadcast of the World Championships to the Soviets was in March 1963 from Stockholm.

In 1964, a very popular movie called *The Hockey Players* appeared on Soviet screens. It not only demonstrated the internal professional problems of Soviet hockey – the different styles and tactics of CCSA and Spartacus, for example – but also claimed the ideological and moral priority of the "Soviet hockey school" over Western-style hockey (or Swedish-style). The same theme is evident even in popular TV cartoons like *Puck, Puck!* (1964) and *Return Match* (1968).

Hockey as Propaganda

The ideological and political context of ice hockey became evident during the Soviet invasion of Czechoslovakia in 1968. This action converted games between the Soviet and Czech teams into moral competitions and expressed the sense of protest against Soviet aggression and the crushing of democracy in Czechoslovakia. Very clearly, it was demonstrated in Stockholm in 1969 when the Czech team won matches against the Soviets with scores of 2–0 and 4–3.

It was clear that ice hockey in the Soviet Union, because of its massive popularity, became one of the most powerful tools of propaganda about the achievements and priority of the Soviet social and political order over what was labelled "the rotten capitalist system." Hockey stands in one line in the mainstream of Soviet ideology with such national features like the victory in the Great Patriotic War (1941–45) and space program, beginning from the *Sputnik 1* era (1957) and Yury Gagarin's first flight (April 1961). In this international hockey competition, the Soviet players had to present themselves like the soldiers of the great empire. The idea of organizing some matches with Team Canada would demonstrate this image at full size (Kolesnikov, 14).

The first contact with Canadians in the World Championships in 1954, when the Soviets won over the East York Lyndhursts (Ontario second division) with a score of 7–2, did not attract much attention. In 1966 in Kalinin in the middle of Russia, the Soviets crushed the Sherbrooke Beavers 15–4. During their tour around Canada in 1969, the Soviet team won ten of ten games against amateur clubs. In Ottawa, they won with a score of 10–2, for example. Anatoly Firsov scored six goals in the game.

But everybody in Soviet hockey – including coaches, players and the public audience – understood then that a real competition between the Soviet national team and the Canadians must be demonstrated first in games with professionals. It became an *idée fixe* of Anatoly Tarasov, who pointed to the opportunity of organizing the matches between the USSR and Team Canada in his book *Coming of Age* (1968). But then, it was still a dream. Only after the Soviet victories in the World Championships in 1970 and 1971 under the coaching team of Arkady Chernyshev and Tarasov could the Summit Series idea become a reality.

The Birth of a Series

The irony was that the Summit Series project was realized by Tarasov's opponent and critic Vsevolod Bobrov. Tarasov was pulled down from the leadership of the national team in 1972 because of intrigues within the hockey bureaucracy.

Among the supporters of the Summit Series idea were high-level political functionaries like Prime Minister Alexey Kosygin (the boat racing champion of Leningrad, in his younger years) and the general secretary of the Communist Party, Leonid Brezhnev, a great amateur hockey player and fanatic supporter of CCSA. A leading party ideology functionary, Alexander Yakovlev met with confrontation by the conservative wing inside the Political Bureau of the Central Committee of the Communist Party of the Soviet Union because of his critical attitude to Stalinism rehabilitation and was forced to go into honourable exile. Ironically, it was an embassy in Canada where Yakovlev had to spend almost ten years before he was brought back to Moscow by Gorbachev. During his stay in Canada, Yakovlev made very important efforts to organize the Summit Series. Later, he wrote an introduction to *Vernost* (*Faithfulness*) by Vladislav Tretiak.

Among the opponents of the Summit Series idea was the powerful propaganda leader Mikhail Suslov. The main argument was the impossibility to win against Team Canada, and the result of this would be the failure of the national prestige in the international arena, not in hockey only, but political failure as well. In the official paper of the Central Sporting Committee, the *Soviet Sport*, an editorial under the title "The Marriage with the Professionals: Who needs it?" was published. But generally, because of the active campaigning by well-known and popular hockey observer and TV announcer Nickolay Ozerov, as well as by the coaches Arkady Chernyshev, Anatoly Tarasov, Boris Kulagin and Vsevolod Bobrov, the project was officially supported by both sport and party officials. The preliminary decision was made at a game in Vancouver in October 1971, where Kosygin and Trudeau agreed about a possible hockey series in general. The loyal attitude of Brezhnev to the project also had a powerful influence. The final official agreement between the National Hockey Association of USSR and the NHL was signed during the World Championship tournament in Prague in the spring of 1972.

In his interview after the Summit Series in November 1972, the coach of the Soviet team, Vsevolod Bobrov, noted: "We went to Canada like the blind kittens. We had only a vague idea of Canadian professionals" (Kolesnikov, 45). But of course, before the trip to Canada the Soviet coaches and players tried to analyze all the strong and weak features of the future competitors. As far back as the summer of 1968, as Vladislav Tretiak writes in *The Hockey Epos*, six-time world champion Boris Mikhailov presented a table with a five-point system that compares features of Soviet players and Canadian professionals. According to Mikhailov, the Soviets had the following advantages: (a) physical preparation – 5:4; (b) team spirit – 5:4; (c) passing – 5:3; and (d) realization of the majority advantage – 4:3. Team Canada was stronger in the following: (a) shooting – 4:3; (b) fighting (force) style – 5:4; (c) goalkeeping – 5:3; and (d) defence – 4:3, 5.

Mikhailov gave equal grades to skating – 4:4; individual puck control – 4:4; shorthanded performance – 4:4; and common game character – 5:5. The average score was 53.5:51.0 in favour of the Soviet team (58).

But of course the Soviet players understood that they would meet with the best professionals in the world, with a high international reputation. The names of the Esposito brothers, Dryden, Orr, Clarke and Cournoyer were familiar to millions of Soviets. After the Summit Series, many members of the Soviet team revealed that bureaucratic authorities and even CGB agents had not believed they could be victorious over Team Canada and had asked them to keep face and lose the games gracefully, and told them not to panic if they failed (Tretiak, 86–87). The Soviet players' psychological state was a key element during their first match in Montreal on September 2, 1972.

Political Contexts

We have to note again that the Summit Series took place under a very complicated atmosphere on the political stage. From one side, we can point to the successful trips of Henry Kissinger and Richard Nixon to Moscow in May 1972 and the beginning of détente policy in the relations between the USSR and USA. From another side, the Soviet officials had enforced the pressure on the so-called dissident movement inside Russia, making a lot of arrests, Vladimir Bukovsky included. In September 1972, the Munich massacre of the Israeli Olympic team happened as a result of Palestinian terrorist activity.

There were some attempts to upset the Summit Series just before the opening ceremony – for example, a former citizen from Czechoslovakia who had immigrated to Canada wanted to get compensation for his private car which had been crushed by a Soviet tank during the Soviet invasion in Prague in August 1968. As well, some emigrant organizations (Czech and Ukrainian) tried to block the transportation of equipment for the Soviet team (Kolesnikov, 44).

The night before the Soviet team left for Montreal, a strange event happened in the Moscow apartment of Vsevolod Bobrov – a new, just-bought crystal chandelier suddenly fell from the ceiling and was broken. When Bobrov's wife called her husband, who was preparing for the flight with the other fellows, and informed him about the incident, Bobrov's reaction was laconic: "It is a good sign, and we'll win" (Kolesnikov, 46).

The Summit Series drama has been described by hundreds of authors from different points of view. Let us note some moments connected with the political and psychological atmosphere during the games. In short, the feature moment or decisive point for Russians was the first game in Montreal on September 2.

The final score of the game, 7–3, not only demonstrated the strong character and high game class of the Russian players but also showed Team Canada clearly how dangerous it could be to be self-satisfied. "Canada Mourns Hockey Myth," Toronto's *Globe and Mail* wrote after the Montreal failure. It was interesting that this sport episode was expressed immediately by local media as Canadian military history metaphors: "Ypres was involved. Dieppe. Dunkirk... these were all overblown, given that hockey games do not cost people their lives, as battles do" (Kennedy, 155).

But even in this harsh atmosphere of misunderstanding and confrontation, there were some good moments as well. Vladislav Tretiak, who was the splendid personage in the event, admitted in his memoirs how valuable the friendly advice of Jacques Plante was for him before the game (Tretiak, *Kogda lidy jarko... [When Ice is Hot...]*, 79).

Game one was broadcast on Russian television in the evening of September 3 because of the time difference between Canada and the USSR (the final score was kept secret all day), and the match was watched by more than one hundred million Soviet people (Kolesnikov, 90).

As for the atmosphere among the players during the Summit Series, we can say that the Russians had two main characteristics—discipline and alertness. The Canadian mood presented a very special combination of direct hate and ignorance. Phil Esposito once said that he liked all the Soviets during the Summit Series except Boris Mikhailov, because of his hockey style, but in his memoirs Esposito directly called the opponents "the Red Bastards." Esposito and Mikhailov shook hands in 2012 only during the anniversary celebration of the Summit Series in Moscow (Kolesnikov, 96). The main hero of the Moscow play, Paul Henderson, underlined the feelings of hate and disgust toward the Soviet political and ideological order that he and all of Team Canada felt. He commented, "I hated then everything connected with them" (quoted in Kolesnikov, 98).

During their stay in Moscow, the Canadians were afraid of new tricks by KGB authorities and searched for "bugs" planted in their rooms in the Intourist hotel. Frank Mahovlich deconstructed some suspicious-looking equipment on the floor of his hotel room, and as a result a crystal candelabrum fell from the ceiling in the conference room downstairs. It was a probably a good sign for the Canadians, but simultaneously it caused great damage to the Intourist hotel. It seems very strange and silly now, but this event demonstrated the atmosphere of common hostility and suspicion that was typical for the Cold War era. By the way, no one asked the Canadians to pay for the destruction (Dubinin).

The Cold War stereotypes were too strong, and both sides were too different from each other. It was freedom versus control, as Brian Kennedy notes in his popular book *My Country Is Hockey* (158).

The Truth about the Soviets

The Soviets, though considered hockey amateurs, were actually mainly professionals because the majority of the national team consisted of military officers who were on service and were paid by the Soviet Ministry of Defence. They had special, comfortable training bases where they spent six to seven months a year, so they reserved eighty per cent of their time for hockey only. They were under strong political and ideological control. Vladimir Petrov was the head of the team party Communist branch, and Vladislav Tretiak was the head of a Young Communist group (Komsomol, quoted in Kolesnikov, 50–51). In the 1970s, Vyacheslav Starshinov successfully defended his Ph.D. dissertation about "the sense of duty and responsibility of Soviet sportsmen" (Kolesnikov, 68). In common the players were part of a closed society with very limited consumer and political choice and opportunities. During a conversation with Boris Mikhailov, Brad Park realized that Mikhailov's annual salary reached $200,000. Mikhailov kindly responded that he had a regular monthly salary, and was not paid only once per year (Kolesnikov, 70). The ironies in this misunderstanding are obvious.

Actually, the leading Russian hockey players were members of a privileged circle of Soviet society. For example, the common monthly salary in the early '70s in the Soviet Union was equal to 90 to 120 rubles a month (1 dollar equalled 0.65 ruble, according to the official rate, but actually you could buy 1 dollar for 4.65 Soviet rubles on the so-called black market). As former goalkeeper Alexey Bogomolov notes, his older colleague Vladislav Tretiak made 410 to 480 rubles a month without benefits. He could get an additional 100 rubles for a victorious game. So generally, his monthly salary was around 600 rubles. In case of a win in the Summit Series, the Soviet players were to get 2,000 rubles each. In reality, they got less. Foreign trips were paid in US dollars

(200 to 300 each). For comparison, around this time a bus ticket cost 5 kopeks (1 ruble equals 100 kopeks), a bottle of beer was 17 kopeks, a pair of shoes was 12 to 17 rubles, a pack of cigarettes was 10 to 20 kopeks, gas (1 litre) was 4 kopeks, and a newspaper was 3 kopeks.

The best players also received gifts from sponsors (the Ministry of Defence, for example), like watches, tape recorders, and so on. Beginning in 1968, the Soviet players could sell some types of hockey souvenirs and gear they brought back from foreign trips. In 1972–73, a Jofa helmet could cost around 30 rubles, and hockey gloves 30 to 50 rubles (Bogomolov).

Another privilege was the opportunity to buy a private car without waiting in the long waiting list that existed in the Soviet Union. Usually ordinary people waited for four to five years, so strong was this desired symbol of personal freedom and privacy. Ordinary hockey players could get a very modest Giguli (the Soviet variant of the Italian Fiat 124) or a Moskvich for the price of 3,500 rubles, and the members of the national team and the leaders of the team could expect to get the more luxurious Volga (5,000 rubles) with personal plates. One more important detail: the best players could get free apartments in prestigious suburbs in Moscow or Leningrad.

The disadvantages of playing on the Soviet team were having to live away from the family home, the impossibility of getting a regular education or a regular profession, and the likelihood of experiencing professional trauma.

The Canadians got around 5,000 dollars each for the victory in Moscow, but more important were the explosion of national spirit and their extremely strong will to win. Sometimes they crossed borders and rules, like when Bobby Clarke broke Kharlamov's ankle. (Russian observers then referred to Clarke as a "hungry vampire.") Exactly at this moment, Nickolay Ozerov pronounced his famous phrase: "Look at this! No, we do not need this style of hockey at all. It is dirty" (Grigoriev).

But there were some funny moments on the hot ice as well. During the first game in Moscow on September 22, Phil Esposito suddenly fell down on the ice and found an effective way out of the embarrassing moment by bowing and sending Leonid Brezhnev regards by waving, getting a friendly smile in return from the general secretary (Dubinin).

Also, the Canadians and Soviets were very different in everyday life. Team Canada seemed very relaxed; they smoked cigarettes and drank a lot of beer after the games (the Russians preferred Coke and natural water). But both sides took in the rich and distinguished cultural programs, such as museums and theatres, when they visited each other's countries.

For Team Canada, the last goal scored by Paul Henderson was the same "moment of truth" as the Zimin and Kharlamov goals for the Soviets during the first play in Montreal. As Colin Howell writes: "When Paul Henderson scored the winning goal with thirty-four seconds left in the final game, thus propelling Canada to victory, the result was an outpouring of national feeling that reminded us what hockey meant to us as Canadians. It was also a defining moment for hockey: from that time on, professional hockey was on the ascendancy, not just at home but around the world" (77).

Brian Kennedy continues the point: "Had Canada lost, maybe all memories of the series would have been buried, too. This happened with the next great series, the 1974 Summit Series of WHA stars against those same Russians. The DVD set of these games is fittingly titled *Team Canada 1974: The Lost Series*. But because Team Canada 1972 won, and in dramatic fashion, September will always be overlaid with memories of those eight games in a pattern that rings true for Canadians who know the (original) Summit Series" (171).

The Soviet mass media did not comment about why the Soviets lost the final game in Moscow. Everyone in the Soviet hockey community agreed that psychologically and technically, Team Canada was the stronger of the two. It was the time for the national Soviet team to go back to studying. And in two years, during the 1974 Summit Series with the World Hockey Association, they proved that they had learned a good lesson in 1972.

Post-1972

After the dramatic events of 1972, Canadian hockey became even more popular among the Soviet audience than before. The names of the Esposito brothers, Dryden, Cournoyer and Henderson were pronounced everywhere. In Canada, they spoke about Valery Kharlamov, Alexander Yakushev and Vladislav Tretiak.

The main result of the Summit Series for Russians was not only sporting experience but also the depoliticization of Soviet hockey in general. It was a real thaw in the relationship between the Soviet national team and the Canadian national team.

The connection became closer and more regular, first theoretically and later in the practical field. In 1975, a Soviet publishing house published Ken Dryden's memoirs with an introduction by Soviet coach Boris Kulagin. Then dozens of publications, including Harry Sinden's memoirs, became available for Russian readers.

In 1982, Victor Nechayev from Spartacus (Moscow) became the first Soviet player to appear on the line of an NHL team. He played two games for the Los Angeles Kings but left because of bad contract conditions. The second Russian player in the NHL was Alexander Mogilny in 1990.

The personal contacts between the Soviets and their Canadian fellows became closer in the early '80s when Gorbachev's Perestroika began in the USSR. Tretiak and Dryden became close friends, as did many others. Alexander Selivanov (a former player from Spartacus, Moscow) married Phil Esposito's daughter, and now there are three grandchildren in the family who speak Russian fluently.

The fact that now Canada and Russia are equal partners and members of the international hockey community is not only a result of political change inside Russia, the dissolution of the USSR, and the crushing of communist ideology but also, strongly, because of the rich socio-cultural and professional experience that both sides had during the 1972 Summit Series. As Vladislav Tretiak noted, "We were the first who held out our hand of friendship to Canadian professional hockey players. They accepted it, and together we broke down the Cold War ice" (92).

Works Cited

Bogomolov, Alexey. "How Phil Esposito kissed Brezhnev." *Sovershenno Sekretno* (*Top Secret*) [Weekly paper], October 2, 2012.

Dubinin, Nickolay. "Vspominaya 1972 [Remembering 1972]." Vesti.ru. September 2, 2012.

Grigoriev, Ivan. "Takoy Hockey nam ne nujen! [We do not need in this kind of Hockey!]." Interfax-West, http://www.interfax.by//article/95275.

Howell, Colin. *Blood, Sweat, and Cheers.* Toronto: University of Toronto Press, 2001.

Kennedy, Brian. *My Country Is Hockey.* Edmonton: Argenta, 2011.

Kolesnikov, Andrey. *Holodnaya voyna na ldu* [*The Cold War on Ice*]. Moscow: Avgust Borg [August Borg Publishing House], 2012. www.chaskor.ru/article/holodnaya_voyna_na_Ldu. September 6, 2011–May 2012.

MacSkimming, Roy. *Cold War: The Amazing Canada-Soviet Hockey Series of 1972.* Vancouver, BC: Greystone, 1996.

Tarasov, Anatoly C. *Sovershennoletie* [*Coming of Age*]. Moscow: Molodaya Gvardia, 1968. http://bookz.ru/authors/anatolii-tarasov/tarasov_anatol01.html.

Tretiak, Vladislav. *Hockeynaya Epopeya* [*The Hockey Epos*]. Moscow: Leonardo, 1993.

———. *Kogda Ldy Jarko...* [*When Ice is Hot...*]. Moscow: Sovetskaya Rossia, 1979.

———. *Vernost* [*The Faithfulness*]. Moscow: Phizskultura I Sport [Physical Culture and Sport Publishers], 1986.

The
Series as
Cultural
Artifact

Media Retrospectives of the Summit Series

🍁

IRI CERMAK

The September 1972 eight-game contest between Canada and the USSR known as the Summit Series endures as a seminal moment in the history of the Canadian game. Until Paul Henderson scored the winning goal in the closing thirty-four seconds of the final matchup, however, the Canadian team, stocked entirely with NHLers, was staring at a certain loss. Henderson saved the day, and, with good reason, media retrospectives of the event refer to the series by way of his heroic tally. Canada Post and the Royal Canadian Mint have also enshrined Henderson's feat in a postage stamp and a silver coin, respectively.

As a live prestige competition with global reach, the series had all the makings of a media event, out-of-the-ordinary television programming of the sort that amplifies the public's nostalgic fascination with the larger-than-life accomplishments of great men (Dayan and Katz, 21, 27).[1] The meeting of the recurring World Championships winner and Olympic gold medalist Soviet national team and Canada's marquee NHL players was a first in the modern history of the international game, and audiences sidestepped daily routines to eagerly watch the proceedings.

Coverage prior to the start of the competition remained narrow, in part due to experts' sunny predictions, which reinforced the expectation that Canada would readily prevail. The presence of legendary *Hockey Night in Canada* announcer Foster Hewitt, who came out of retirement to call the contests, emphatically relayed to viewers the premier status of the event. Hewitt attested to the pivotal character of the meeting via statements such as, "This will be the most important game in the history of our national pastime," and "Tonight we're making hockey history."[2] As a trusted authority, the play-by-play icon framed the series for audiences as a momentous cultural juncture for the nation. The critical nature of the event pointedly struck home as widespread alarm over game one's loss set in.

Throughout the years TV documentaries, miniseries and other sports programming have reiterated the series' mythic stature. Projects like *The Canada/ Russia Games 1972: Hockey's Series of the Century* (1987); Ken Dryden's *Home Game* episode "No Final Victories" (1990); *Summit on Ice* (1996); *September 1972* (1997); *Sport Journal's* "1972 Summit Series Anniversary" segment (1997); *Les grands duels du sport*, "Hockey sur glace: Canada/URSS" (2005) and the *Hockey: A People's History* episode "Soul of A Nation" (2006) today serve as commemorative documents that also influence the event's meaning by emphasizing, minimizing and even blotting out various aspects of the competition.[3] In putting forth specific views of the national character and the opponent, these productions not only distinctively update the series but retool it as part of the nation's memory work.

Team Canada and National Character

According to myth, the hockey player represents Canadians' successful adaptation to the immensity and harshness of the environment of the North. Because as a civic nation-state grounded in legalistic principles Canada has few identity myths with which to rally citizens, public discourse relies on the robust northern nation motif to produce Canada out of difference with its global neighbours. The chronicle, first fielded by Canadian nationalist movements of the mid 1800s, is based on environmental determinism, which links climate and geography with national character. Hockey features closely in this account as substantiation of muscular Canadians successfully navigating the northern frontier landscape.[4]

The Summit Series texts likewise dramatize hockey through the twin variables of northern climate and geography as the very essence of Canadian identity. *Summit on Ice's* narrator asserts that "we carved this game from the ice and snow. It was ours, who we were, who we are. And a world that didn't know much about us knew one thing for certain: we could play hockey better than anyone." Michael McKinley in "Soul of a Nation" reiterates that "Canadians grew up with very few national myths, things we can readily grab out of the hat and say 'This is us.' And one of the most dependable has always been hockey. It's our game.... We gave it to the world in all forms." The texts zero in on landscape and climate to ground mastery of hockey as part of the Canadian heritage. In deploying the myth of northernness to naturalize the game as Canadian, these statements veil hockey's long history as capital investment and the documented conflicts between social groups and organizations that paved the way for the NHL's rise (Gruneau and Whitson 132–33).

National discourse also commonly deploys the notion of Canada as northern enclave to depict the country as "small, rural, innocent and old-fashioned" vis-à-vis larger, more powerful nations (Hughes-Fuller, 26).[5] Eva Mackey reiterates the point when she notes that "northern wilderness and...cold climate remain constant images in public representation and myth" to differentiate Canada from more influential global powers (40, 48). This iconography amplifies Canada's colonial history, calling up images of the Dominion as a site for resource extraction largely for the benefit of powerful outside interests.[6] The northern outpost paradigm consequently fashions Canada as small and pastoral, lacking in the *savoir faire* and cunning of influential global others.

These ideas surface in the films, as Ken Dryden in "No Final Victories" notes that "there can often seem in Canada a shortage of world events...the kind of moments that make time stand still." He adds that, although "there is much that is special about Canada...surrounded by countries richer, older, more powerful, we cling to every symbol. We had to win this series." The episode fashions Canada as accidental Cold Warrior,[7] very much in the context of inexperience and innocence, as Dryden amplifies that the series permanently changed the country because "Canadians knew little of the world in 1972... uncomfortable in anything but our own backyard." Phil Esposito echoes the notion of players as innocents swept by the course of the events when he tells Dryden, "I remember my brother Tony saying, 'Why? Why are we going? Why are we doing this? Who [are] we playing?' And I says, 'I don't know. We're playing the Russians. How good can they be?'" To distinguish Team Canada from the Soviet opponent, then, the texts deploy the nation's organic ties to the landscape to reaffirm players both as northern exemplars and in line with assumptions of Canada as an unblemished, guileless social formation.

The preceding blueprint contradicts the portrayal of the Canadian squad as the elite of the hockey world. Brushing off notions of Canada as small northern enclave, archival footage upholds players' celebrity status, depicting them signing autographs for adoring fans, leisurely filing out of expensive hotels, and sporting sunglasses as they board a plane bound for Moscow (*September 1972*; Summit on Ice; "Soul of a Nation"). The narration also buttresses NHLers' standing in the culture by portraying the contest as an opportunity to once and for all prove Canadian supremacy in hockey:

> **"Soul of a Nation," Narrator:** Canada has never been able to send NHL players to the World Championships because the International Ice Hockey Federation has a ban on professional players.

> **"Hockey sur glace: Canada/URSS," Paul Henderson:** You know, this was going to be so wonderful that we were just going to put these Russians in their place. Finally establish that, you know, they're beating our amateur teams and at the Olympics but they've never played the big boys.

> *September 1972,* **Bobby Clarke:** All these great stars on our club. I couldn't believe anybody could be as good as we were going to be.

> *Summit on Ice,* **Narrator:** We had the NHL. A star-studded league of all-Canadian boys dazzled and shone.
> **Phil Esposito:** I defy anyone on that team, on that bench, to tell me that we weren't going to walk over those guys like crazy.

> *Canada/Russia Games 1972,* **Alan Eagleson:** We, the press, and everyone in Canada were so convinced we were gonna win eight games in a row, all we felt we had to do was show up, step on the ice, and beat the Russians eight straight.

The imperative to represent players both in line with Canada's image as northern outpost and as NHL stars results in an inconsistency that is difficult to resolve. This conceptual mismatch entails fashioning hockey's cream of the crop as simple and inexperienced sorts and defining Canada not as undeveloped Northern territory but as chief producer of a pricey commodity: the marquee elite-level hockey player. The practice of linking NHL ice to the icescape of the North also complicates the issue of identity because it implicates capital in the formation of national character and detracts from the idea of hockey as an organic expression of a northern people.

The projects also define the Canadian squad by way of emotion and resolve, particularly during the final stages of the series. These twin abilities confer advantage by generating a surplus of energy that moves the team forward and expedites play through the dying stages of the game:

> *Summit on Ice*, **Jean Ratelle:** We are very emotional type of players. Everything that we do is emotional....We won because of emotion.
> **Serge Savard:** They could not come at the same level emotionally that we did. And that's why we won. You cannot play this game without emotion.
>
> *September 1972*, **Wayne Cashman:** The '72 series set an example that Canadian hockey players live by. They know down inside somewhere there's something a little extra they can give. I think it came out in that series.
>
> **"Soul of a Nation," Pierre Plouffe:** I'm so proud to be a Canadian. Our character, our will and our refusal to surrender...[are] something I will remember for the rest of my life. This is our legacy.

These attributes, which come up in the narratives virtually as variants of skill, work to differentiate Team Canada from the Soviet opponent. Resolve references Canadians' ability to endure and thrive in the harsh environment of the North, while emotion aligns the team with the values of the West and its respect for the individual.

Otherwise, the Summit Series texts describe Team Canada largely through adversarial conditions that loop back to the Soviet opponent. The texts elaborate on players' insufficient preparation and poor conditioning, and detail the outfit's inadequate scouting and resultant underestimation of the adversary. However, all these references occur in the context of Soviet subterfuge, whether express or accidental. John Ferguson repeatedly observes, "did we ever get fooled" (*September 1972*), and "we were extremely fooled and stunned and shocked" (*Summit on Ice*), a point that the narrators in both films ratify despite the insertion of sequences that confirm coach Harry Sinden's call for vigilance because of prior experience with the Soviet national team. The inventory of adversarial conditions also includes uneven playing field motifs that work against the Canadian team's success. The Soviet practice of keeping national teams together under schedules and routines not seen in the West, the incompetent officiating of European referees unfamiliar with the Canadian game and the absence of Bobby Orr and Bobby Hull, which effectively shortened the Canadian bench,[8] all script obstacles in the heroic path of the team.

Curiously, the projects allude to injuries sustained by Canadian players on the roster, like Serge Savard's fractured ankle, only in passing, if at all. Complaints by Canadian players about the insufficiency of ice time also merit comparatively few references. Ice size, a common motif in marquee event broadcasts, which determines the extent to which Canadians can play the body, likewise earns a lone mention in "Hockey sur glace: Canada/URSS," where Yvan Cournoyer comments that the ice size in Moscow changed the shooting angle and forced the team to adapt. These omissions corroborate that the texts choose to expressly direct the viewer's attention to the Soviet opponent's multiple pivotal advantages.

The great number of hurdles that the Canadians must face, especially as portrayed in "No Final Victories," *Summit on Ice*, *September 1972* and "Soul of a Nation," certainly make for added drama. But notably they serve to transform the team into underdogs in line with sport genre conventions. Fictional and non-fictional sports programming that enlarges on the feats of national teams tends to reproduce the mythical overtones of the hero journey, which formulates the protagonist as "smaller and weaker" than his opponents (Landau, 265). Deborah Tudor argues in her work on sports films that "a major part of the ideological project of athletic films [is]…to ensure that the hero…operates within the Western heroic tradition," which entails constructing a "flawed hero…who suffers temporary disgrace or loss of skill" (46). This convention is in keeping with the practices of Canadian networks, which harbour a predilection for "turn-around situations…[in] which…underdogs come from behind [to]…

win," in line with "the entertainment imperative of current North American television" (MacNeill, 117). The negative conditions that Team Canada must face, which the projects funnel through the motif of purposeful or accidental entrapment, work to minimize the stature of the players as NHL stars, turning them into underdogs in good melodramatic form.

The Soviets

Since the texts position the Soviet opponent as the source of difficulties facing the Canadians, they also convey the adversary as an "internal other." Stephen Frosh argues that "the 'internal other' radically disturbs the…sense that each of us is 'master' of himself" by working to break down confidence and suggesting that the individual's consciousness "has been infiltrated by something subjectively inexplicable that the 'self' is not" (393). Phil Esposito expresses this view in "Hockey sur glace: Canada/URSS" when he notes that Soviet captain Boris Mikhailov and defenceman Alexander Ragulin "made me do things I didn't like in myself. They all did. I did things in that series that I never did before and I never did after." In "No Final Victories," Ken Dryden also observes that the series evoked uncharacteristic reactions from his team-mates: "What happened in that series? A lot of people did strange things in that series. I mean, Rod Gilbert was fighting; Jean-Paul Parise was threatening referees. I mean, what happened? Why did all those strange things happen?" Dryden does not blame the Soviet opponent for the actions of his squad, but his comments nonetheless suggest the presence of an internal other. Hélène Joffe observes that casting accountability on an outside source springs from individuals' capacity to comfortably associate only certain attributes with self and the in-group, prompting them to displace undesirable traits and conditions onto the out-group. This is especially the case when individuals react to danger, which allows for the protection of the in-group by exteriorizing the threat (1, 13).[9] Because the Soviet opponent acts as an internal other, this projection obscures the notion that hockey can quickly devolve into mayhem and violence. Indeed, as Richard Gruneau and David Whitson observe, the hockey exemplar can operate outside the rules of the game when the situation requires it (191). The Canadian hockey code consequently conceives of a model of masculinity that the norms of wider social theatres cannot always check. However, the aforementioned projection authenticates the Canadians as innocents and the Soviets as a menace, as attested by their power to sway the psyche.

Representation of the Soviet team as a dangerous outfit also comes through in recurrent imagery of USSR militarism. The texts delineate the Soviet Union as a sinister superpower by way of archival footage and dramatic re-enactment. Imagery of gates fronted by soldiers, barracks, massive impersonal buildings ("No Final Victories") and shadowy hallways ("Soul of a Nation"), tanks leading military parades (*Summit on Ice*), Lenin's statue, the Kremlin (*September 1972*) and Red Square ("Hockey sur glace: Canada/URSS") rehash familiar iconography of the Soviets as material threat. While a majority of the texts humanize the Russian players that took part in the series, the collective Soviet persona remains largely embedded in the Cold War formula, a geopolitical construct that conveyed the East-West confrontation as a zero-sum game.

In "No Final Victories," Dryden's USSR emerges in the midst of a tug-of-war between the old and the new. The Red Army is "the owner of the world's most successful hockey team," and the old order remains fronted by Viktor Tikhonov, for whom a majority of the project's criticism is reserved, reminiscent of early 1990s North American sports reports and game commentary about the coach.[10] Even as Dryden is concerned that "money is allowed to matter" almost to excess, it is clear that Russian league managers' and promoters' insufficient free market experience also preoccupy him. In "No Final Victories," the structures of the old order relegate the needs of the individual to the mandates of the state, and Dryden's comment that "things here were always definite, traditions, expectations, immutable, some things right, the rest always wrong" recapitulates the Cold War image of the USSR by relaying sport as an arm of the autocratic state and by subsuming culture under the rubric of politics.

Similarly, *Summit on Ice, September 1972* and "Soul of a Nation" highlight the Soviet Union's harsh repressive aspects by way of the Canadian outfit's harassment and surveillance, as well as the theft of their goods and dubious one-upmanship during the Moscow leg of the series. The texts formulate the Soviet team and the state through references to shadows, spying, secrecy and hidden agendas. In addition, they repeatedly allude to the Soviet contingent through its reified "machine" image, which assigns players a robotic essence and ultimately reiterates the idea of sport in line with the propaganda imperatives of the Soviet state.

All the programs nevertheless allow Soviet players to express their opinion to provide balance in line with documentary practice, likely because the great majority were produced after the fall of the Soviet Union in 1991. In *Summit on Ice*, for example, Vladimir Petrov explains the Russian perspective on hockey, noting that the team's robotic image in the Western media amounted to a compliment because "in Russia the word 'robot' is a derivative of work, hard work. And without a doubt we were working seriously, like robots, working very hard." Other projects also emphasize Soviet contributions to the game in positive terms. In *Canada/Russia Games 1972*, Serge Savard praises the Soviet team for raising the calibre of the game, even as NHLPA President Alan Eagleson remarks on the "shenanigans" pulled by Soviet officials during the Moscow leg of the series. The 1987 production showcases the goals of the series, almost to the exclusion of the contest's physical battles at a time when the Soviet Union, albeit immersed in the *perestroika* and *glasnost* reforms of the Gorbachev era, very much remained a political force in the international arena. Sports Journal's "1972 Summit Series Anniversary" special, for its part, updates the state of Russian hockey for viewers. The program corroborates the Cold War image of the Soviet state through motifs such as sport as propaganda, as well as poverty, crime and the decline of youth hockey programs, alongside Russian players' influx into the NHL. The piece nonetheless humanizes the team by incorporating a greater number of Russian voices into the narrative as well as by quantifying the Soviet game by way of its iconic team orientation and superior skating skills.

"Hockey sur glace: Canada/URSS" similarly gives Russian players an equal if not a greater voice than their NHL counterparts, reflective of the roots of the French/European production company. The film defines the Brezhnev era as a period of extreme retrenchment in Soviet political history, despite the détente and the rapprochement efforts of the Canadian and Soviet governments, and spotlights the USSR as a coercive and dilapidated police state. However, Team USSR players in the film also act as counteracting agents on issues of Soviet politics and culture. For example, although familiar imagery of the Soviets as machine team puts in an appearance, the narrative widely contextualizes the

Soviet school of hockey as a tradition, an appellative more typical of Western sporting practices in North American media texts. Retorting to Phil Esposito's statement, "Nobody smiled, nobody, it was like there was no emotion; they were robots to us, it was over here, over here, over here," the narrator clarifies that "the Russians were not robots but athletes made in the great Soviet mould, complete, well-rounded athletes shaped according to the great communist tradition."

Russian players also express frustration about North American assumptions that construct the Soviet "other" in the context of primitivism and "flawed development" (Dahlgren and Chakrapani, 53). For example, goalie Vladislav Tretiak, whom "Hockey sur glace" introduces as a member of the Russian Duma, attributes mistaken Canadian assumptions about the USSR to the atmosphere of fear bred by the Cold War: "In the United States and Canada people were afraid of the Soviet Union. It was the first time players came over to our country. They expected to find bears in Red Square. They thought Moscow was a bit like Siberia.... This was a different planet." Canadian innocence and inexperience in "No Final Victories" summarily transforms into provincialism and ignorance in "Hockey sur glace." The documentary accordingly situates Soviet/Russian culture in the context of greater European culture, a discursive stance about the USSR that is rarely aired even today.

While Russian voices and viewpoints contribute to a more personal portrayal of the team, the majority of Summit Series texts add little to the sketch of the Soviet Union as totalitarian state. Representations of geopolitical "others" put forth by image generators typically express in political, economic and cultural terms needed to mediate national interests,[11] and as such are susceptible to variation and incongruity because these interests alter with the historical context (Breger, 260). However, the Soviet image in the Summit Series texts emerges virtually frozen in time. Indeed, only the French production "Hockey sur glace: Canada/URSS" allows for distance from this image by deploying lighthearted sound effects, at times resembling the NHL's blooper plays of the week, to amplify the physical action of the series and connote the Soviet Union as a historical artifact that belongs in the past. Because TV lends an aura of presentism to historical material – in Gary Edgerton's words, "television's unwavering allegiance to the present tense is...one of the medium's grammatical imperatives" (3) – the efforts of "Hockey sur glace" stand alone in reproducing the Soviet past as "a category of experience" rather than as steeped in the prevailing present tense of televisual texts. The monolithic character of USSR representation in the Canadian projects conversely suggests that these texts recall Soviet contributions to hockey as jeopardizing Canada's ownership of the game.

The Summit Series: A Crisis Point for the Nation

Because the Soviet outfit started off the eight-game contest by winning, they quickly transformed into a threat, and Summit Series productions fore-ground textual representations of Team Canada as motivated by a sense of crisis. Crises have the effect of raising anxiety levels, and hockey's standing as the preeminent Canadian cultural resource that must be protected at all costs only aggravates the team's apprehension over its piracy. Joffe posits that during times of crisis the out-group morphs from "mildly threatening, a change to the core values of the society, to…a purveyor of chaos" (21). Since public discourse constructs hockey as essential to Canadian identity, losses to the Soviet team present the prospect of undervaluing the game as Canadian cultural form. It is not unexpected that while the Summit Series, as its original "Friendship Series" moniker suggests, was conceived to broaden relations between the Pierre E. Trudeau and Leonid Brezhnev governments, the projects fail to pursue any narrative threads about the role of the series in the service of international diplomacy. Instead, the confrontation in these texts insistently registers as an ideological conflict informed by the Cold War:[12]

> **"No Final Victories," Phil Esposito:** To me it was war.… I've never shot anything in my life…but there's no doubt in my mind I think would've killed to win.

> *Summit on Ice*, **Narrator:** The series was going to be a war led by warriors like Phil Esposito.
> **Phil Esposito:** It wasn't a game. It wasn't a series. It was our society against their society.
> **Alan Eagleson:** In those days the Soviet Union was the Big Bad Russian Bear, the home of communism, the enemy of democracy.

Red Berenson: At the time there was absolutely no question that it was a battle of lifestyles or beliefs.

Serge Savard: It was like a communist country winning over us, a communist country sending the world a message that our system is better than yours.

September 1972, **Serge Savard:** Two systems want to show the world that their system is the best.... It was no longer sports.

Rod Seiling: It was a war. This was the Cold War. This was our way of living versus their way of living.

Ron Ellis: Our belief system against their belief system.

Phil Esposito: As I skated out after the interview, some guy was yelling out, I mean, really adamant....That's when I really realized, "Man, we are in a war here. This is no game. This is society. This is war. And we better damn well get ourselves together."

"1972 Summit Series Anniversary," Sports Journal, Bill White: It turned into a war. And we used to come out the same as them to go on the ice in Moscow. There wasn't too much said, but the looks were pretty intimidating on both sides.... So you could just feel another war as you'd come out.

"Hockey sur glace: Canada/URSS," Phil Esposito: For me it became a war. And that's when I really started to bear down.... And I knew that I had to get myself together...and we had to become a team.

Paul Henderson: They were taking over the world. Obviously now they're invading our ground.... It was war. It got carried away, like all of us got carried away.... It's just a game. And you tell yourself that. But...it was more than a game. It was our Canadian pride, our way of life and everything.

"Soul of a Nation," Phil Esposito: It was a war, a real-life war. It wasn't a game anymore. It was society against society.

Narrator: In this war, both sides do whatever is necessary to win.

Jean Beliveau: There was a lot of tension. They were telling me, Jean, if you only knew the pressure we have on the ice. One said, "It's a war out there." And I could see and...feel [it].

Summit on Ice and *September 1972* especially underline violence by Canadian players as well as the actions of Harry Sinden, John Ferguson and Alan Eagleson in the context of the critical need to counteract the Soviet threat. Recurring images of Canadian team members involved in harsh physical play, and coaching staff skirmishes with Soviet officials, militia and European referees, all point to the struggle to protect the Canadian game.

Because the Canadian culture of hockey supports the distinct model of aggressive masculinity embodied by '72 team members, which defenceman Gary Bergman evokes in his observation, "We don't have a responsibility to answer to anybody else. This is how we play hockey.... We play it rough and skillful" (*September 1972*), it is only logical that the players should have parlayed physicality in defence of the Canadian game. However, echoing cultural fissures over the way hockey should be played,[13] the Summit Series texts also struggle with evenhandedly portraying Bobby Clarke's slash on Valery Kharlamov.

September 1972 frames the slash as a result of increasing friction between both teams. "With more than half the game left to play, animosity [erupts] on both teams. Frustrated by the one-sided officiating, Team Canada lashes out," the narrator observes. Assistant coach John Ferguson explains that he instructed Clarke to break "the guy's ankle" because "I mean, this guy is killing us." Clarke, for his part, notes that Kharlamov "gave me a little dig with his stick and then turned and took off the other way." This rendition of the slash constructs the act as part of the hard man's approach to the game, one which Ferguson alludes to when he asserts, "That's the way I played the game. I wouldn't expect that from anybody else...but I'd talk to Bobby Clarke and he'd do it." Statements that articulate the Canadian players' sense of duty also precede the depiction of the slash: "So in war you do whatever you have to do" (Paul Henderson) and "It wasn't fun. It was *not* fun!" (Phil Esposito). The assumption, then, is that Clarke's actions align with the team's mission to defend Canada's game from Soviet assailment. This version of the slash is not unexpected given that *September 1972* is co-sponsored by both Canadian Hockey and the 1972 Canadian players, who as a rule voice support for the physical game. Not coincidentally, of all the projects, this film devotes the greatest amount of time to physicality issues through verbal and visual cues that legitimate robustness as part of the Canadian game.

While clearly labelling the slash "a piece of infamy," *Summit on Ice* likewise deploys the motif of Canadian anxieties over losing to contextualize the move. The narrator underscores the act both verbally and visually, noting, "Watch the stick," as a slow motion view of Clarke striking Kharlamov's ankle appears on the screen. However, Foster Hewitt's commentary, "This game is reaching a fever pitch…and they're really hitting each other hard, tempers flaring," which does not coincide with the action shown, attenuates Clarke's act by positioning it in the context of the fierceness of the proceedings, even as the piece presents views from Ferguson and Clarke that the slash was carried out in a premeditated manner.

In similar fashion, even while remarking on "the vicious slash," the narrator of "Soul of a Nation" asserts that "Bobby Clarke and Valery Kharlamov have been mixing it up all game." The piece visually amplifies Clarke's actions by way of a medium shot of the player inciting Kharlamov, followed by a slow-motion visual that spotlights the slash and a medium shot of Kharlamov bent over in the vicinity of the Soviet bench. The narrator amplifies that "Kharlamov is gone with a broken ankle. State filmmakers compile a gallery of images that will portray the Canadians as thugs." Even though the film pronounces an indictment of the act, references to the Soviet record, one sullied by its pronounced propaganda aims, mediate the slash's portrayal and ultimately distract from the rebuke. Accusations that "the Soviets had their own dirty tricks" (narrator), not shown, and Phil Esposito's remarks that "it was a war, a real-life war; it wasn't a game anymore, it was society against society," reinforce the point.

Sports Journal's "1972 Summit Series Anniversary" segment alone expresses unequivocal condemnation of the slash and denounces the Canadian team's physical excess as acts of transgression,[14] as the narrator notes, "Apparently the formula for capturing the series was to win ugly. Bobby Clarke's slash on Valery Kharlamov in game six broke the ankle of the brilliant winger who had been dominating the Canadians throughout the series. The piece shows the slash and pairs it with a medium shot of Clarke putting up a glove in Kharlamov's face and the Soviet player shoving it back. While Bill White remarks, "Well, it took a big man out of their lineup," Terry Mosher, the *Montreal Gazette*'s cartoonist known as Aislin, firmly rejects the assertion by amplifying, "We looked very bad, I think, in the process. I spent a fair amount of time wandering around the stadium, and the Russians were appalled by this sort of behaviour."[15]

The balancing act performed by these productions and their disparate rendering of Clarke's actions mirror the ongoing debate about the physical strategies the Canadian team deployed during the series. On the one hand, the notion of crisis assumes that during junctures "decisions have to be made, decisions with very real effects…[which] suggest the necessity of human agency," as Mary Ann Doane argues (283). Per this reading, Clarke's slash and the team's acts of excessive physicality are critical and necessary to protect Canada's game from Soviet encroachment. However, these works also show that physical excess remains contentious. While allowing that mounting frustration with Soviet officials' subterfuge and players' desperation to win led to extreme demonstrations of hostility, the films also articulate the slash as maladaptive and un-Canadian. Albeit Clarke's actions were consistent with the '70s game, which the player hints at in *September 1972* when he notes, "At the time everybody thought it was a pretty good thing to do," the productions do not make room for contextualizing the slash as such. It is also significant that almost half of the projects – *The Canada/Russia Games 1972*, "No Final Victories" and "Hockey sur glace: Canada/URSS" – sidestep the controversy by erasing the slash from their texts. These differences show that although in times of crisis leaders may take actions that fall outside a community's values, in public discourse the slash and the game of excess remain informed by the Canadian cultural divide, which opposes skill and propriety to physical force and mayhem.

Because the eight-game series quickly transformed into a crisis for the Canadian game and the nation, the films also exhibit a preoccupation with national unity. Roger Fowler notes that the ideology of consensus "assumes, and in times of crisis actually affirms, that within the group, there is no difference or disunity in the interests and values of any of the population or institution" (49). While *Summit on Ice* and "Soul of a Nation" devote national unity the greatest amount of running time, all the programs tackle the issue in one way or another. Except for *Summit on Ice*, which alludes to the political unrest in Canada during the 1960s – "We struggled as the '70s begun. The FLQ crisis, soldiers in Montreal. Separation was the issue. We faced the '72 issue preoccupied with unity, questioning even back then our identity (narrator)" – the texts largely unhinge unity concerns from their regional or historical contexts. For example, none of the projects underscore booing by fans during game four by way of Canadian regionalism, in the manner that the CBC TV miniseries *Canada Russia '72* conveys in a scene in which Toronto-based broadcasters castigate Vancouver fans for characteristic disloyalty. This exclusion is unsurprising because the Summit Series texts prioritize the event as having national implications, and regionalism, a so-called problem that remains unsolvable, militates against the very idea of Canadian unity.

In the same vein, none of the Canadian productions amplify fan disenchantment with the team because of sympathy with the ideals of the Left. In "Hockey sur glace: Canada/URSS," Phil Esposito suggests as much when he observes that after game four in Vancouver "there were three or four young guys about eighteen to twenty-five…up in the stands. And they were yelling obscenities at me: 'The commies are better. The communists are better. Why don't you admit it? It's a better lifestyle.'… And I thought, 'Wow! That's what this is all about.'" Like regionalism, fan affinity with the values of the Left, while consonant with the political backdrop of the '70s, which critiqued commodity culture and situated cultural nationalism outside the market's directives (Ebron, 208–9), constitutes a potentially unmanageable fissure between team and nation. Indeed, the ideological divide between Left and Right is particularly damaging because it exposes a rift between the capitalist, market-driven values of the team and the more radical, progressive values of the nation it represents.

It is not unexpected, then, that to centralize the narrative thread the productions consistently reroute fan disillusionment to differences over playing styles, because doing so keeps the subject matter sports-specific and less philosophically burdensome. After the Vancouver game, Phil Esposito observes in *Summit on Ice*, "We were called the Canadian mafia. We were called the goon squad." Similarly, in *September 1972* Wayne Cashman notes, "They started to attack our style of hockey, that style that was successful in winning. They thought that [the] Russian [approach], that's the new style of hockey, that's how you play the game." Because films formulate the Summit Series as a crisis point that necessitates a resolution, complex subject matter like regionalism and the Left-Right ideological divide are not only troublesome but also outright unpalatable, particularly to a genre that deploys the resolute actions of the sports hero as a form of social capital for the community.

Predictably, the texts tidily resolve the problem of disunity through imagery of Canadian fans who travel to Moscow to cheer their team at the Luzhniki Ice Palace. The texts identify this group as indefatigable in their support of the Canadian squad, shoring up players' spirits and modelling for the rest of Canada the meaning of patriotic fervour. The theme of three thousand Canadian fans out-shouting eleven thousand Soviet fans in Luzhniki appears in all the projects, reinforced by close-ups of Canadian flags and "Go Canada Go" signs brought into the arena. References to telegrams signed by thousands that arrive in support of the team ("No Final Victories," "Soul of a Nation," *Summit on Ice*) also reiterate the ideal of a nation finally coming together. Likewise, Alan Eagleson's entanglement with the Soviet militia and his ostensible rescue by the Canadian team and staff appears in almost every storyline under the motif of a united bench and a nation rallying against Soviet subterfuge and heavy-handedness.

Paul Henderson's goal in the final thirty-four seconds of the eighth game provides for the ultimate reconciliation of differences, and for this reason all productions make the point to foreground it. Henderson's goal is pivotal because of the anxieties evoked by the prospect of the Soviet "other's" appropriation of the game. As Phil Esposito makes clear in *Summit on Ice*, "All I cared about was winning and winning. Had to win, had to win." Referring to Richard Lipsky's discussions of the hero figure, Deborah Tudor ascribes "the worship of the sports-hero to the importance of winning, of success, in fact, to 'any threat' to moral and community values." She notes that in crisis situations, in particular, the hero's "courage disposes of the threat of humiliation… and symbolizes the possibility of human control" (103). The projects therefore present Henderson's goal as a symbol of Team Canada's redemption, a moment of restoration that, as Tudor suggests, fundamentally communicates the hero's power "to momentarily unite the fragmented culture" (184). Comments consequently spotlight the contest's ability to unite the nation: "Nothing, ever in my opinion, touched this country coast-to-coast the way September 28, 1972, did" (Alan Eagleson, *Summit on Ice*); "for the first time, the whole country was behind one team" (Serge Savard, *September 1972*). These statements feature

Canadian culture and identity as an inherently fractured and contested realm that necessitates a unifying force, and the films imply that the Summit Series was precisely such a force, even though the skill-versus-physicality debate remains contentious and unresolved.

It is evident that the memory work performed by the Summit Series projects is diverse and, in ways, contradictory. The eight-game contest came down in history as an event that changed hockey, but the films only allude to this transformation in passing,[16] suggesting that this is not their main concern. Instead, the memory work of the Summit Series appears to be split between the Russian and Canadian versions of the event. While the Russian contingent credits the series with enabling progress in hockey,[17] none of the Canadian players echo this argument. Instead, Canadian voices in these texts contextualize the series as a juncture for the nation, a crisis that Team Canada settled by winning: "the '72 Series defines hockey ultimately as Canada's sport" (Dowbiggin, "Soul of a Nation"); and "Canada is still able to produce the number one best player" (Bobby Clarke, *September 1972*). Gary Edgerton posits that "popular uses of memory have less to do with accuracy…than using the past as a kind of communal, mythic response to current controversies, issues" (5). In these televised projects, then, Canadians eulogize the Summit Series for dramatizing the power of hockey to define and bring the nation together; in short, for authenticating the game as Canadian.

* * *

The writer wishes to extend heartfelt thanks and appreciation to Jean-Patrice Martel of the Society for International Hockey Research (SIHR), without whose assistance work on this chapter would not have been possible.

---

[1] Daniel Dayan and Elihu Katz first defined the concept of media event as an exceptional occurrence that television commonly relays through mythical overtones.

[2] Hewitt made these statements to introduce game seven and game eight, respectively.

3 *The Canada/Russia Games 1972* is a production of Labatt, owner of film rights for the contest, which released the home video for the fifteenth anniversary of the series. "No Final Victories" is an instalment of the six-part series *Home Game* (1990), produced by Ken Dryden and Roy MacGregor. *Summit on Ice* is a CBC presentation broadcast in September 1992 on the twentieth anniversary of the series and released on VHS in 1996. *September 1972*, a production of Eye Entertainment in conjunction with Canadian Hockey and Team Canada 1972, is a CTV presentation broadcast on the twenty-fifth anniversary of the series. *Sports Journal*'s "1972 Summit Series Anniversary" segment is a commemorative special that also updates viewers on the state of Russian hockey in the mid 1990s. "Hockey sur glace: Canada/URSS" is an episode of *Les grands duels du sport*, a 2005 production by Ethan Productions and Arte Films. "Soul of a Nation" is an instalment in the series *Hockey: A People's History*, released in 2006. While each project dramatizes the series as a self-enclosed narrative, considering the projects together casts light on the event's commonsensical understandings as well as its major points of contention.

4 For more on the topic, see Scott MacKenzie's and Michael Robidoux's discussions of the paucity of Canadian myths and the significance of the North in organizing Canada's narrative of identity.

5 Hughes-Fuller notes that this construct specifically references the United States as Canada's powerful political and economic "other." During the Cold War, however, the Soviet Union operated as a compelling Canadian "other," especially in the hockey arena.

6 Economic historian Harold A. Innis first put forth this view, but this perspective also informs the writing of Northrop Frye and the survivalist literature of Margaret Atwood.

7 Doug Beardsley expresses similar sentiments when he writes, "Hockey is an allegory in our life in Canada and of our role in society and our role in the world. We are in between the world's superpowers, skating in circles at centre ice" (36).

8 Bobby Hull was bypassed by the NHLPA because he jumped to a new rival league, the World Hockey Association (WHA), while Bobby Orr was sidelined by an injury.

9 Soviet captain Boris Mikhailov in *Summit on Ice*, in contrast, apologizes for kicking and bloodying Gary Bergman during game seven. While like Canadian players he also attributes his actions to the heat of the moment, he observes, "I have never felt good about it.... I never meant to hurt him. And I did not act as a professional. I acted like an amateur." Mikhailov's comments are possibly in keeping with cultural differences.

10 See, for example, Cermak's discussion of coach Tikhonov's depiction in CBS and CTV's 1994 Winter Olympic broadcasts in "Seeing Red: Images of Soviet and Russian Hockey in US and Canadian Olympic Broadcasts."

11 Canada's political alignment with the US likely also has something to do with this portrayal, even while contravening the narrative of tolerance that public discourse associates with Canadianicity. Stephen Randall observes of Canadian foreign policy during the Cold War that even when Canada stated distinct opinions and sought different

strategies, owing to "Canadian-American military and economic partnership during World War II…[and the] growing integration of the two economies…foreign policy adhered to American Cold War designs" (269).

[12] Game one in Montreal, for example, was conducive to finalizing an agreement for Canadian wheat sales that the Soviet government had coveted. Despite Team Canada's 7–3 loss to the Soviet team, Trudeau's reported good mood enabled both parties to hash out the details of the new compact by game's end (Joukova).

[13] Highbrow sensibilities express a predilection for the aesthetic and didactic features of hockey consistent with the Victorian amateur reading of sport, which formulates athletics as civilizing social agent. Popular or lowbrow tastes, on the other hand, favour physicality as genuine masculine expression (Gruneau and Whitson, 110, 189).

[14] In his essay film *Valery's Ankle* (2006), Brett Kashmere aptly submits that in exalting the Summit Series, social memory has obscured the significance of the slash, and that the act should have as much weight as Paul Henderson's goal in contemplating how the event expresses Canadian identity.

[15] Unlike the 2006 CBC miniseries *Canada Russia '72*, these programs do not depict Soviet players or staff giving their reactions to the slash. A 1976 report by Mark Mulvoy on an upcoming friendly game between the Philadelphia Flyers and the Central Army Club procures a glimpse of how the Soviet team regarded the episode. Kharlamov observes during the interview that Clarke "hunted me down…and intentionally put me out of the game." In Moscow to observe Soviet hockey training methods, Mulvoy is also advised by interpreter Felix Rosenthal, "If you want the people here to be friendly, you will not mention the name of Boo-by Clarke…. Boo-by Clarke is what we call a no-no'" (25).

[16] Phil Esposito notes in "Soul of a Nation" that "hockey as we knew it would never be the same again." Ken Dryden also hints at change when commenting in "No Final Victories": "We had won, but it seemed we could never win again." However, none of the projects expressly state how the series modified the manner in which "Canada looked at the game and how it developed its players," as *The Hockey News* writer Ken Campbell notes (69).

[17] The Russian players, as well as the writers, analysts or narrators of the documentaries, rather than the Canadian players, express this view. In an article that commemorates the Summit Series, regular contributor to the International Ice Hockey Federation (IIHF) newsletter Klaus Zaugg similarly observes that given the influence of "Don Cherry's philosophy, Fred Shero's 'Broad Street Bullies' in Philadelphia or Harry Sinden's and Tom Johnson's 'Big Bad Bruins' in Boston," without Russian contributions to the game today "hockey would resemble…earth…ruled by dinosaurs" ("Don't Cry for Russian Hockey"). In contrast, Phil Esposito in Claude Mailhot questionne notes: "I get very, very angry when I hear, 'Oh, they taught us the Soviet way of hockey.' Who gives a crap!… In fact, as far as I'm concerned…we should have stayed more on our own path."

Works Cited

Beardsley, Doug. *Country on Ice*. Toronto: Paperjacks, 1988.

Breger, Rosemary Ann. *Myth and Stereotype*. New York: Peter Lang, 1990.

Campbell, Ken. "What Was a Bigger Moment: 1972 or 1980? Do You Believe in Miracles?" *The Hockey News,* Great Debates Special Issue, 2004.

The Canada/Russia Games 1972: Hockey's Series of the Century. VHS. Produced by Morningstar Entertainment. London, ON: TV Labatt, 1987.

Canada Russia '72. DVD. Directed by T. W. Peacocke. Montreal: Maple Pictures, 2006.

Cermak, Iri. "Seeing Red: Images of Soviet and Russian Hockey in US and Canadian Olympic Broadcasts." Ph.D. diss., University of Washington, 1996.

Dahlgren, Peter, and Sumitra Chakrapani. "The Third World on TV News: Western Ways of Seeing the Other." In *Television Coverage of International Affairs*, edited by William C. Adams, 45-65. Norwood, NJ: Ablex, 1982.

Dayan, Daniel, and Elihu Katz. *Media Events: The Live Broadcasting of History*. Cambridge: Harvard University Press, 1992.

Doane, Mary Ann. "Information, Crisis, Catastrophe." In *The Historical Film: History and Memory in the Media*, edited by Marcia Landy, 269–85. New Brunswick, NJ: Rutgers University Press, 2001.

Ebron, Paulla. *Performing Africa*. Princeton, NJ: Princeton University Press, 2002.

Edgerton, Gary, R. "Television as Historian: A Different Kind of History Altogether." In *Television Histories: Shaping Collective Memory in the Media Age*, edited by Gary R. Edgerton and Peter C. Rollins, 1–16. Lexington: University of Kentucky Press, 2001.

Esposito, Phil. Interview by Claude Mailhot. Claude Mailhot questionne. TV. Montreal: RDS, September 30, 2002.

Fowler, Roger. *Language in the News: Discourse and Ideology in the Press*. New York: Routledge, 1993.

Frosh, Stephen. "The Other." *American Imago: Psychoanalysis and the Human Sciences* 59.4 (2002): 389–408.

Gruneau, Richard, and David Whitson. *Hockey Night in Canada: Sport, Identities and Cultural Politics.* Toronto: Garamond, 1993.

"Hockey sur glace: Canada/URSS." *Les grands duels du sport.* TV. Directed by Jean-Christophe Klotz. Paris: Arte, 2005.

Hughes-Fuller, Patricia. "'Am I Canadian?': Hockey as 'National' Culture." In *Culture and the State: Nationalisms*, edited by James Gifford and Gabrielle Zezulka-Mailloux, 25–39. Edmonton, AB: University of Alberta Press, 2002.

Joffe, Hélène. *Risk and 'The Other.'* Cambridge, MA: Cambridge University Press, 1999.

Joukova, Marina. "Players Didn't Know They Were to Make History." Faceoff.com, August 25, 2002. http://www.faceoff.com/news/20020825/020825117177.html (site discontinued).

Landau, Misia. "Human Evolution as Narrative." *American Scientist* 72 (1984): 262–68.

Lipsky, Richard. *How We Play the Game.* Boston: Beacon, 1981.

Mackenzie, Scott. *Screening Québec: Québécois Moving Images, National Identity, and the Public Sphere.* Manchester, UK: Manchester University Press, 2004.

Mackey, Eva. *The House of Difference: Cultural Politics and National Identity in Canada.* Toronto: University of Toronto Press, 2002.

MacNeill, Margaret. "Networks: Producing Olympic Ice Hockey for a National Television Audience." *Sociology of Sport Journal* 3 (1996): 103–24.

Mulvoy, Mark. "Boris and His Boys Prepare for a Few Friendlies." *Sports Illustrated*, January 5, 1976.

"No Final Victories." *Home Game.* TV. Produced by Ken Dryden and Roy MacGregor. Ottawa: CBC, 1990.

Randall, Stephen J. "Divergent Visions, Common Problems: Canadian and American Foreign Policy Traditions." In *Canada and the United States: Differences That Count*, edited by David Thomas, 380–406. Peterborough, ON: Broadview, 1993.

Robidoux, Michael A. "Historical Interpretations of First Nations Masculinity and its Influence on Canada's Sport Heritage." *The International Journal of the History of Sport* 23, no. 2 (2006): 267–84.

September 1972. TV. Created and produced by TV Eye Entertainment. Toronto: CTV, September 28, 1997.

"Soul of a Nation." *Hockey: A People's History.* TV. Produced by Marc Starowicz. Ottawa: CBC, 2006.

"1972 Summit Series Anniversary." *Sports Journal.* TV. Produced by Terry Walker. Ottawa: CBC, September 21, 1997.

Summit on Ice. TV. Produced by Robert MacAskill, Ian Davey and Dave Toms. Ottawa: CBC, September 1992.

Tudor, Deborah V. *Hollywood's Vision of Team Sports.* New York: Garland, 1997.

Zaugg, Klaus. "Don't Cry for Russian Hockey." *The Summit in 1972* (blog), 2000. http://www.chidlovski.com/personal/1972/speakers/dontcry.htm.

(Mis)Deeds of Gods and Heroes: Religion and the Suspension of Disbelief in the Summit Series

✤

JAMIE DOPP

> [An analysis of the Summit Series] has to account for why a country could be brought so low by the loss of Game One and sail over the moon with joy in delight by the victory in Game Eight…. [It would have to account for the way] Game Eight wiped away all that happened on September 2nd in Montreal.
>
> Jack Ludwig, *Hockey Night in Moscow*

One of the most telling facts about the Summit Series is this: Team Canada's victory is perhaps the most celebrated event in Canadian hockey history, and yet, until Paul Henderson's last-minute goal in game eight, the series had been felt widely in Canada to be a disaster. With the golden goal, depression turned to elation and, as David Whitson and Richard Gruneau describe it, Canadians went into a frenzy of "self-congratulation" about the triumph of the "Canadian virtues" of "individualism, flair, and most of all, character" over the machine-like Soviets (263). Across the country, there were untold incidents of flag-waving, anthem singing and cries of "We're number one!" One group of about thirty-five celebrants even paraded in front of the Soviet embassy shouting, "Phil Esposito for Pope!" and "Phil Esposito for Prime Minister!" ("Horns blow"). The *Globe and Mail* front-page headline for September 29, 1972, nicely summarizes the view of Team Canada after the victory: "From Russia with Glory" (Proudfoot).

Even more telling than the jubilation after Team Canada's victory is the historical revisioning that followed. After game eight, much of the angst Canadian hockey fans had felt about the series was forgotten. Later discussions of the event, as Brian Kennedy has pointed out, were mostly repetitions of "the cries of victory" (55). So complete was the revisioning that popular accounts, like Roy MacSkimming's *Cold War: The Amazing Canada-Soviet Hockey Series of 1972*, could, without a trace of irony, make claims like "the series did more for national unity than a dozen royal commissions and any number of constitutional conferences" (157).

How to account for the remarkable psychological ups and downs triggered by the Summit Series? And, more significantly, how to account for the historical revisioning that followed?

To date, scholarship on the series seems to contain two possible answers to these questions. Henk Hoppener, in *Death of a Legend*, suggests that the extreme ups and downs were rooted in the fragility of Canadian national identity. "Canadians have had few assists to nationhood through history," Hoppener writes. "National unity, integrity and purpose are abstract political propositions that lose out to bread and butter issues.... But, for years, the majority of Canadians have been united at least in their irrepressible belief that hockey was their cause, their common fascinating attraction, their visible symbol of pre-eminence in the world" (1). Hoppener's analysis anticipates the claims about hockey that Whitson and Gruneau make in *Hockey Night in Canada* in 1993. According to them, the famously problematic nature of Canadian identity has given hockey "even greater symbolic currency" as one of those institutions that Canadians cling to as "truly Canadian" (277). Seen from this point of view, both the despair and the elation inspired by the Summit Series are reflections of a pathologically heightened Canadian investment in hockey. If what it means to be Canadian is so dependent on superiority at hockey, to lose claim to this superiority is truly a national disaster.

Brian Kennedy, in "Confronting a Compelling Other: The Summit Series and the Nostalgic (Trans)Formation of Canadian Identity," adds a more psychologically based line of explanation. According to Kennedy, one of the things the Summit Series did was to expose how dependent national self-definition – like individual self-definition – is on the construction of "a visible 'other'" (45).

The near disaster of the series forced Canadians to confront the Soviets as a compelling "other," and in particular to confront how their own identities were not autonomous and independent but interdependent on this "other" to whom they were connected. The recognition of this interdependence was very uncomfortable. Fortunately (or unfortunately) the final victory allowed for the chance to repress the connection, which is why so much of the discomfort triggered by the encounter was quickly forgotten. Kennedy explains the mechanism by way of this passage from Stephen Frosh: "[Awareness] of the extent to which what is other dominates our existence is too painful, too terrifying, to be maintained; instead, both the subject and psychoanalysis itself 'wander' back from the momentary vision of this truth, to the fantasy of completeness, of narcissistic selfhood" (quoted in Kennedy, 46).

Both of these explanations, it seems to me, have considerable merit. In what follows, I'd like to build on them by exploring two further approaches to the aforementioned questions. The first is rooted in the religious quality of sport; it explores how the series unfolded in a way that was particularly ripe for religious-like responses in Canadian fans. The second explores how the series occasioned a particularly illustrative version of the "willing suspension of disbelief" that seems necessary for the pleasurable consumption of both spectator sports and works of literature. These approaches build on some of the ideas of Kennedy, Hoppener, et al., but also, I hope, throw some additional light on these very interesting issues.

Religion

One of the enduring clichés about hockey is that it is "a religion" in Canada. Most of the time this claim is simply a way of saying that Canadians are passionate about the game, in keeping with the well-worn expression that identifies anything that anyone is really passionate about as his or her religion – as in, "money is his religion." Sports discourse in general contains a lot of overwrought religious metaphors. The need for "sacrifice" and "faith," the idea of great players as "gods" and great plays as "miracles" are all part of the standard sport lexicon. Hockey discourse is no different. Sometimes the use of religious metaphors is accompanied by a jokey self-awareness about combining the sacred and the profane, like the invocations of Shakespeare in hockey writing, which always play, at least in part, on the irony of high-culture language being used in reference to something so widely thought of as part of low culture.

Yet there is a way in which sport operates in a more serious way as a form of religion. Michael Novak, in *The Joy of Sports*, offers an impressive analysis of the parallels between major Western religions and major American sports, how they all involve rituals and customs, the idea that character can be developed by "patterns of self-denial, repetition, and experiment," the invocation of aging and death, the consecration of certain hours and days, the use of a "pattern of symbols and myths" and so on (29–31). Novak's primary focus is on baseball, football and basketball, but when he writes that "the ceremonies of sports overlap those of the state on one side, and those of the church on the other," he could very well be writing about hockey in Canada (19).

What the various elements Novak describes have in common is the way they express a desire for meaning. Humans are meaning-seeking creatures. From very early on in our history, we have invented stories to try to explain ourselves to ourselves, and especially to explain the fundamental mysteries of what it means to live and die. Religious stories place our lives in a larger setting and connect us to some kind of underlying or overarching pattern, in order to reassure us that, against a lot of depressing evidence to the contrary, our lives do indeed have meaning and value. "Myth," according to Karen Armstrong in *A Short History of Myth*, "is nearly always rooted in the experience of death and the fear of extinction...[and] all mythology speaks of another plane that exists alongside our own world, and that in some sense supports it" (3–4).

As part of this meaning seeking, religions contain within themselves a vision of what a good life would look like, along with a vision of the human self that would go along with or be necessary to this life. The religious power of various cultural institutions – whether secular or religious in the more traditional sense – has to do with the vision of the good life they project and the practices they promote for the development of the human self associated with this good life. James Smith, in *Desiring the Kingdom*, puts it this way: "[What] makes us who we are is shaped by what we ultimately love or what we love *as* ultimate.... [And what we love] is a (largely implicit) vision of what we hope for, what we think the good life looks like." For Smith, there is an "element of ultimacy" in our vision of a good life that is "fundamentally *religious*" (26–27).

Sports – including hockey – do not contain within them the kind of developed cosmology evident in Christianity, Judaism, Islam, Buddhism or any other world religion, but they are nevertheless expressions of the religious impulse in the more general sense I have outlined. Playing sports, or being a fan of them, involves a vision of a hoped-for good life, connects the individual with something larger than the individual self, and responds, in a ritual and symbolic way, to certain ultimate questions.

How do sports respond to ultimate questions? A starting point would be to think about those of us whose love of sports began in childhood. This love was almost inevitably accompanied by fantasies about becoming a star player – an NHL hockey player, in my case, as with many Canadian boys of my class and generation. Why? Quite simply, I think, the fantasy was driven by a belief that to become a star would "solve" certain larger questions of life. How am I going to make a name for myself? To find love? To earn money? To be a man? To be a rich and famous hockey player, the fantasy suggests, offers a ready answer to all these questions. When you are older, at least for the large majority of us, the fantasy of becoming a player disappears but the dynamic of being a fan remains. To be a fan means to share vicariously in the success of a favourite team or player. If your team is a champion, or your favourite player a star, then you yourself, in the reflected light of being a fan, are a champion and a star. This vicarious success doesn't address the larger questions in the same direct way as the fantasy of becoming a player, but there is still a lingering belief that the success of your favourite team or player will have a real effect on your life.

The ultimate mystery of human existence has to do, of course, with death. How can sports be understood as a response to the fact that we die? It's not very hard, I think, to imagine that athletes – young, bursting with vitality and virility, capable of acts that seem beautiful, heroic, even transcendent – are, for the fans, ritual actors and that their accomplishments can be read as "ritual triumphs of grace, agility, perfection, beauty over death" (Novak, 48). There is indeed something about great athletic achievements that seem to defy time; they do seem to involve, as Novak suggests, a "momentary attainment of perfect form – as though there were, hidden away from mortal eyes, a perfect way to execute a play, and suddenly a player or a team has found it and sneaked a demonstration down to earth" (Novak, 5). For this reason, the euphoria of winning is accompanied by "the sense of one's inflation by a power not one's own" (48). To win "is to have destiny blowing out one's sails" (49); or, to put it in a more traditionally religious way, to win is to appear to be a favourite of the gods – chosen. It is precisely because of these associations – the athlete as the embodiment of youth and vitality, athletic achievement as a ritual triumph over death – that the image of the aging athlete is so poignant to us (much like the image of the aging movie star, whose fame has the same mythic resonances as that of the star athlete). It seems not possible somehow that such a person should die, and when they do, as they inevitably must, it seems particularly tragic. How could death (also) come to those who have been so favoured by the gods?

These kinds of analysis have to be done with caution, of course, since the more you emphasize the mythic resonances of sports, the more you elide the material conditions in which sports actually takes place. As Roland Barthes famously put it, "myth is constituted by the loss of the historical quality of things" (131). Nevertheless, there is something useful in taking the religious resonances seriously; they help to explain some of the deep roots of sports and offer a model to explain the passions that sports can inspire. How is it that people can feel such joy or despair over a mere game? Even accounting for the affective power of spectacle and the way tribal identifications have of magnifying emotion, there remains something unexplained about the extremity of the passions inspired by sport that hints at deeper (and largely unconscious) psychic forces at play.

So many aspects of the Summit Series are conducive to a religious reading. The buildup to the series, over the spring and summer of 1972, made it clear that the stakes in this "friendly" competition were enormous. The series was not just about Canada redeeming itself after years of losses in international hockey because of our having to use amateurs, but about pitting the Canadian way of life against that of the Soviets. A key reason we believed we would dominate was because we thought our team would play hockey expressive of our superior way of life. We thought the Soviets would be robots, well trained but lacking in personal initiative and creativity; that they would lack the heart of Canadians and would not be able to handle the Canadian slapshot (which, somehow, seemed connected to the idea of personal initiative – a Canadian prerogative). That there were still a lot of Cold War sentiments of the "Soviets are godless communists" variety around didn't hurt either. It was as if our vision of the good life was about to be tested by an encounter with an evil "other."

I remember, as a fifteen-year-old, being unusually worked up in anticipation of the series. In particular, I had a great deal of anxiety at the prospect that Team Canada might lose. If the Canadians failed, would it reduce the quest for the Stanley Cup – the focus of so much of my hockey fantasy life – to a consolation prize? If Canadian hockey turned out to be no better than, or not as a good as, Soviet hockey, would it even matter who our champion was anymore? The predictions of an eight-game sweep that so dominated the buildup to the series offered some comfort (surely, if we were so favoured in the series, we had to win), but they also created another anxiety. If we were expected to win all eight games, would even one loss be considered a failure? Did we have to meet such a standard of perfection in order to justify our claims to supremacy?

When I think back about my anxiety over these questions – an anxiety that led directly to my own despair at the results of the early games in the series – it seems to me that it was about much more than the usual bragging rights. Truth be told, at the age of fifteen, I didn't have much in the way of attachment to Canada as a nation per se. What my anxiety had to do with, at root, I think, was the religious nature of my attachment to my favourite team and players, the idea – vague but powerful – that their success would connect me to something larger that would have a real effect on my life. If the value of that success was diminished, the connection to that something larger might be lost.

The way the series itself unfolded was also important. Both the intense passions inspired by the series and its later canonized status are direct (and ironic) results of how badly things started off for the Canadians. Had Team Canada won eight games in a row, as predicted, the series would have gone down as only another in a long line of events at which Canadian teams dominated European opponents in hockey. Many people would probably have tuned out halfway through. As it was, the unexpected loss in game one, followed by the ups and downs of the next four games, set the stage for a mythic drama of truly classical proportions.

From a mythic point of view, two moments in the Summit Series particularly stand out. One is the heartbreaking loss in game five, in which Team Canada blew leads of 3–0 and 4–1 to lose 5–4, leaving themselves down 1–3–1 in the series and with only the slimmest margin left for a possible victory. The dire circumstances Team Canada found itself in after this game were like the lowest point in a heroic tale, when the band of heroes find themselves in a seemingly impossible situation. By this point, Canadian media representations of the Soviets had shifted. At the beginning of the series, the Soviets were presented more or less as adolescents, brush-cut schoolboys about to be taught a lesson by the masterful Canadians (Kennedy, 50); by the time of Team Canada's loss in game five, the Soviets had become powerful, better-trained opponents backed by sinister allies (the KGB and the seemingly "crooked" referees). In other words, the Soviets had taken on the characteristics of mythic monsters. They had started out the series demonized as the Communist "other," of course, but only as they started winning games did they acquire the characteristics of a monster-like threat. Conversely, as in a mythic tale, the Canadians were transformed by losing into plucky underdogs, an extremely ironic reversal, given the earlier predictions of an eight-game sweep.

This is what set the stage for the other key moment from a mythic point of view, which was, of course, the victory in game eight. Paul Henderson's goal put an exclamation point on a three-game winning streak that featured a third-period comeback from two goals down in game eight. Christopher Booker, in *The Seven Basic Plots*, his monumental study of the recurring patterns in narrative, points out that escape from seemingly certain defeat by a miraculous feat of ingenuity and/or strength is a staple of all quest-like literature (44–48). Whether it is Dorothy throwing water on the wicked witch, or James Bond turning the tables on a supervillain just in the nick of time, or Luke Skywalker becoming one with the Force at just the right split second to destroy the Death Star, the pattern is the same. Sometimes, as in H. G. Wells's *The War of the Worlds* or the Bible's book of Jonah, escape is the product of assistance that is beyond human control, but the basic pattern – the buildup to a nightmare stage where defeat seems certain, followed by a miraculous reversal – is the same.

Brooker argues that, at the most basic level, the pleasure of such quest-like tales has to do with the physical effect of constriction and release that they trigger. If we identify with a hero, we feel tense as he or she faces ordeals or comes under threat, and then, when the threat is lifted, we relax (49). It is easy to see, however, how such a pattern would also intensify the experience of a ritual triumph over death, which Novak has identified as a feature of winning at sports. Indeed, the threat by a powerful foe that precedes the escape would play into our sense of vulnerability in the face of death in the way that crushing a weaker opponent never could. In any case, whatever the actual mechanism of the escape from seemingly certain defeat, there would always be a sense of destiny blowing out our sails in such triumphs, a sense of being a favourite of the gods (or, literally, of God, in the case of Job).

Interestingly, Paul Henderson, who in later life has become a devout Christian, has written about his last-minute series-winning goal in fate-like terms:

> Even today, Henderson has no idea why he called Peter Mahovlich off the ice, or why he jumped on in his place. Was divine intervention involved? "I'll tell you what," he said. "I was not a Christian in '72. I'm a very devout Christian today and when I get to heaven and have a chance, I'm going to say, 'Okay, tell me about this goal back in '72.'" (Henderson and Prime, 56)

It's hard to know how seriously Henderson intends this description. Certainly it would be the worst kind of religious chauvinism to think that the Christian God intervened in the Summit Series to make sure Team Canada was victorious. Henderson's account, though, does point to the way in which moments leading to victories in sports, like the victories themselves, tend to acquire, in retrospect, a sense of being fated. After the fact, it is easy to believe that a victory was meant to be, somehow – that it was an expression of some underlying or overarching force or pattern. Winning has a way of eliding the elements of chance and uncertainty that are part of a game. From the point of view of Canadian fans, the sense of fate in the heroic conclusion of the series would have given psychological permission for the revisioning that was to follow. It was as if, despite the thrill ride of the near escape, the underlying pattern – the mythic truth of Canadian dominance at hockey – revealed itself, in Paul Henderson's goal, to have been there all along.

Two Material Conditions

In *The Joy of Sports*, Novak acknowledges that in addition to the religious aspects of sports there are also darker elements. The two most prominent of these are the role of money in professional sports and the way competition can reinforce a chauvinistic version of masculinity. Novak calls these darker elements "corruptions." For him, they are not what is essential. To dwell on these corruptions is to fail to appreciate "the deep springs" from which sports come and to offer "a vision not deep enough for the reality" (24).

Novak, I think, makes too neat a distinction between "the reality" of sports and the "corruption" of the so-called darker elements. His starting point is his own love of sports, and in his analysis he naturally wants to concentrate on those elements (the mythic and the religious) that speak to him of the deep sources of his love; but to understand the so-called darker elements only as "corruptions" is to oversimplify the reality of sports – particularly the major team sports about which Novak is primarily concerned. Recall Barthes's analysis of how myth elides the historical quality of things. The kinds of elements Novak calls "corruptions," I would argue, are actually part of the material conditions in which sports take place.

One of the things the Summit Series did was to present a stark demonstration of some of the material conditions of hockey – especially of the elite hockey for which the series was to be an exemplar and over which, in North America, the NHL has asserted a monopoly. The conditions most directly exposed by the series are related, in fact, to the two darker elements Novak identifies as corruptions: the series exposed tensions between the commercialism in hockey, represented by the NHL, and the desire to preserve the game as part of Canadian national heritage; and it exposed tensions within the game itself between the speed and skill that are so much a part of the game's beauty and the violent ugliness that may or may not be necessary to win.

The commercial dominance of the NHL at the time of the series was most immediately demonstrated by the so-called Bobby Hull affair. When the roster for Team Canada was announced in July 1972, Hull – who had just come off another fifty-goal season for the Chicago Blackhawks and was considered by many to be the best winger in hockey – was left off of it. It turned out that the agreement between Hockey Canada and the NHL brokered by Alan Eagleson to allow for the series to take place stipulated that all members of Team Canada had to hold signed contracts with the NHL. Hull had recently signed a contract with the fledging World Hockey Association (WHA). When his exclusion from the team was revealed, it caused a furor across the country that included leading Canadian politicians. Prime Minister Pierre Trudeau even cabled Clarence Campbell, the president of the NHL, to protest (Hoppener, 4).

It would be naïve, of course, to think that the owners of the NHL – mostly Americans with teams based in American cities – would not be concerned about how the Summit Series might affect their investments. They would have been reluctant in the first place to risk injury to their players for a series of international "exhibition" games. On top of that, to allow a WHA player on Team Canada would create advertising for a business competitor. In reply to the outcry over Hull's exclusion, Clarence Campbell was blunt: "There is no reason why we should put on parade the showpiece of the other side. You don't show off the competition's best product" (quoted in Hoppener, 8).

Where Clarence Campbell's argument breaks down is that the series was promoted explicitly as a non-commercial event. The original idea was to allow Canada to play an international series with its best players at a time when the amateur requirement barred these players from the World Championships and the Olympics. The team name – Team Canada – evoked the tradition of the Canadian national team (a non-commercial enterprise). The players themselves agreed to play for free, exactly like amateurs, and to give up part of their summer for no reason except the love of country (a fact referenced by Phil Esposito during his anguished comments after game four). Any profits from the series were to be split among the Canadian Amateur Hockey Association (CAHA), Hockey Canada and the NHL players' pension fund. These elements fuelled the outrage over Bobby Hull's exclusion. An editorial in the *Globe and Mail* was particularly scathing, insisting that Team Canada "was not a commercial venture" and that competition between the NHL and WHA should have been irrelevant (quoted in Hoppener, 5). The *Ottawa Citizen* seconded the protest and added, "Could we not at least eliminate the hypocrisy by renaming it Team NHL, instead of Team Canada?" (quoted in Hoppener, 5).

A more insidious – and sordid – aspect of commercial interests came to light only years later. This had to do with the primary organizer of the series: Alan Eagleson. After the victory in game eight in Moscow, Eagleson was hailed across Canada as a hero on the same footing as Esposito and Henderson. Scott Young's chapter on the Summit Series in his 1976 book *War on Ice* opens with a quote from Harry Sinden: "Al Eagleson, more than anyone else, should take the bows for Team Canada" (159). As Young details it, Eagleson was involved in so many aspects of the series that it is impossible to define his exact role. He started out as but one member of the Hockey Canada steering committee charged with organizing the event, but he assumed single control of the Canadian end of things by force of will. At the same time, as executive director of the NHL Players' Association, Eagleson was charged with looking out for the best interests of the players. Exploiting his combined roles, he was the one who set up the deal to split profits for the series among Hockey Canada, the CAHA, and the players' pension fund (165). He arranged for Sinden and his assistants to be paid for their work but, in a seeming act of patriotism and altruism, worked himself "for nothing but…expenses" (164).

Years later, however, it became evident that Eagleson's role in the Summit Series, as well as in the later Canada Cup tournaments that built on the success of the series, was anything but altruistic. It is impossible in a short essay to detail all the self-serving actions by Eagleson, but the basic facts are that he used his multiple roles as organizer of the international tournaments, executive director of the NHLPA and player agent for the financial advantage of himself and his friends. His friends included NHL owners. After years of complaints by players behind the scenes, Russ Conway, a reporter for the *Eagle-Tribune* in Lawrence, Massachusetts, did a series of exposé articles in 1990 on Eagleson, alleging that he had skimmed money from the international tournaments through companies controlled by him set up to get advertising revenue, had made loans to associates from the players' pension fund, had shown favouritism to players he represented as agent while acting as executive director of the Players' Association, and had made various sweetheart deals with NHL owners who were also friends. *The Canadian Encyclopedia* entry on Eagleson takes the story from there: "In 1993 a grand jury in Boston held hearings into Eagleson's affairs and indicted him in 1994 on charges of racketeering, fraud and embezzlement.

On 3 December the RCMP finally charged Eagleson with fraud and theft. He pled guilty to fraud in Boston on 6 June 1998 and in Toronto the next day, receiving a sentence of 18 months in prison."

Conway eventually published his research into Eagleson in a book entitled *Game Misconduct: Alan Eagleson and the Corruption of Hockey*. Though it was not one for which Eagleson was held criminally liable, one of his most sordid actions, as detailed in *Game Misconduct*, was how he handled the finances and last contract of his most famous client, Bobby Orr. Orr, in 1975, was a free agent who very much wanted to finish his career in Boston. The Bruins, it turns out, also wanted him to finish his career in Boston and made a very generous contract offer of $295,000 US a year for five years guaranteed, plus an 18.5% ownership share of the team (or $925,000). Eagleson hid the offer from Orr. He told Orr the Bruins had written him off as damaged goods and signed him instead to his friend Bill Wirtz's Chicago Blackhawks team for ostensibly $300,000 a year. The money was supposed to be guaranteed, but when Orr had to retire early because of his knees, Wirtz refused to pay and Orr had to sue to get what he could. The court costs and Eagleson's mismanagement of Orr's other finances left Orr virtually bankrupt at the end of his career (146ff.).

The other condition revealed by the Summit Series had to do with violence. Part of the attraction of hockey, from the beginning, has been the way it combines rough physicality with speed and skill. The traditional masculine characteristics embodied by hockey players – physical strength, toughness and the ability to succeed by force of will – has had a strong resonance in Canada over the years. Because of the nature of the game, however, the questions of how much violence is acceptable and which acts violate "the code" of the game have also been perennial ones.

One of the things that happened in the Summit Series is that the Canadians, encountering an unexpectedly strong opponent and faced by the possibility of a humiliating loss, resorted to physical intimidation and other bad behaviour. Beginning with game one and continuing throughout the series, Team Canada's play more than once crossed the line into goonery. A minority of commentators after the series victory decried the Canadians' tactics. A *Globe and Mail* editorial pointed out that "the spectacle came to involve Canada's honour, often in unpleasant ways" and that there were "ruthless tactics" because

"Canada's superiority had to be asserted at all costs" (quoted in Hoppener, 93). John Robertson in the *Montreal Star* summarized all the negative aspects of what he called "Team Ugly" that included goonery and vulgar antics and a belief that "anything goes in word, gesture or antics as long as we score more goals than the other guy" (quoted in Hoppener, 95–96).

The ugly side of needing to win at any cost was perhaps best illustrated by Bobby Clarke's slash on Valery Kharlamov in game six. At the time, Team Canada was in a do-or-die situation, needing to win three games in a row to salvage the series. Kharlamov was arguably the most skilled Soviet player. In the video of the slash, you can see that Clarke follows Kharlamov into the Team Canada zone and, after Kharlamov has passed off the puck, takes a two-handed swing with his stick. The stick hits Kharlamov on the outside of the ankle, breaking the blade, and also breaking Kharlamov's ankle. After the play is called, other Canadian players go after Kharlamov, as if he had been the one at fault, and Foster Hewitt, in his play-by-play, seems surprised that Clarke has been assessed a penalty: it's as if the penalty call is just one more of many made against the Canadians by the biased referees. Kharlamov, after the slash, tried to play on in the game and series but was not the same – and this almost certainly contributed to Canada's comeback victory.

Over the years, for those who have tried to advance a counter-narrative to the celebration of the Summit Series, Bobby Clarke's slash has become emblematic of the darker side of Team Canada's play. Jason Blake calls the slash an "on-ice nadir" of the series and the embodiment of "winning ugly" (156). Michael Buma sees the slash as "the ultimate expression" of the myth of Canadian manhood acquired through hockey violence (186). Brett Kashmere, in his documentary *Valery's Ankle*, takes a similar line to Buma and argues that an analysis of the slash could disrupt the seamless transmission of the version of aggressive masculinity that seems so much a part of hockey culture.

An important point to emphasize is that the Bobby Clarke slash was not part of a "corruption" of hockey in the way that Novak might want to define it. Instead, the slash was one of those incidents, of which there have been many over the years, in which certain material conditions of hockey are exposed in an unusually overt way. Hockey, like every other competitive sport, contains within itself a tension between the "desire to win at all costs" and the imperative to play "within the rules" (whether these are the formal rules or the unwritten "code" that defines what breaking of the rules is honourable or not). The desire to win inevitably creates moments of ugliness. In the more physical sports, like hockey and football, these moments of ugliness more often than not take the form of incidents of overt violence.

To support the idea that incidents like the slash lay bare certain material conditions, it is necessary to refer to the evolution of sports like hockey. Obviously I don't have the space to go into this in great detail here. Suffice it to say that the literature about the evolution of sports tends to contain two quite distinct theories. One theory, perhaps most influentially articulated by Norbert Elias in *The Civilizing Process*, sees in the evolution of sports a gradual development of rules, of a code of conduct, that reflects the imperatives of a more civil society. Early sports like jousting were extremely violent, often leading to fatalities, but as sports developed regulations came into effect to enforce "restraint" so that victory "is enforced less and less by direct physical force." In this process, Elias sees a parallel to the evolution of society as depending less and less on raw violence for its order and more on, for example, the rule of law (157–58). Over against this theory is the claim, by Marxist theorists like Jean-Marie Brohm and others, that sports are a way of perpetuating, by other means, the capitalist underpinnings of Western society. According to Brohm, sports – especially the more violent ones – are training grounds in the core values of patriarchal capitalism, in which both players and spectators are conditioned to be consumers and capitalists, with the emphases on virility, symbolic and physical violence, chauvinism, racism and sexism that go along with this (15). This kind of critique – with or without the Marxist edge – is quite common in contemporary society. Novak has clearly encountered versions of it himself, probably in more feminist forms, for in *The Joy of Sports* he tries to preempt criticism about his love of sports by defending, in particular, his love of football. "Say, if you like, that men *ought* to be less primitive, less violent, less mesmerized by pain and injury," he writes, "[but] football makes conscious to me part of what I am…[and what it makes me conscious of is] not half so ugly as… beautiful" (xv).

The truth about sports like hockey, I would argue, lies not in the "beauty" of the game separated from the "ugliness" – nor vice versa. Hockey – like football

– has evolved with a built-in tension between the thrill of a combat-like activity and the risk of real injury or death, just as it has a tension between the desire to win and the requirement to restrain that same desire within certain rules. How to maintain the thrill while keeping the risk of "ugliness" at an acceptable level is a perennial issue. The built-in tension, however, means that "ugliness" – whether revealed overtly in any given moment of play or not – is a condition of possibility of the game.

The Willing Suspension of Disbelief

What to do, then, with the way that the "glory" of game eight of the Summit Series seemed to "wipe away" all the "ugliness" exposed by the loss in game one? This historical revisioning, I'd like to argue, offers a particularly illustrative version of the "willing suspension of disbelief" that seems necessary for the pleasurable consumption of sports as well as literature and other cultural products.

The phrase "the willing suspension of disbelief" was first used by Samuel Taylor Coleridge in 1817 in chapter XIV of the *Biographia Literaria*. Here are Coleridge's exact words: "[It] was agreed, that my endeavours should be directed to persons and characters supernatural, or at least romantic; yet so as to transfer from our inward nature a human interest and a semblance of truth sufficient to procure for these shadows of imagination that willing suspension of disbelief for the moment, which constitutes poetic faith" (452). Coleridge is alluding here most directly to his fantastical poem "The Rime of the Ancient Mariner" and trying to distinguish its poetical aims from those of the more realistic poems of his friend William Wordsworth, which deal with subjects "chosen from ordinary life" (452). The idea of suspension of disbelief, however, has come to be applied more broadly over time to describe how readers have to repress or ignore elements in order to enjoy literature in a certain way. A good analogy might be a puppet show. If you are too distracted by the strings that move the puppets, you won't enjoy the show. There are a number of assumptions about the nature of reading – and the nature of the pleasure of reading – behind this that I can't go into here. The broad circulation of the belief, however, is suggested by the number of encounters those of us who are critics have with readers (including our own students!) who say they prefer not to analyze literature because to do so "spoils" the fun of reading for them.

There is a connection, I think, between the suspension of disbelief and the process of commodification of both sports and art. Marx's famous chapter on commodity fetishism in *Capital* describes the basic mechanism of commodification as a separation of "material relations" from the thing becoming a commodity. "The existence of things *qua* commodities," Marx writes, "[has] no connection with their physical properties and with the material conditions arising therefrom" (77). In other words, part of what makes things into the objects of desire that commodities are is that the process by which the things are made is hidden. A good example is meat in a grocery store: Beef in a grocery store tends to come in bloodless cuts neatly wrapped in styrofoam and plastic. If consumers had to witness the killing of the cow each time they bought a steak (or, worse, had to participate in the killing), there would be much less beef sold.

Something similar, I think, happens during our consumption of sports. The process of commodification goes beyond the obvious aspect of money paid and received for a product. It has to do with how sports become objects of desire, alluring places where players, would-be players and fans invest their yearning for something like "the good life" (interesting how the word "fan," though derived in the first instance from "fanatic," also has a connection to "fantasy"). As consumers of sports, we can't look too closely at the process of production without affecting the allure, so when we are faced with evidence about that process (which, like the slaughterhouse, inevitably contains a lot of raw ugliness), we tend to not want to dwell on it too much. If collisions on the ice remind us too strongly of the bodily cost of professional hockey – like the recent widespread problems with concussions – it disrupts our viewing pleasure. Or, to put it another way: even though a part of us might be aware of the uglier possibilities of hockey, we have to suspend the disbelief this might cause if we are going to enjoy the spectacle of the game.

Why do we do this? The simple answer, I think, is that the needs fulfilled by being a fan of sports are, for those of us who are fans, profound. The needs, as I argued earlier, are indeed religious-like in nature, and for that reason fans have a strong psychological tendency to protect the view of the game that allows for the projection of those needs onto the game and their subsequent, possible fulfillment in fantasy (rather like adherents to a religion tend to be inured to demonstrations of contradictions within that religion). Doug Beardsley has suggested that passion for hockey in Canada has to do, in part, with how it has supplied Canadians with heroes – and that we all need heroes. "The hero," he writes, "has the ability to make us feel we live a larger life. He gives our lives significance, connects us to the great possibilities that lie within us, to the hope that we could be the exception" (109). There is an important truth in this claim – and, it seems to me, the mechanism for constructing heroes who might allow for the satisfaction of the needs Beardsley identities is no more evident than in the historical revisioning associated with the Summit Series.

Let me end by commenting on a development in the world of professional sports that perhaps offers a counter-narrative to the argument I have put forward here. This has to do with what a 2013 article by Bill Briggs called "scandal apathy" in major professional sports.

The fact is, since the Summit Series in 1972 all of the major sports in North America have gone through high-profile problems that have exposed, sometimes in wrenching detail, the "ugliness" that is implicated in the alluring surface they attempt to present. Racism and sexism, drugs, violence on and off the fields of play, sordid financial dealings: all of the major sports have gone through scandals that have exposed these darker aspects of their products. The NHL has had a number of instances of extreme violence since 1972, including many on-ice brawls during the heyday of the Philadelphia Flyers and later incidents like the Marty McSorley stick swing and the Todd Bertuzzi sucker punch, as well as numerous examples of sordid financial dealings, some exposed in books like David Cruise and Alison Griffiths's *Net Worth*, others revealed in the parade of owners – Bruce McNall, John Spano, William Del Biaggio and Henry Samueli come immediately to mind – who have had financially related legal troubles. And yet, as the Briggs article points out, despite all this ugliness, the revenues of professional sports have only continued to grow (Briggs).

The recent NHL lockout is a particularly interesting example. The lockout offered a glaring example of the ruthless side of the business of professional hockey and triggered a vast amount of negative press for the league. Internet comment sections were filled with vitriolic denunciations of both owners and players, generally along the lines of "Millionaires arguing with billionaires – who cares!" and vows made by many fans that they would never watch another NHL game. And yet, instantly with the return to play, fans returned in even greater numbers than before.

One way to interpret this "scandal apathy" is as a continuation of the psychology I discussed earlier: the needs fulfilled by sports are so strong that fans are willing to overlook any sort of ugliness in order to get their fix. This suggests a continuation of – or intensification of – the suspension of disbelief revealed by the historical revisioning after the Summit Series, as well as a continuation of – or intensification of – the fragile sense of identity that Hoppener and others proposed as a root cause of this behaviour. Do fans today have an even more fragile sense of identity than fans during the era of the Summit Series did? Does this lead to even greater extremes of euphoria, depression and denial than in years past? Certainly the vitriolic denunciations followed immediately by the loyal return of the fans during the NHL lockout seem to have strong parallels to Canadian fan reaction in September 1972.

There is a more disturbing explanation, however. I do think that, rightly or wrongly, people today perceive the world to be more complicated and difficult to navigate than in years gone by. There is a widespread sense (evident in phenomena like the Occupy Wall Street movement) that the globalized economy keeps getting more and more cutthroat and that it is getting harder for the average person to achieve prosperity and happiness. In this environment, are fan identifications with sports stars changing? Is there less of an inclination to idealize athletes into the kinds of heroic-godlike figures Novak reveres? This is a hard thing to measure, but it does seem to me that certain changes in attitude have taken place since 1972. Perhaps fans are just more comfortable with the idea of flawed, more human-seeming heroes, in keeping with our increasingly secular age; or, perhaps sports is just so much bigger than any athlete or event that the scandals don't matter. Or – and this is the disturbing alternative – perhaps fans of sport are following the lead of fans of television shows like *The Sopranos*. Why do people identify with antiheroes like Tony Soprano? Ultimately, I think, it is because – despite the ugliness and violence that is so much a part of his character – Tony is by turns very human and entirely able to be ruthless in getting what he wants. In a world seemingly ruled by winning-at-all-costs attitudes, a character who is willing to do anything to win is a hero

235

even if what he does is ruthless or illegal (especially if he is a seemingly regular guy the rest of the time). Tony Soprano, like a certain type of hockey player, is willing in his work to "go to the dirty areas" to succeed. Perhaps Bobby Clarke's slash on Valery Kharlamov offered more of a vision of the future of sports than any of us recognized at the time.

Works Cited

Armstrong, Karen. *A Short History of Myth*. Toronto: Vintage, 2006.

Barthes, Roland. "Myth Today." In *A Barthes Reader*, edited by Susan Sontag, 93–149. New York: Hill and Wang, 1983.

Beardsley, Doug. *Country on Ice*. Winlaw, BC: Polestar, 1987.

Blake, Jason. *Canadian Hockey Literature: A Thematic Study*. Toronto: University of Toronto Press, 2010.

Booker, Christopher. *The Seven Basic Plots: Why We Tell Stories*. London: Continuum, 2004.

Briggs, Bill. "Scandal Apathy: Revenue Soars for Sports Franchises despite High-Profile Problems." *NBC News*, August 5, 2013, http://www.nbcnews.com/business/business-news/scandal-apathy-revenue-soars-sports-franchises-despite-high-profile-problems-f6C10825511.

Brohm, Jean-Marie. *Sport, A Prison of Measured Time*. London: Ink Links, 1978.

Buma, Michael. *Refereeing Identity: The Cultural Work of Canadian Hockey Novels*. Montreal: McGill-Queen's University Press, 2012.

The Canadian Encyclopedia. S.v. "Alan Eagleson." Last modified February 3, 2014. www.thecanadianencyclopedia.com

Coleridge, Samuel Taylor. "Selections from *Biographia Literaria*." In *English Romantic Writers*, edited by David Perkins, 448–90. New York: Harcourt Brace Jovanovich, 1967.

Conway, Russ. *Game Misconduct: Alan Eagleson and the Corruption of Hockey*. Toronto: Macfarlane Walter & Ross, 1995.

Elias, Norbert. *The Civilizing Process*. Oxford: Blackwell, 2000.

Henderson, Paul. *How Hockey Explains Canada*. With Jim Prime. Chicago: Triumph, 2011.

Hoppener, Henk W. *Death of a Legend*. Montreal: Copp Clark, 1972.

"Horns blow, fans howl as Canada wildly celebrates hockey triumph." *Globe and Mail*, September 29, 1972.

Kennedy, Brian. "Confronting a Compelling Other: The Summit Series and the Nostalgic (Trans)Formation of Canadian Identity." In *Canada's Game: Hockey and Identity*, edited by Andrew C. Holman, 44–62. Montreal: McGill-Queen's University Press, 2009.

Ludwig, Jack. *Hockey Night in Moscow*. Toronto: McClelland & Stewart, 1972.

MacSkimming, Roy. *Cold War: The Amazing Canada-Soviet Hockey Series of 1972*. Vancouver, BC: Greystone, 1996.

Marx, Karl. *Capital*. Vol. 1, *A Critique of Political Economy*. Translated by Samuel Moore and Edward Aveling. Edited by Frederick Engels. Moscow: Progress Publishers, 1954.

Novak, Michael. *The Joy of Sports: End Zones, Bases, Baskets, Balls, and the Consecration of the American Spirit*. Lanham: Hamilton Press, 1988.

Proudfoot, Dan. "From Russia, With Glory." *Globe and Mail*, September 29, 1972.

Sinden, Harry. *Hockey Showdown: The Canada-Russia Hockey Series*. Toronto: Doubleday, 1972.

Smith, James K. A. *Desiring the Kingdom: Worship, Worldview, and Cultural Formation*. Grand Rapids, MI: Baker, 2009.

Valery's Ankle. Independent digital video. Directed by Brett Kashmere. 2006.

Whitson, David, and Richard Gruneau. *Hockey Night in Canada: Sport, Identities, and Cultural Politics*. Toronto: Garamond, 1993.

Young, Scott. *War on Ice: Canada in International Hockey*. Toronto: McClelland & Stewart, 1976.

Lessons from *Valery's Ankle*

🍁

BRETT KASHMERE

> Hockey is part of life in Canada. Thousands play it, millions
> follow it, and millions more surely try their best to ignore it
> altogether. But if they do, their disregard must be purposeful, one
> in conscious escape, for hockey's evidences are everywhere....
> In Canada, hockey is one of winter's expectations.
>
> – Ken Dryden and Roy MacGregor, *Home Game*

Valery's Ankle, a thirty-three-minute video essay about the spectacle
of hockey violence and its representation in North American media, which
I completed in May 2006, takes Bobby Clarke's breaking of rival Russian
star Valery Kharlamov's ankle during the 1972 Summit Series as its point
of departure and site of research. Working outwards from there, the video
examines the series' circuitry, from development and staging to transmission
and historicization. The video views the event through the filters of
Canada's political and cultural histories, the history of hockey violence, the
particular circumstances of the Summit Series and its semiotic function in
the mediascape and collective memory of Canadians. *Valery's Ankle* attempts
to unearth contradictions regarding our national identity and to redress the
function of hockey in Canadian culture. Hockey has often been employed as
a symbol of national unity, an indicator of Canadian values and an instrument
of foreign policy. To question or renounce our common assumptions forces one
to become conscious of what might have been automatically and habitually
accepted before. Consider hockey: increasingly unrepresentative of Canada's

multi-ethnic mosaic, the power of its imagery in the national imagination is nonetheless impossible to deny.[1]

Having grown up in a hockey-obsessed, small-town prairie culture, my involvement with the sport is deeply entwined with my identity, providing a rhetorical frame for the evidence that I present in *Valery's Ankle*. Utilizing a self-reflexive, investigative voice, I fashion an argument from the viewpoint of a participant-observer, one that interrogates the trope of violence in hockey while also affirming the symbolic and unifying potential of hockey as Canadian popular culture. Avoiding a simple repetition of spectacle, which Bill Nichols describes as "an aborted or foreclosed form of identification where emotional engagement does not even extend as far as *concern* but instead remains arrested at the level of *sensation*" (234; emphasis added), I treat images of hockey violence as troubled and troubling texts that gain magnitude and meaning through excess accumulation and enumeration. The Summit Series becomes the prime trope, the ur-text, that allows for the following conclusion: that hockey violence is a cyclical, social problem that has been normalized, even glamorized, through its perpetuation in mass media, rather than a series of unrelated "sporting incidents." Celebrating the end result – a narrow victory in an eight-game hockey exhibition – while repressing the political forces and brutal actions that enabled the result, has caused, in my view, a hairline fracture of our national self-image. That is, an almost indiscernible breakage, a subtle psychological splitting, an elision.

Winters of Discontent

At the beginning of *The Death of Hockey*, which positions the late '60s US corporate takeover of pro hockey as an affront to Canadian nationalism, Bruce Kidd and John Macfarlane assert that "hockey is *the* Canadian metaphor, the rink a symbol of this country's vast stretches of water and wilderness, its extremes of climate, the player a symbol of our struggle to civilize such a land. Some people call it our national religion" (4; emphasis added).[2] Others have called it our national game, our popular theatre, our common passion, the game of our lives, the best game you can name, the Canadian universal and the Canadian specific. Apocryphal or not, hockey remains a socializing force;

it also plays a significant role in the formation, production and representation of Canadian identity. As the only mainstream culture we didn't import, the unifying potential of hockey's collective representation remains strong. Hockey's mythic function, however, reached its zenith during the Summit Series, one of the most dramatic sporting events ever staged. Still, one doesn't have to back check forty years to find evidence of the game's ongoing social relevance: over the past decade, Todd Bertuzzi's blindside revenge assault on Colorado Avalanche forward Steve Moore, Don Cherry's persistent, bigoted comments regarding Europeans and French Canadians, Mike Danton's failed murder-for-hire plot against his agent and former coach, and the recent, tragic deaths of Derek Boogaard, Rick Rypien and Wade Belak have inspired international media coverage and community debate.[3] More important, these incidents have thrust issues of hockey-related violence, racism, sexual abuse and mental health into the mainstream discourse.[4]

The Death of Hockey was published shortly after the Summit Series' conclusion. As Michael Robidoux writes, "the most celebrated hockey and, in turn, Canadian story occurred on September 28, 1972, when Paul Henderson scored the winning goal in the final of an eight-game series against the Soviet Union" (3). Samir Gandesha claims – seriously, I believe – that "the single most important historical event in this country after the British North America Act of 1867 was not the two World Wars nor the October Crisis, but rather the Canada Cup series [*sic*] of 1972" (14).[5] Ken Dryden contends that Henderson's goal is the "one wholly Canadian event that has left a similar trail of memory" as John F. Kennedy's assassination (193). It's estimated that ninety-five per cent of Canadians followed the Summit Series on radio or television, with over sixteen million tuning in for the deciding game.[6]

Footage of Henderson's last-minute goal, transmitted via the Soviet Union's unstable video signal, has been remastered and rebroadcast ad infinitum on the collective Canadian mindscreen. In Canada it remains the epoch's enduring moment, an audiovisual loop made even more memorable by its stark, unavoidable colour. Foster Hewitt's coterminous commentary likewise invokes instant recall, engendering a shared sense of nostalgia. But as Gary Genosko observes, "The unanalysed replay is visual fast food. It becomes a domain of analysis when it is played in slow and stop motion and presents the opportunity for expert and colour commentary.... It is...a kind of moving blackboard open to the analysis of otherwise indecipherable patterns and flows" (122).

In *Valery's Ankle*, I utilize televisual techniques such as instant replay, freeze frame and slow motion as tools for analysis. The filmmaker and theorist Peter Gidal writes, "slow motion is a technical invention, *inseparable from analytic work on representation*" (11; emphasis added). "Analysis" means to break something down to its component parts. To Clarke's breaking of Kharlamov's ankle, I apply a forensic approach, isolating and magnifying each frame as if it were a molecular structure, a social nerve cell. Frame by frame, I deconstruct and re-present this action, teasing out new potential or hidden meanings; questioning how it functioned in the past (as absence), and how it should be understood in the present; rendering the images textual and allegorical. A broken ankle, the synecdoche for a nation's unspoken psychological crisis.

When dealing with iconic (or missing) cultural images, it's important to also recognize the power dynamics of mass media. The selection and repetitive distribution of images by socio-technological apparatuses (like the CBC) function to construct and reproduce political ideology. The limitless "instant" replays and rehashing of Henderson's goal have produced an extended ideological effect – stirrings of patriotism.[7] Isolating less celebrated evidence from the series, slowing it down, shuttling it forwards and backwards through time, helps us to understand *why* the desperate, paranoid aggression carried out by Team Canada during the Summit Series has been narratively recast as heroic, noble and necessary.[8]

Like anyone born after 1970, I have no *authentic* memory of the Summit Series. I remember the *replays*. Like a short film loop, the image and sound of Henderson's winning goal remain etched in my mind; I can picture it clearly, easily recalling Hewitt's high-pitched account. How has this "memory" been constructed, and what is its relationship to the historical record? Whose version of the series is being imprinted on my consciousness? Players, sportswriters, politicians and historians have manufactured an official public memory that has become "shared cultural knowledge by successive generations" (Confino, 1386) but that serves a narrow political agenda: to advance the idea of a successfully democratic and unified nation. The construction and reception of memory is a tightly closed circle. Evidence cannot speak for itself; it needs to be deciphered, mediated. Accordingly, cinema is often employed as an architectural support, and metaphor, for human memory. The ethnographic filmmaker and theorist David MacDougall observes that "films have a disconcerting resemblance to memory.... Sometimes film seems even more astonishing than memory, an intimation of memory perfected" (260). As *technologies* of memory, film and video are incredibly powerful tools for addressing issues of signification and representation (including their impossibility),[9] cultural amnesia and delayed remembrance. By focusing attention on an intentionally forgotten (or repressed) aspect of the Summit Series – Clarke's breaking of Kharlamov's ankle – by re-enacting it, repeating it, re-photographing it, stretching out its duration, I hope to burn a new image-loop into our collective memory.

The story of Team Canada's violent performance during the series requires greater scrutiny and discussion. A nation's identity, mythology and collective conscience are at stake. I would argue that Clarke's slash is an action equivalent to Henderson's series-winning goal, now considered a moment of national historical importance. Millions of Canadians skipped work, crowded department store windows, and gathered in school gymnasiums to bear witness to a victory that was enabled by a deliberate, premeditated act of violence, which was, at least in part, determined by the political context of the series.

A History of Violence

The history of Canadian hockey is simultaneously a history of de-sublimated violence, which has, over the decades, resulted in an increasingly unsafe workplace for its professional players. But even in its early days of the late 1800s and early 1900s, as a recreational pastime, hockey had a reputation for brutality. The speed of the game, the legality of body contact, and the inherent dangers of the hockey stick all contributed to an atmosphere of injury and aggression (Howell, 43–46). A number of times the violence in hockey has escalated to dangerous levels, on rare occasions resulting in death.[10] The first phase of NHL expansion greatly contributed to the increase of violence, *as a form of spectacle,* that culminated in the 1970s with the success of the Philadelphia Flyers.[11] Dubbed the "Broad Street Bullies," the Flyers were the first professional hockey franchise to employ intimidation as an instrument of winning. Led by Bobby Clarke, the Flyers became the first expansion team to win a Stanley Cup. The expansion era is also, notably, the backdrop against which the Summit Series was conceived and realized.

As Clarke admits, the kind of unconcealed attack that he visited upon Kharlamov rarely occurred in the NHL: "It's not something I would've done in an NHL game, at least I hope I wouldn't," he said years later. "But that situation…at that stage in the series, with everything that was happening, it was necessary" (quoted in Morrison, 151, 167). In Canada and the United States, all male hockey players acquiesce to a de facto code designed to protect stars.[12] This method of self-policing and ritualized retribution sacrifices players like Steve Moore – young, hardworking, limited in pure talent and easy to replace.[13] As a member of the NHL's lowest class, Moore was quickly cast out of the league, barred from even rehabilitating his injuries at his team's facilities.[14] His decision to sue Bertuzzi and related parties surely contributed to Moore's banishment. This underscores the fact that pro hockey is a highly controlled, homosocial labour environment that doesn't tolerate subversive or insubordinate behaviour, and which contributes to an atmosphere of domination, control and intimidation.

Evoking Walter Benjamin's conception of history – where the past is revealed in the present at critical moments – Clarke's slashing of Kharlamov's ankle was once again brought to light in the image of Bertuzzi's 2004 attack on Moore.[15] The Bertuzzi incident released an entire historical constellation of abject Canadian aggression into the televisual sphere. The resultant montage of blindside slashes and crosschecks, crashes, concussions and fractured skulls revealed that nearly all of the previous half-century's most vicious hockey incidents were instigated by Canadian professionals. The conclusion I draw from this assembly, conveniently organized by an omniscient television media, is that corporate and public pressures to win at all costs not only shape but also encourage hockey violence. Although such violence has been a domestic problem going back to the game's amateur beginnings, its political stakes were raised during the Cold War, providing Canada with a rare opportunity to transcend its international middle power status.

Fear of a Red Planet

Beginning in the mid 1950s, Canada's reputation as the world's premiere hockey power encountered its first serious challenge. After the Russians' upset victory over the East York Lyndhursts (Canada's amateur representative) at the 1954 hockey World Championships, the nation was scandalized.[16] This loss eventually led to the creation of the '72 Summit Series, marking the first time a team composed of NHL pros faced off against the Soviet nationals. Primarily, the eight-game challenge tournament presented an opportunity for Canada to regain its number one status. Set amidst the rhetoric of an ideological war, the international media seized on the contrast of democratic and socialist values and styles, pitting Team Canada's flair, individuality and long hair against the Soviet Union's disciplined, systematic team play and uniform military grooming. Many North American experts predicted a Canadian sweep, but the Soviets' early domination, including their decisive 7–3 victory in the first game, recalls Trinh T. Minh-ha's claim that the assumptions of specialized knowledge need to be constantly scrutinized and counteracted. "The waning of the hegemonic professional ethos is a necessary condition for the emergence of new relationships and complex forms of repressive subjectivities," she writes (227).

The Soviets entered game six needing a win to clinch the series; for Canada it was sudden death. Midway through the second period, with Canada ahead 3–1, Bobby Clarke received a special assignment from Team Canada assistant coach and former NHL tough guy John Ferguson. Perhaps fearing a replay of game five, in which the Russians stormed back from a three-goal deficit in the final period to win the contest, Ferguson prompted Clarke to injure Kharlamov, the Russian star. As Ferguson admits, "Kharlamov was hurting us all the time. So I called Bobby Clarke over…and asked him to try to tap that ankle of his and break it" (quoted in *Summit on Ice*). "I chased him down and gave him a whack across the side of the ankle," Clarke recalls, adding Kharlamov "wasn't an effective player after that" (quoted in *Summit on Ice*).[17]

Occurring in the heart of the Communist Empire under the spectre of the Cold War, Clarke's transgression resonates with distinct political overtones. As the populist commentator Don Cherry argues, the Summit Series wasn't about hockey at all, "This was WAR!" (quoted in *Canada's Team of the Century*).

Critics and participants on both sides of the Atlantic have made similar observations. Kidd and Macfarlane conclude that "In the end the stars of the NHL had not played better than the Russians, but they had shown more desire – which may have *little* to do with hockey but everything to do with winning" (95). "To me, it *was* war," Phil Esposito said years later. "There's no doubt in my mind that I think I would have killed to win" (Dryden and MacGregor, 211). "I am convinced that Bobby Clarke was given the job of taking me out of the game," Kharlamov maintained after the series. "Sometimes I thought it was his only goal. I looked into his angry eyes, saw his stick which he yielded like a sword, and didn't understand what he was doing. It had nothing to do with hockey" (quoted in Pelletier). Thirty years later, Paul Henderson called Clarke's slash "the low point of the series" and compared it to "shooting a guy in the hallway" (quoted in Stevens). Clarke justified the penalty by explaining, "If I hadn't learned to lay on a two-hander once in a while, I'd never have left Flin Flon [Manitoba]" (which is a small mining town located along the Saskatchewan border) (quoted in Stevens).

These comments bring to mind Roland Barthes' observation about Canadian hockey, that "the great players are heroes and not stars" (75).[18] Barthes wrote the line as accompanying commentary for the overlooked National Film Board of Canada production *Of Sport and Men* (1961). Conceived and directed by Hubert Aquin, *Of Sport and Men* is a film essay covering five national sport spectacles: Spanish bullfighting, the Tour de France, American sports car racing, British soccer and Canadian hockey. The film was one of several hockey-related projects produced at the NFB between 1953 and 1967,[19] a period marked by nuclear escalation, Cold War anxiety, a second Red Scare, widespread censorship and the emergence of television. At the same time, Canada's dominance in the hockey arena was being challenged by the Soviets. Like the United States, Canada previously defined itself against the communism and state power of the Soviet Union, with hockey substituting for the space race as a primary instrument of anti-communist propaganda.[20] For English Canada, cultural anxiety was triply determined by the machine-like Soviet system, materialized in their hockey successes; the ideological dominance of America's entertainment industry – namely Hollywood; and the insulated autonomy of *Québécoise* culture.

Like other hockey films of the postwar era, *Of Sport and Men* reconstructs and reaffirms the mythic image of the rugged, vigorous Canadian hockey player, signified here by Maurice "Rocket" Richard.[21] Over shots of Richard scoring, we are reminded by a voice-of-God narrator that "a goal scored proves the virility of the attackers," and that "hockey is an offensive game where the joy of the attack justifies every risk." Cutting to a skirmish after the whistle, the film implicitly conflates hockey with combat. As an incredulous Richard is thrown from the game for slashing an opponent, a riot erupts in the stands. Meanwhile, outside the arena, another riot is in full bloom. As fans tussle with police amid the chaos of flames, protests and sirens, the narrator reminds us that "sport is what separates combat from riot." Ironically, in this case sport *doesn't* separate combat from riot: it perpetuates the worst riot in Canadian sports history, the infamous Richard Riot of 1955, later interpreted as a catalyst for Quebec's Quiet Revolution.

The only Canadian hockey-themed feature to appear prior to 1972 is George McCowan's *Face-Off* (a.k.a. *Winter Comes Early*) (1971). Set during the NHL expansion, *Face-Off* follows Billy Duke (Art Hindle) through his debut season with the Toronto Maple Leafs, including a road trip to hippie-era California. Before that, though, Duke falls in love with a peacenik folk singer played by Trudy Young (looking like a young Joni Mitchell), who breaks up with him after witnessing the violence during a game and soon becomes a drug addict. The conversations between Duke and the real-life Maple Leaf captain George Armstrong (appearing as himself) are striking. Nicknamed "Chief," Armstrong was one of the first minorities to transgress the NHL's unspoken colour barrier. In their final exchange, he explains to Duke, "You're a slave by choice. We all are. Haven't you figured that out yet? Great white hunter say 'jump,' we jump. Great white hunter no like Billy Duke, sell Billy Duke new master," at which point Duke quits the team.[22] The systematic racism implied in Armstrong's statement belongs to the same sports-industrial nexus that sanctioned Team Canada's aggressively dirty play and out-of-control behaviour during the Summit Series. Time and again, hockey violence has been motivated by a fear of the other, whether political, racial or class-based.

The mythic construction of Canadian hockey reached its apotheosis during the Summit Series. One outcome has been an increasingly complex representation of Canadian identity, gender and masculinity in hockey-themed films, and which was initially foretold in *Face-Off*. In *Perfectly Normal* (Yves Simoneau, 1990), the hero Renzo Parachii (Michael Riley) works in a brewery, plays goal for the company team, and drives a taxicab at night. In one climactic scene, the coach's nurse, played by Patricia Gage, urges the team to victory by challenging their manhood, while Renzo's American friend, the gregarious chef Alonzo (Robbie Coltrane), oversees the opening night of their opera-themed Italian restaurant, at which Renzo will later perform Bellini's *Norma* in full drag.

Like many of the Canadian films produced after 1972 that foreground hockey, including *Paperback Hero* (Peter Pearson, 1973), *Strange Brew* (Rick Moranis and Dave Thomas, 1983), and *Les Boys* (Louis Saia, 1997),[23] *Perfectly Normal* features working-class amateurs rather than NHL pros. Janice Kaye points out, "*Perfectly Normal* constructs the Canadian male character as more feminine than masculine, with Renzo assigned traditionally female characteristics…slim, reserved, polite…sexually reticent, shy [and] passive"; he's also fond of opera and averse to hanging out at the local strip club (67). In several ways he's Maurice Richard and Bobby Clarke's opposite number. *Perfectly Normal* also signifies ironically on *Of Sport and Men's* statement that "the *goalie* is ultimately responsible for the good name of the team" by appearing indifferent towards winning – he doesn't take part in the team's victory celebrations – and by publicly performing his transvestism in their presence. Questioning the terms of heroic masculinity as it's determined in popular media representations of Canadian hockey prior to 1972, *Perfectly Normal* negotiates a more complex relationship among playing hockey, being Canadian and being male than any of its pre–Summit Series film predecessors. In this sense, the Summit Series might be seen – thankfully – as a breaking point for the physical, reticent, hockey-warrior stereotype in Canadian culture.

A Glitch

The Summit Series occurred at a moment when video was becoming an *international* broadcast medium; the poor technical quality of the cameras and television facilities used in Moscow, provided by the Soviet Union, caused several moments of temporary picture loss during the final four games. Besides pointing to obvious economic and technological disparities between the countries, these technical glitches also denote the forgotten juvenile misbehaviour that occurred throughout the series. But of all Team Canada's numerous on-ice transgressions, Clarke's premeditated slash of Kharlamov's ankle during game six carries the greatest *symbolic* significance.[24] By aggressively challenging the way we characterize ourselves as a country, Team Canada's performance throughout the tournament, and Clarke's two-handed slash in particular, signify a discernible "glitch" in the production of Canadian nationalism, identity and masculinity. This fissure disrupts Canadian self-identification as polite, peaceful and sportsmanlike and enacts a shadow identity as hostile, frustrated and vengeful.

A video glitch is a form of low frequency interference, appearing as a horizontal bar moving vertically through the picture; a technical mistake from the bygone analogue era; a visual "artifact" that can't be erased, only ignored or overlooked. Incidents of hockey violence are like video glitches in the collective Canadian memory/archive. Go back to the tapes, and you'll find plenty of both. But we don't want to be reminded. Obsolete technologies are a safe house for unwanted memories. In *Valery's Ankle* the glitch acts as a metaphor for nearly imperceptible visible evidence, such as Clarke's slashing of Kharlamov. At regular speed, thirty frames per second, it's almost impossible to discern Clarke's stick as it strikes Kharlamov's ankle. Only by slowing the footage down, by splitting the second and freezing the frame, can we actually *witness* the act of violence. Contact occurs at one-thirtieth of a second. Blink, and you miss it. Like a video glitch, ignoring the almost unseen is easy. Blink, and it's gone, but not erased.

* * *

> There is an awesome, rushing beauty to this game. Even from this perspective, patterns emerge, fade, shift, change, fade and form again. A rhythm sets in, as the play flows back and forth, eases off, gets broken and picks up. For an immeasurable instant, a gap appears.
>
> — Peter Gzowski, *The Game of Our Lives*

Valery's Ankle is a dense, synthetic video. Because hockey is a fast, transitional game, each sequence is intended to overload viewers with interrelated images, ideas and data. In order to best represent its speed and flow (also the cause of its violent collisions), I built a montage that moves quickly and transparently between sections and time periods. Like swift skating strides, short bursts of images build momentum then recede, imbuing the video with circular, hockey-like rhythms. Gzowski's description of hockey's fluidity sums up my editing strategy for *Valery's Ankle*. The gaps, however, provide opportunities to ask questions. I say in the video that an image can cover up as much as it reveals. Too often, we blindly trust what we see. As with the ubiquitous image of Henderson's goal, its mass reproduction informs and obscures at the same time.

---

[1] Drawing on Benedict Anderson's notion of imagined communities, Mike Gasher explains that "the national imagination is a collective sense or feeling, most powerfully articulated through the cultural expressions of a community's artists and intellectuals" (95). According to Anderson, they are imagined because the members of even the smallest nation will never know a majority of their fellow citizens, while a sense of common unity still persists. See Benedict Anderson, *Imagined Communities: Reflections on the Origin and Spread of Nationalism* (London: Verso, 1989).

[2] At the end of their book, Kidd and Macfarlane maintain the only way to "save" hockey from degenerating into crass entertainment spectacle, along the lines of professional wrestling, or extreme sport is to sever its ties to US capital. "If we cannot save hockey," they write, "we cannot save Canada" (163).

[3] In November 2005, CBC's *the fifth estate* aired a documentary about the Danton case that casts light on the controlling relationship David Frost had with Danton and how he encouraged Danton's estrangement with his parents, as well as an alleged incident where Frost and a group of his players abused Danton's younger brother.
Danton's situation eerily recalls the story of Sheldon Kennedy and his former coach, Graham James. Kennedy was coached by James as a junior-level hockey player in Winnipeg, and then during the late 1980s on the Swift Current Broncos of the Western Hockey League. Between the ages of fourteen and nineteen, Kennedy was sexually abused by James twice weekly from 1984 to 1990. In 1997, James was sentenced to three and a half years in prison for sexually assaulting Kennedy and another unidentified player. After the sentencing, Kennedy went public with his story, effectively ending his hockey career. In 1998, he enrolled in a substance-abuse program sponsored by the NHL for continuing drinking and drug problems.
For more on Boogaard's story, see the three-part *New York Times* feature "Punched

Out: The Life and Death of a Hockey Enforcer," by John Branch, published December 3–5, 2011 (http://www.nytimes.com/2011/12/04/sports/hockey/derek-boogaard-a-boy-learns-to-brawl.html).

4 The NHL's colour barrier is addressed in Daniel Cross and Mila Aung-Thwin's documentary *Too Colourful for the League* (2001). See also Gary Genosko, "What Is the Plural of Hockey?" Fuse 18, no. 4 (1995): 46–47. For more on the problem of sexual violence in hockey, see Laura Robinson, *Crossing the Line: Violence and Sexual Assault in Canada's National Sport* (Toronto: McClelland & Stewart, 1998).

5 Regarding the '72 series, Gandesha concludes, "It was at this time…that Canadians came close to *imagining* themselves as part of a single national community" (14, emphasis added).

6 This fact is remarkable considering the game was televised on a Thursday afternoon, when a large segment of the population was presumably in school or at work. See Clarence Campbell, "Hockey: Is It the Only Thing We're Famous For?" *Canada and the World* 38, no. 4 (December 1972): 17. Cf. Ken Dryden and Roy MacGregor, Home Game, 212; Harry Sinden, *Hockey Showdown: The Canada-Russia Hockey Series* (Toronto: Doubleday, 1972), photo insert; Tim Burke, "Campbell Favors Russian Renewal, Eagleson Less Keen," *Gazette* (Montreal), November 10, 1972, 33.

7 Henderson participates in the ideological whitewashing, stating, "When I scored the final goal, I finally knew what democracy was all about." Quoted in Dick Beddoes, "The Backbone of Team Canada," *Weekend Magazine*, November 11, 1972, 29.

8 If the public saw Phil Esposito's or Gary Bergman's gestures of intimidation and aggression repeated as often as Henderson's fortunate, face-saving goal, the Summit Series' central place in our collective cultural representation would be more difficult to endure.

9 Alain Resnais' harrowing film essay *Night and Fog* (1955) deals with the impossibility of representing Nazi concentration camps. "Is it in vain that we try to remember?" the film asks, infusing the *necessity* of remembrance with skepticism and doubt. The answer is to reflect, to ask questions, to examine the record.

10 During an eastern Ontario hockey game in 1905, Alcide Laurin was killed after being hit by a stick. His attacker, Allan Loney, known as an excessively violent player, was charged with murder but was acquitted. Two years later, during an Amateur Hockey League game, Cornwall star Owen McCourt received a severe blow to the head from the stick of Ottawa Victorias' Charles Masson. McCourt died in hospital several hours later. A murder charge against Masson was reduced to manslaughter, but at the trial evidence showed that another Ottawa player had also struck the victim. Because of the uncertainty over which player had administered the fatal blow, the judge acquitted the defendant.

11 NHL expansion, which began in 1967, constituted a clear shift in the balance of ownership and power. Expansion was motivated by prospects of a US television contract,

an enterprise later blamed for promoting violence to uninitiated audiences. Many fans, especially those in untraditional hockey regions like California, southern Florida, the Carolinas and Tennessee are still attracted by the potential for fighting, which is used as a marketing tool. Coupled with the portrayals of hockey violence in Hollywood films such as *Slap Shot* (George Roy Hill, 1977) and *Youngblood* (Peter Markle, 1986), fighting has produced an expectation of dangerously aggressive behaviour on the part of mainstream, casual fans.

[12] Basically, the code ensures that any player guilty of questionable conduct (such as injuring another team's best player) is physically punished for it on the ice. Unique to this continent, such a system doesn't exist in other hockey-playing cultures. However, I sense that the intricacies of this archaic code, propped up by dinosaurs like Don Cherry, have been lost on a younger generation of players who grew up watching glamorized highlights of hockey fights on TV (not to mention Cherry's "Rock'em Sock'em" series of hockey tapes). For insight into this disjunction, see Charles Foran, "The Trials of Marty McSorley," *Saturday Night*, November 4, 2000, 22–32.

[13] One of the more fascinating hockey anecdotes concerns a similar player, Bill McCreary, Jr. McCreary is most remembered for his open-ice hit on Wayne Gretzky on January 14, 1981. It was one of the first times that Gretzky – then the NHL's brightest superstar – had been hit hard in his young career, and it left him on the ice for several minutes. The incident received considerable press and was widely publicized in the newspapers. The next day, McCreary, a rookie with only twelve games under his belt, was shipped down to the minors. He never played another NHL game.

[14] Adding insult to injury, Moore's team, the Colorado Avalanche, signed Brad May to replace him. While a member of the Canucks, May issued a public bounty against Moore after he injured May's teammate Markus Naslund with a clean hit, leading to Bertuzzi's revenge attack later that season. Moore's crime did not follow the unwritten code protecting star players.

[15] For a contextualized account of the Bertuzzi-Moore incident, see James Deacon, "No End in Sight," and Charlie Gillis, "Bad for Business," *Maclean's*, March 22, 2004, 18–25.

[16] The outcome of this loss is documented in *The Day We Beat the Russians* (Nick Bakyta, 1983), produced by the NFB. In the film, Bill, Dick and Grant Warwick – "three Depression-era kids from Regina" – discuss their Penticton Vees' victory over the Soviet national team at the 1955 world hockey championship in Krefeld, Germany. The Warwick brothers admit to being "consumed with anti-Communism," claiming, "hockey is the only thing we're good at." Cf. Les Rose's 1974 NFB documentary *Thunderbirds in China*. Released two years after Richard Nixon's famous visit, *Thunderbirds in China* follows the University of British Columbia Thunderbirds to Beijing for a set of exhibition hockey games. In one scene, the Canadian and Chinese players come out for a game holding hands!

[17] Despite this, I believe the Clarke-Kharlamov rivalry has been overplayed in the popular media, especially in the CBC miniseries *Canada-Russia '72* (T.W. Peacocke, 2006). At the end of the real game eight, Clarke and Kharlamov exchange sticks with one

another, implying a mutual respect. It's worth underlining that Clarke's slash was done at the suggestion of his coach and was not personally motivated.

[18] Barthes wrote this text in Montreal between January 15 and January 25, 1961, while consulting a finished work print of the film. For more on *Of Sport and Men*'s production history, see Scott Mackenzie, "The Missing Mythology: Barthes in Quebec," *Canadian Journal of Film Studies* 6.2 (1997): 65–74.

[19] The others are *Here's Hockey* (Leslie McFarlane, 1953), *Un jeu si simple* (Gilles Groulx, 1964) and *Blades and Brass* (William Canning, 1967). Of these, only Canning's film deviates from the form and structure of the prescient wartime documentary *Hot Ice* (Irving Jacoby, 1943). Intercutting between children playing shinny on a frozen lake with a game between the Toronto Maple Leafs and New York Rangers as they "fight to break a tie score," *Hot Ice* (subtitled "The Anatomy of Hockey, Canada's National Game") concludes with a return to the outdoor rink and a restatement that hockey is Canada's game.
    1967 is also notable for the formation of the Canadian Film Development Corporation (CFDC), Canada's first government-subsidized feature film initiative (now Telefilm Canada). It's important to note there was very little independent and experimental film production in Canada during the '60s. This may account for the lack of Canadian hockey films produced outside of the NFB prior to the early '70s.

[20] A poster produced by the Canadians for Fair Play Committee in 1972 announces "SPORTS AND POLITICS ARE JUST THE SAME to the RUSSIANS so LET'S BEAT THEM TODAY for a change." Questioning the disproportionate number of Russians on the Soviet national team, the poster implores Hockey Canada to investigate the "present 'Soviet' representation." Thanks to J.W. Fitsell for supplying the document.

[21] One of Canada's most enduring hockey legends, Richard is the subject of several NFB productions, including Pierre L'Amare's collage film *Mon numero 9 en or* (1972), Sheldon Cohen's popular animated film *The Sweater* (1980), based on Roch Carrier's famous short story, and Jacques Payette's composite documentary *The Rocket* (1998). When Richard passed away in 2000, it is estimated that 115,000 Montrealers paid their respects, thronging the arena where he laid in rest. In 2005, *Maurice Richard*, a fictionalized account of Richard's career, directed by Charles Binamé, was released to both critical and commercial success in Quebec.

[22] Duke's epiphany corroborates Michael Robidoux's claim that "professional hockey players' identities are *shaped and defined* through the labour process" (5, emphasis original).

[23] A thematic precursor to *Perfectly Normal, Strange Brew* and *Les Boys* is Serge Morin and Guy Dufaux's short film *De l'autre côté de la glace* (1983). Foreshadowing the convergence of detached irony in Canadian narrative and documentary hockey films following the Summit Series, Morin and Dufaux's film combines elements of fantasy, cross-dressing and theatrical performance with realistic scenes of the Acadian national team, Les Aigles Bleus.
    Slap Shot fits a similar paradigm. Arguably the best known and beloved hockey film ever made, *Slap Shot* takes the depiction of sports violence to an extreme level. As Harvey Mark Zucker and Lawrence J. Babich point out, "the new permissiveness in the

[post-Hays code] cinema allowed for depiction of violence in hockey and roller derby films" (301). See Harvey Mark Zucker and Lawrence J. Babich, *Sports Films: A Complete Reference* (Jefferson, NC: McFarland and Co., 1987). The Hays code, known formally as the Motion Picture Production Code, was replaced in 1968 by an advisory rating system.

[24] For instance, in the seventh game Phil Esposito threatened the Russians with throat-cutting gestures. During the eighth game Rod Gilbert fought with Evgeny Mishakov; Bill White shot the puck at a referee; Jean-Paul Parise, angered at being penalized, faked an attack on the referee with his stick; coach Harry Sinden threw a chair on the ice; and team official Alan Eagleson, about to be ejected from the arena after a melee with Soviet militia, gave Moscow fans the finger at centre ice.

Works Cited

Barthes, Roland. "Of Sport and Men." Translated by Scott MacKenzie. *Canadian Journal of Film Studies* 6, no. 2 (1997): 75–83.

Canada's Team of the Century: 1972 Canada vs. USSR. DVD insert booklet. Willowdale, ON: Universal Studios Canada, 2002.

Confino, Alon. "Collective Memory and Cultural History: Problems of Method." *American Historical Review* 102, no. 5 (1997): 1386–403.

Dryden, Ken, and Roy MacGregor. *Home Game: Hockey and Life in Canada.* Toronto: McClelland & Stewart, 1989.

Face-Off (Winter Comes Early). Video. Directed by George McCowan. Scarborough, ON: Agincourt Productions, 1971.

Gandesha, Samir. "PreText." In *Contest: Essays on Sports, Culture and Politics,* edited by Gary Genosko, 11–15. Winnipeg: Arbeiter Ring, 1999.

Gasher, Mike. "Decolonizing the Imagination: Cultural Expression as Vehicle of Self Discovery." *Canadian Journal of Film Studies* 2, no. 2–3 (1993): 95–105.

Genosko, Gary. *Contest: Essays on Sports, Culture and Politics.* Winnipeg: Arbeiter Ring, 1999.

Gidal, Peter. "Theory and Definition of Structural/Materialist film." In *Structural Film Anthology,* edited by Peter Gidal. London: BFI, 1978.

Gzowski, Peter. *The Game of Our Lives.* Toronto: McClelland & Stewart, 1982.

Howell, Colin D. *Blood, Sweat, and Cheer: Sport and the Making of Modern Canada.* Toronto: University of Toronto Press, 2001.

Kaye, Janice. "*Perfectly Normal,* Eh?: Gender Transformation and National Identity in Canada." *Canadian Journal of Film Studies* 3, no. 2 (1994): 63–80.

Kidd, Bruce, and John Macfarlane. *The Death of Hockey.* Toronto: New Press, 1972.

MacDougall, David. "Films of Memory." In *Visualizing Theory: Selected Essays from V.A.R. 1990–1994,* edited by Lucien Taylor, 27–36. New York: Routledge, 1994.

Minh-ha, Trinh T. *When the Moon Waxes Red: Representation, Gender and Cultural Politics.* New York: Routledge, 1991.

Morrison, Scott. *The Days Canada Stood Still: Canada vs. USSR.* Toronto: McGraw-Hill, 1989.

Nichols, Bill. *Representing Reality: Issues and Concepts in Documentary.* Bloomington: University of Indiana Press, 1991.

Of Sport and Men. Video. Directed by Hubert Aquin. Montreal: National Film Board of Canada, 1961.

Pelletier, Joe, ed. "1972 Summit Series Quotations." A September to Remember website. http://www.1972summitseries.com/quotes.html (accessed March 2014).

Perfectly Normal. VHS. Directed by Yves Simoneau. Shelburne, VT: Academy Entertainment, 1992.

Robidoux, Michael. *Men at Play: A Working Understanding of Professional Hockey.* Montreal: McGill-Queen's University Press, 2001.

Stevens, Neil. "Henderson Candid on Clarke's Slash." *Gazette* (Montreal), September 17, 2002, B7.

Summit on Ice. Directed by Robert MacAskill. Malofilm, 1996.

Valery's Ankle. Independent digital video. Directed by Brett Kashmere. 2006.

Unintentional Epic:
Ken Dryden's Struggle with Words and the Myth of Team Canada

♦

BRIAN KENNEDY

Ken Dryden lost games one and four of the 1972 Summit Series, and he ended up playing four games (one, four, six and eight) and letting in nineteen goals for a 4.75 goals against average (GAA). Pretty grim numbers indeed, though not so bad when one considers the average statistics shared by NHL goaltenders of the time.[1] In game eight of the series, he had allowed five goals by the end of the second period, putting his team down 5–3 and nearly costing them the ultimate victory. Or perhaps that should be said the opposite way: Dryden's anti-heroics in the first two periods of game eight set up the situation where a come-from-behind win made the series the epic event it is often viewed as today.

In the shadow of the series, Dryden wrote the first of his hockey books, *Face-Off at the Summit* (1973), which purports to give a goalie's-eye view of the series and its inner workings. What he beclouds in the book is that he must have known how good the Soviets would be, because he was with the Canadian National Team during 1969–70, and he played in the hockey World Championships in 1969. As such, he would have seen the Red Army team and understood their skill, and logically, he should have recognized their conditioning advantage and their potential strategic superiority. For someone as observant as the Ivy League–educated Dryden, there was no excuse not to realize that the Canadian team of 1972 was in trouble before game one. But if he knew, he did not speak up at the time, and because he did not, and because the NHL-based Team Canada believed, as did nearly everyone else in

Canada, in the country's hockey superiority, the series took on the look of an epic struggle when Canada had to come from behind to win.

Dryden's book reinforces the myth of the series, but not without winding through a series of contradictions. What renders it ironic is that *Face-Off at the Summit* allows Dryden to build the myth of the Series though it might never have had the meaning it did but for his poor play. In turn, giving the series a mythic quality allows his weak goaltending to be eclipsed in fans' memories. The strategy the book uses replicates the struggle in the collective imagination in Canada during the Summit Series as the country wrestled with the dynamic definition of the word "professional." Dryden's ongoing discussion attempts to solve the shock of the Soviets' strength and Canada's near loss first by discussing his own coming to terms with the Soviets' skills and then by unpacking the multiple and shifting contexts in which the term "professional" was now resonant.

Who Knew?

"Who on Team Canada knew?" Andrew Podnieks asks in his recent fortieth-anniversary volume commemorating the Summit Series (16). He throws the question out without expecting a specific answer but rather as an exclamation that there was no one who anticipated what would turn into the "head-on collision at the Forum on September 2, the start of the greatest eight games ever played" (16). In fact, that need not have happened except for a crucial miscalculation on the part of Team Canada (and almost every other observer in Canada as well, from journalists to fans). That mistake has always been described as one of *perception*, as Team Canada failed to recognize the skills of their opponent. However, it might be more accurate to see this failing as one of *definition*. Team Canada had to come from behind to win the Summit Series because from the outset Canadians had enacted a series of linguistic slippages surrounding the word "professional," first by creating a binary definition of the term and assuming that the superior part of the duality belonged to their players exclusively. This definition was allowed to linger even as the series showed the Soviets' hockey strength, and then, quite late in the going, it was exploded as Team Canada admitted that it was not inherently superior but would have to work as hard as possible to prevail. With that lexical admission arrived a change in hockey strategy, which some observers describe as coming as late as game six, with each of the last three contests being a must-win for Canada.

In fact, if "Who knew?" is not rhetorical but an honest question, the answer is in the record. Of the thirty-five players on Team Canada's roster going into the Summit Series, many had international hockey experience. Players' prior experiences against the Russians had come as follows: Seiling as a member of the 1964 Olympic team; Berenson at the 1959 World Championships; Glennie at the 1968 Olympics; Savard as a member of the Montreal Junior Canadians in the mid 1960s, and with Orr as players on loan to the Toronto Marlies to play the Russians; Lapointe in an exhibition with other pros in 1968; Perreault and Clarke as junior players; and Dryden in the 1969 World Championships.[2]

Other players also claimed knowledge of the Russians' skills, including Bill White (Podnieks, 97), Mickey Redmond (49), Vic Hadfield (42), Don Awrey (102) and Peter Mahovlich (69). This awareness had come through various means, including playing European teams other than the Russians while in the Canadian amateur ranks. Coach Harry Sinden, in addition, had played the Russians as a member of the Whitby Dunlops in two different tournaments, the 1958 World Championships and the 1960 Olympics.

That, then, totals forty per cent of the Team Canada roster, plus their head coach, with either direct or clear indirect knowledge that the team they were to face in the Summit Series was skilled enough to put up a battle with Team Canada. Two questions thus arise. First, why, with this much shared knowledge, did they and the rest of Canada get so badly fooled by the Russians? Second, why didn't any of these men speak up to quantify the Russian threat?

In fact, only one person sounded the alarm bell before the series. Red Berenson said, "The disadvantage our team faces is that we're going against superbly conditioned athletes who have played as a team unit in competition and who have a much greater national stake in what they are doing. They have a lot more to prove" (Podnieks, 14). Why didn't anybody hear this?

Sinden has more recently explained that he had a singular knowledge of the threat, saying, "I don't think anyone, except me, realized how good the Russians were going to be when we made that promise" (that each person who came to camp would play in at least one game). Yet almost as soon as he says this, he takes it back with, "Even as impressed as I had been all those years, I thought the best NHL players would be able to beat them" (Podnieks, 20).

Last-minute wrangling over the birth of the World Hockey Association complicated the matter of how Team Canada was defined, because once the WHA players (notably Bobby Hull and Gerry Cheevers) had been declared ineligible, the attitude in Canada had to realign itself with this reality. Thus the team was not, as Phil Esposito points out, Team Canada at all, but Team NHL (Podnieks, 207). This did not bother anyone, however, since the definition of "professional" in the public mind (and the players' minds), even when restricted to "NHL professional," equated to "we will win no matter who plays for us, or who we're missing."

Most accounts of the events of September 1972, and particularly of game one, go the same way: The Russians took Canada by surprise. After getting over their initial awe in Montreal and going down by two goals in the series' first period, the Russians took over, their superior conditioning and unfamiliar style of play completely overwhelming the Canadian team as they posted an initial game score of 7–3. The failure of the Canadian team in this game and in the first half of the series, and the squad's eventual redemption, made for a memorable series. But why should it have been that way at all?

A Problem of Definition

The problem, I would like to argue, was not one of intention or function so much as of definition. The words the Soviets deployed to describe themselves, and the words Canadians used to describe both themselves and the Russians, were what set Team Canada up for the fall it took. In particular, the issue centred on the word "professional," which for Canada both had absolute meaning and contained a series of slippages. Seemingly, this is impossible; meaning is either fixed or it is not. In fact, without acknowledging the fact, Canadians wanted it both ways. They wanted the Russians to admit that their teams were professional, not amateur, and thus competing unfairly in the various world tournaments (World Championships, Olympics) that they had dominated since 1954. And yet they wanted to see them as amateurs for the purpose of evaluating them against the best (i.e., Canadian professional) competition. Scholar Dave Holland explains: "In the decade leading up to [the series], the mounting defeats at the world championships and Olympics were continuously accompanied by the public's concessions that the Soviets were no match for Canada's professionals" (113). Alan Eagleson describes his thoughts about the definitions of terms in this way: "Listen, you have proved that you have the best amateur hockey players in the world even though I don't agree with your definition" (Henderson and Prime, 89).

The Russians, whether by calculation or accident, had deployed this linguistic slippage to their advantage. They called themselves amateurs, though everyone in the hockey world thought otherwise of them. The facts were plain: their team played hockey as a job, training nearly all year round.[3] They had no other professional responsibilities as members of the Soviet military. The problem (or the loophole they created for themselves) was that the semantic reach of their language had no room for the definition of a "professional" when it came to hockey players (or at least, that was their claim). With no category called "professional," their players were, at least to them, de facto amateurs. Paul Henderson and Jim Prime explain: "The Soviet Union found a clever way to get around this restriction [against pros in the World Championships]. There was no doubt that hockey was their full-time profession, but these elite athletes were given other job descriptions, most notably as soldiers in the Central Red Army" (Henderson and Prime, 91–92).[4]

After wrangling for years, trying to change the rules of the International Ice Hockey Federation to allow at least some Canadian professionals to play in tournaments like the yearly World Championships, the country finally gave up and offered the chance for an exhibition series, Canada's best players against the Russians' best, call them what you like. From the Soviet perspective, this was a good thing, because they knew that their (ab)use of the term "amateur" limited them. As scholar Markku Jokisipilä puts it, "Up to the early 1970s, the international successes of the Soviet national squad were shadowed by the fact that they had played only against the amateurs" (47). Yet they valued the reputational gain that playing against the best in the world would bring them. "Ice hockey was the only team sport where they were capable of challenging the best Western professionals. This is why hockey became Moscow's weapon of choice in Cold War sports propaganda" (38).

In agreeing to the series, both Canada and the Soviets made a semantic move that by definition put the Soviet team into the category "professional." This happened because both sides were admitting that the Russians paralleled the Canadian pros in skill more than they paralleled any prior (amateur) Canadian opponent. The goal was simple: "Canada's amateur representatives had begun to lose habitually to superior Russian teams as early as the 1950s. By allowing players from the NHL [i.e., pros] to compete against the Soviets, the hockey powers in Canada thought the question of global hockey dominance would be soundly put to rest" (Wilson, 272).

Yet having made this invisible concession, Canadians then made another linguistic/psychic shift – they split the term "professional" into a binary, with one side being reserved for the Russians and the other the Canadians. In seeing professional/professional as an opposition of terms with space between the words, Canadians, to cite Derrida's term, were focusing on "differance," meaning at once "difference" and "deferral." Thus while the word for each side, had it been spoken, would have sounded the same, Canadians reserved a special connotative category for their pros. This happened because the Canadians saw one type of professional – their players – as superior, despite the binary itself not betraying a qualitative difference between the two.

Brad Park's statement highlights the distinction: "We knew the Russians beat our amateur guys, but in the back of my mind that didn't matter. We're pros. We have the best players in the world" (quoted in Podnieks, 65). Sinden echoes that when he says, "I had seen them play a lot, but against amateur teams, so you think, what would they be like playing against pros, and you don't have a high regard for the way they were piling up wins" (Podnieks, 20). Ditto Cournoyer, who said for the fortieth anniversary book, "We knew the Russians were winning a lot of international tournaments, but they were playing against our non-professional players, guys who were strictly amateur" (quoted in Podnieks, 211). In each case, the distancing of the Russians from their amateur opponents puts them in the "professional" category, but without allowing for their being good enough to beat Team Canada.

Put simply, Canadians wanted to define the Russians as pros for the purpose of governing who they played but to reserve the true strength of that word for their pros. However, this argument was made in a vacuum, without reference to external facts – obvious ones about how good the Russians had been, how prepared they were (and how much Team Canada was not), how many Team Canada personnel knew this, and how Hockey Canada even acknowledged it. Player Ron Ellis elaborates on this theme: "I think as that series went on, it became very clear that this wasn't just a friendly international match like it was billed, and that the Russians were not coming just to learn from the Canadians, absolutely not, and we know we've talked to some of those Russian players, and they've told us, years later, that they thought they were going to win from day one, that's how prepared they were."

In fact, what Team Canada found out in game one and the contests to follow is that the Russians were in better condition than their players, which formed a huge advantage. In addition, they had strategies of play that worked against Team Canada, particularly fooling starting goalie Dryden by moving the puck side to side and catching him coming out too far to cut down angles. Sinden has since claimed that the Soviets "were on the same level as the NHL players" (Henderson and Prime, 94), and Serge Savard agrees, "Things had changed in the 10 or 12 years from '58, '59, even '60.... They were just too good; they were actually as good as we were, no question about it" (Henderson and Prime, 103). He points particularly to the first game, in Montreal, as the moment where the definition shifted. To state it another way, this was when it became clear that the Russians weren't just professionals in the way Canada had been defining them. They were professionals in the way that Team Canada defined themselves; in fact, maybe more so.

Why was this? Because they trained eleven months a year, and they had been working out without a break all summer to prepare for the Summit Series. Canada's players, by contrast, had had a three-week camp following their summer vacations. It has often been said that the Team Canada training camp was not terribly rigorous, nor as demanding as it should have been, or, in the words of player Marcel Dionne, "maybe there was a lack of intensity..., but it was three weeks of training camp, and everyone wanted to start playing games. We put the team together like it was an All-Star Game" (quoted in Podnieks, 127). Peter Mahovlich said that the Russians' conditioning in 1972 created a culture change in professional hockey in North America, prompting players to come to camp in shape, rather than to work their way into condition (Podnieks,

69). Sinden apparently admitted to the Russians after a couple of vodkas that Canadian players would never agree to the Russian-style rigid training regimen: "It simply wasn't part of their tradition" (quoted in Martin, 117).[5] So which team was the professional one?

In fact, Canada's early losses prompted a series of explanations that started to move the definition of "professional" in an entirely new direction. A source from the time said, "Here [in Canada], the professional hockey player is also a businessman; who could ask him to spend his afternoons on the ice practicing; but with the salaries paid to those professional athletes, one could expect them to be in better physical shape" (Terroux, 78). Another commentator, whose apparently cynical tone is actually sincere, judging by its context (it comes from a hagiography of Alan Eagleson), says that Eagleson turned "lumps of muscle [and] guts" into "highly polished, million-dollar skating machines; then he sent them into international arenas to test their performance" (Clayton, 110). Russian goalie Tretiak commented after the series that it seemed that "the Canadian professionals' principal interest appears to be money" (31).

Tony Esposito says it simply: "We weren't ready, physically." And he blames it on Canadian ignorance: "Canada was represented by senior hockey players [internationally] then. There were no pros allowed. Basically, it was like Tier II Canadians, but the Russians were like pros" (quoted in Podnieks, 191). As the series went on, it would become apparent that the Russians weren't *like* pros. They were pros, and not in the sense that Canadians had used the definition against them. They were pros in that their preparation was sincere. They were pros in a way that the Canadian players were not. They had taken control of the definition of the term "professional hockey player," and by virtue of their success, the definition should have been flipped on its head, with the Russians taking the dominant position in the lexical binary and Team Canada the inferior. Tretiak himself articulated this a few years later when he said, "The first series against the NHL players showed that there are no invincible professional teams." He further said that "no longer [is there] such a myth connected with Canadian pro hockey" (85). The use of the word "professional" and its shortened version indicate the pejorative attitude he takes toward the notion that equated "Canadian" with "professional" unquestioningly.

Perhaps the boos that rained down on Team Canada as they left the ice after losing game four in Vancouver suggested that in the minds of the Canadian fans the definition had been reversed. Johnny Esaw's interview of Phil Esposito after this game, and Espo's impromptu speech delivered into the TV camera, in fact focus on the linguistic distinction that had earlier held the two teams apart, redrawing the definition of professional back into a singularity that now included the Russians.[6] Esaw said, "I must say that, ah, probably, since everything is relative – we know how good you people are, but the people didn't realize how good the Soviet team was. And now we've found how good they are, I think we can appreciate how good both teams are" (quoted in Podnieks, 92). In other words, the binary that had motivated the Canadians to get into the series in the first place and that had sustained their early overconfidence was now collapsed.

Esposito famously replies that the team was disappointed and that they would be heading to Russia with a renewed sense of purpose in defending the honour of their country. However, in truth, at least according to their coach, their motivation was not nationalism but, in the terms I am using in this argument, the need to regain control over the definition of "professional." Coach Sinden claims that it was their reputation as hockey players, rather than as Canadians, that motivated the team to win the series. "They were playing on…the pride of being so-called the best players in the world from the NHL. Upholding their own personal reputations as the greatest hockey players in the world had much, much more to do with it" than did "national pride," no matter how much people want to hear otherwise (Henderson and Prime, 107). What they were doing was reintegrating the definition of the word "professional" with the notion of being an NHL player. If that also corresponded with being Canadian, then so be it.

By the time the series moved to Moscow, nobody who followed hockey could fail to recognize that the definition of "professional" extended to include the Soviets, not because they played as much hockey as the Canadian pros did (they played more), but because they played it as well as the Canadians did, or better. Yet as the series wrapped up and in the time after, much of this lesson was either forgotten or ignored as Canadian mythmakers took over. Now, the Summit Series was not seen as a necessary corrective to Canadian hubris, but as an event that took on the epic contours of good triumphing over evil.

Dryden's Deliberations Over "Professional"

One early contributor to the Summit Series myth was Ken Dryden, entering his second full year as Montreal's starting netminder in the fall of 1972. His effort came in the form of the 1973 book already mentioned, written with the express intention of being "an honest diary. I will not plug things into holes just so they will fit. What happens on a Tuesday will not be inserted into a spot on Friday just to make good reading.... I want the book to record not only my final feelings but also all the feelings that contributed to that end," as he described his purpose to his co-author, Mark Mulvoy (viii–ix).[7] The result is what looks like a day-by-day account of the series from an insider's point of view. However, taking the book at face value overlooks the fact that Dryden's memories are shaped by an agenda that seeks to rehabilitate his reputation as a goalie by shifting the lens from his own failures to his team's ultimate accomplishment.[8]

That Dryden went into the series unaware of how good the Russians would be seems hard to imagine, given that he had seen this same Soviet team dominate in the World Championships in Prague in 1969. Yet if he knew how good they were, why did it take him so long to adjust to the Soviet style of play, which saw him lose badly in games one and four? His failures were described in his own words after game six: "I've always been a goalie who slid out toward the play to cut down the angles.... I realized the Russians were getting behind me with quick passes, so I consciously began to drop back into the goal and stay there" (quoted in Podnieks, 158). Podnieks says, "Dryden's best effort was game six. This was the game when he clearly changed his style of play, staying in the net and taking away the backside pass the Soviets used to such great effect" (179).[9] Others also point out that it took Canada at least until game five, which they also lost, with Tony Esposito in net, to figure out how the Soviets moved and how they played the puck (Bidini, 66–67).

Contrary to the evidence suggested by his play, Dryden hints that he knew that his team was in trouble from the start, doing so by toying with the linguistic divide at the heart of this series. Discussing the situation where the WHA players were going to be left off Team Canada, he says, "The series between Canada's pros and Russia's amateurs had been desired for a long, long time." He goes on, "I felt we should have the best possible team ready to play against the

Russians, who would be sending their best players against us" (6). He unquestioningly uses the professional/amateur dichotomy that the Russians favoured, yet in also using the word "best" to describe both sides, he bends each team towards the other, perhaps indicating that the Russians fit the definition of professional excellence that most Canadians assumed was the province of their players alone. This is further complicated when he says, "Team Canada would not be Team Canada. It would be Team NHL and lack some of Canada's best players" (6) because they were ineligible due to their WHA contracts. Hence "best" becomes a term that has singular meaning when applied to the Russians but works as a duality – best being set against the lack of the best – when applied to Team Canada, a linguistic trick by which Dryden can suggest that he knew Team Canada was not going to perform well.

He continues, "Obviously, the NHL felt that its chances of winning would not be hurt by the absence of Hull, Sanderson, Tremblay and Cheevers" (6). Dryden's tone suggests that he disagrees. He also indicates his insider knowledge in what follows: "Certainly we were not looking at the ideal situation for turning back the Russian invasion. We did not have the best possible team available for the games; we would not be playing these games at the best possible time of year for Canadian professionals" (7).[10] But if he felt this way, why did he not say anything in August? Perhaps Jim Coleman's explanation of the general mood of self-deceit at the time provides context for Dryden's silence: "The general public didn't worry about any shortage of conditioning.... They and the Canadian news media had brainwashed themselves.... The prevailing opinion was that, in the past, the Soviets had been able to overpower North American teams of amateurs or retreaded minor league professionals. Our genuine major league professionals were another story" (141). In fact, Dryden cites the common belief in August of 1972 that Team Canada would win all eight games by wide margins, doing nothing to dispel the myth (10–11). However, he also suggests his own superior knowledge by offering his assessment of why people say this. It's not because it will be patently true. Rather, Dryden claims that they say it because they feel pressure; they feel challenged, in the sense of being threatened (11–12).[11] That can only be so, however, if the challenge is real. And if the challenge is real, then Dryden's poor performance in net might be forgiven.

A second possible reason for his silence was that Dryden did not have the nerve to speak up, given the often tenuous position goaltenders occupy with respect to their relationships with teammates. Ron Ellis explains:

> We respected goalies; as a forward, you always knew they had their…idiosyncrasies…. Terry Sawchuk, on game days, you didn't want to converse, so you left him alone. You have to learn what that goalie does to prepare…. And once you understand how they prepare, you give them their space if that's what they want. Kenny, though, was pretty good [i.e., not hampered by his routines] I thought. Tony Esposito had his routine, and you'd better not interrupt it. You [Interviewer Kennedy] have a point that possibly Kenny, having played against them for Team Canada [in 1969]…might have had a little bit of an idea, but I think Kenny's style just wasn't conducive to playing against the Russians. Kenny liked to come out and cut the angles, and the Russians did a lot of cross-crease passing. And Tony seemed to adapt to that a lot quicker than Kenny…. But for some reason, he [Sinden, in game eight] must have went with his gut or whatever, and I must say, in that third period, Dryden made some great saves. He made some great saves for us.

Sinden elaborates on the leave-the-goalie-alone syndrome as he talks about the pressure on the netminders as the series went on: "They are kind of a separate entity from the rest of the players, and they kind of live in their little cocoon before the game and have a different mountain to climb every night" (Podnieks, 21). But if goalies are silent and apart, prizing their alienation from teammates, why did Dryden go to the attention-seeking level of putting out a book on the series in the year after it was played? Because it serves to build the myth of the series, which in turn positions Dryden not as the incompetent who lost games one and four and posted an abysmal 4.75 GAA over his four games, but as a member of the "professional" squad that squashed the "evil other" and preserved the Canadian way of life.

As he continues to portray the events of the series, Dryden's strategy in coming to grips with what happened sees him interrogating the definition of the term "professional," realizing its multiplicity and carving out a space wherein both the Russians and the Canadians can be looked at as deserving of it. The book develops two complementary themes in pursuing this end. The first is how Dryden has failed dismally against the Russians both in the Summit Series and in earlier encounters, and his questions about whether and how he can improve; the second is Dryden's work as a proxy for all Canadians who were struggling with how the Soviets should be defined as professionals. The story becomes a quest, with the journey moving in two directions – into Dryden's mind as he probes his goaltending weaknesses, and into various physical places where Soviet players and coaches learn and practise hockey. Finally, he solves the question of how to code the Soviets. Right after that, it's time for game eight, and it is only in that contest that his question about his own abilities is finalized.

The series' eighth game offers the payoff that absolves Dryden of his doubts in his ability to play the Soviet team and win. Earlier, he more than once cited his poor performance against the Russians in 1969 and wondered whether his style is ill-suited to the Russian attack (35, 84). When he finally says that he has solved the problem by adopting a style that has him staying back in the net (a lot like the one his teammate Tony Esposito used naturally, he says), Team Canada is down 5–3 after two periods of game eight (173).[12]

It might seem inopportune to suggest that a strategy is working when five goals have been scored and the other team is solidly in front with slightly over twenty minutes to go. But if it appears curious that at this point Dryden is congratulating himself on stopping Shadrin's shot with "probably the best save I made in the entire series" (173), his statement is made with the hindsight of one who knows that Team Canada would eventually score six goals in the game to take the victory. Yet if this moment is the crisis point of his narrative, how compelling is the book? Given that readers would have been well aware, in 1973, of the outcome of the series and of Dryden's part in it, it seems unlikely that they would have been gripped by this suspense over his style, especially since the best one might say is not that he won the series for Canada but that he didn't lose it, though he was close. Nor would they have been captivated by the self-absorbed nature of Dryden's musings in the book as a whole. What intrigue is there in this: "I've been thinking about it for a few days now, however, and I'm definitely going to change my style. I'm going to stay in my net, like Tony and E. J. [Eddie Johnston, the other Team Canada goalie]" (70). Really? Wouldn't the coach have simply been better off assigning one of the team's other two goalies the starts in games six and eight? Even Dryden thinks so (128).

Thus it becomes necessary for *Face-Off at the Summit* to pursue a second theme, not focused so narrowly on Dryden himself – how to understand and categorize Soviet hockey. The trajectory of this quest begins with Dryden naming the Russians "a good hockey team" after he and his Team Canada mates watch video of them prior to game one (34). He reiterates this after the second period of that game, at which time the Russians were up 4–2. "The Russians had proved over two periods that they were a good hockey team," he says (49). But having lost the game, he turns that on its head: "We obviously did know what to expect from the Russians, and to a man did not dream they were as good as they proved to be in Montreal. Everything we heard, everything we saw, led us to believe they were not that good" (51). So they are variously good, better than the usual expectation of good, and assumed before the fact to be not that good. Unstated in this logic, however, is that "good" is a relative term, its definition shifting depending upon the outcome of play, and that the reason he is having a crisis of meaning with the word is that the Soviets had been categorized already as inferior, the word "amateur" standing for "lesser" as well as "unpaid player." Now that they have demonstrated themselves in fact as superior, he has no language for that.

However, Dryden also invokes the term "professional" – albeit in the negative – in discussing game one. He says that Team Canada, as they began to lose, acted like "the frustrated Canadian professionals trying to be victorious" by being nasty (50). Later, Dryden suggests the professional/amateur dichotomy in talking about various Canadian teams the Russians had faced up to that moment: "I never dreamed they'd be as effective against NHL players [pros] as they were against the National Team players [amateurs] three years ago" (53). Then he speaks of semantics directly: "I…have lost the feeling that the Canadian professional hockey player, by definition, is superior to all other hockey players in the world" (55).

Other commentators at the time also dissected the notion of the Canadian professional, as Dryden recounts. The *Montreal Star* called Team Canada "pampered professionals" and asked why "our pros [must] act like bush-league soreheads when they skate into the world arena and lose?" (60). Perhaps the

Russians had the answer. Dryden says that one of their players told reporter Rick Noonan that "it took us about ten minutes of the game to realize the Canadian professionals are ordinary human beings like us" (64). So while the Canadians were having to refigure their definition of the word "professional" to bring the Russians up to that orbit, the Russians were seeing it the opposite way. Those who had been hockey gods were now mortal.

As Team Canada moves to Stockholm to play two games, Dryden is still mulling over its identity. Prior teams, amateur ones, who had been in Sweden had created a reputation for dirty play. In these games "the Canadian players stopped the Swedes with some violent physical tactics. The next day the papers would be filled with cartoons depicting the Canadians as animals" (96). Dryden hopes that things will be different with Team Canada 1972, invoking familiar language to code this: "But we are the pros, not the amateurs and not animals, and the Swedes have invited us" (96). Of course, things go distinctly downhill as games one and two progress. Team Canada wins game one 4–1, which Dryden explains by saying that the home team perhaps "lacked confidence, or were afraid of the aggressive professionals" (102). When game two ends with Wayne Cashman's tongue split in two and Swedish player Lars-Erik Sjoberg stabbed near the nose by a high stick in a 4–4 tie, "we are animals once again" (107). The progression from animals to professionals to aggressive professionals and back to animals reinforces the European notion that Canadian players, of whatever level of income, would stop at nothing to win.

As the Moscow portion of the series unfolds, Dryden continues his quest to define his team as he diverts his nervous attention from his own poor play by studying the Russian methods of training and game preparation. Observing warm-ups, for instance, he says, "The Russians…have a highly disciplined, highly organized series of drills that would tire out a lot of professional teams" (119). Of course, he is throwing out the term "professional" as a synonym for "NHL," but in doing so, he is also ignoring a point that he should recognize by this stage: that the Red Army team are as professional as NHL players, and more so if preparation and excellence form the foundation of the word.

His movement toward an inclusive definition of the Russians as professionals begins with the axiomatic question of whether they play for money. His explorations of hockey in the USSR allow him to explode the

Russians-as-amateurs myth and offer proof that the Russians do play hockey as a job, with a salary, even though they explain that away as being army pay (138–39). Scholar Jokisipilä confirms this, saying, "With hockey as their only military duty, the Soviets were every bit as much professionals as their North American counterparts in the National Hockey League" (38).

At this late stage, with game six (and his change of style) just behind him, Dryden has admitted that the Russians are professionals, adding to the criterion that pros make a living playing the notion that being a pro is also about competing at a certain level, which itself is a product of thorough preparation. But even in giving them credit for being pros, Dryden turns the definition back on its head. He responds to Russian coach Kulagin's criticism that Canadians are not as serious about the game as the Russians are by saying, "I can't see hockey becoming an eleven-months-a-year job for our professionals" (149). This because they need time off to prepare themselves for their post-hockey lives, he says.

Think about that. Dryden is now saying that the Canadian pros are the players they are because of what they do *not* do, because of the gaps in time that they have when they are *not playing hockey*, which is their profession, but preparing for whatever it is they will have to do for work after their hockey careers are over. In this interesting turn, what defines the Canadian pro is not how much hockey he plays, but the limits to his playing. In this moment, the grand dance of presence/absence that has characterized this discussion of the definition of "professional" has been thoroughly deconstructed.

Where the absence of money and skill marked the Russians as not-pros before the series and the presence of money and skill marked the Canadians as pros, now the opposite condition prevails. The Russians are better prepared, they are paid and they play more. Their skills by this point have been recognized as equal to those of their opponents. By any measure, they have surpassed the definition of "professional" that Canadians held up as true at the beginning of the series. And at that very moment that this is recognized, the definition changes. Now it's about what one does not do, rather than what one does. Dryden admits this late in the book: "Our concept of the Soviet player, of course, is that he is more professional than the North American professional, because he spends forty-eight weeks a year in training" (155–56). He follows that with the admission, "We do have a lot to learn" (156).

As games seven and eight unfold with Canadian victories, Dryden being in net for the last contest, he summarizes the series succinctly, but in so doing takes back some of what he has admitted earlier. "I, for one, don't believe that we are *that* superior," he comments while talking about the aftermath of game eight (180, emphasis added). The trouble is that this runs counter to his admission of the Soviet excellence at the game and his admiration of their training methods, which he has taken great pains to describe and document (137–49). However, if this last pronouncement crashes against the historical facts he has presented in *Face-Off at the Summit*, it also points up the lexical crisis that the series presented to him, and all Canadians, and suggests that even as the series, and the book, ends, the binary of terms that had prompted the creation of the series continues to mystify onlookers even as it multiplies and fragments.

What's a "professional"? That is less clear at the end of September 1972 than ever. Scholar Andrew C. Holman puts it simply when he says that in the series that pitted "the new perennial Olympic Champion Soviet Union and a collection of Canada's best professionals from the NHL in September 1972, the Canadian pros won by only the slimmest of margins, pushing relieved Canadians to re-examine their estimations of their hockey and themselves" (461).

The feeling that "Canadians are unquestionably the best in the world and that our style is right because we invented the game…now seems to have changed to an awareness that the Russians have something going," Dryden admits (185). It might not be the radical change of mind that he seemed to be verging on, but it does show that to the end, he, and Canada, have struggled with the crisis of language that had created the series in the first place. If there is no resolution offered, at least there is the sense that "both the Russians and the Canadians have an amazing amount to learn" (185). Not the least, one might add, lessons about how the definition of a word can have drastic, worldview-shifting implications.

---

[1] Dryden's NHL numbers, by the way, were far better, with a 2.24 GAA.

[2] Detailed in Podnieks and elsewhere.

[3] In fact, Lawrence Martin notes that Coach Tarasov had been ousted after the Olympics in part because he defied officials and let players take the equivalent of two hundred dollars each to play two exhibition games before the Olympics in 1972. So they were, in one sense, professionals, if money is the defining factor.

[4] Even later in the 1970s, an External Affairs pamphlet described the genesis of the Summit Series by saying that "years of negotiation between hockey officials of the Soviet Union and Canada culminated in September 1972 in an agreement that a series of eight games would be played between Canadian professionals from the National Hockey League and the amateur world champions from the U.S.S.R." (4). It further notes, in the kind of bland government-speak that might be expected, that the Canadians "were ill-prepared for the first half of the series" and lost two of the first four games (4).

[5] My archival research into newspaper commentary of the time yielded just one negative prediction regarding Team Canada's conditioning. The *Toronto Sun* said on September 2 that the team's three-week program would not give them a VO2 uptake comparable to the Soviets' (37).

[6] Of course the speech is often read as inaugurating the political dimension of the series in the consciousnesses of the players, something they had not been so plugged into up to this moment. See Abelson, 65, for instance.

[7] In fact what Dryden does is replicated to a degree decades later in scholar Megan L. Popovic's autoethnographic work on hockey, albeit in Dryden's case the approach is less authentic in that it appears more carefully edited.

[8] Dryden's engaging tone and manner, for one, are disputed by his opponent in goal, Tretiak. He read Dryden's book in translation in 1975 and took issue with Dryden's claim that he wishes he could have spoken with the Russians. "They looked down on us. It took time for you to respect us," Tretiak challenged (123).

[9] Tony Esposito, by contrast, picked up on this strategy more quickly, though he had no prior experience playing the Soviet team or watching them. "I never came way out anyway. I didn't have that much of an adjustment," he said (quoted in Podnieks, 192).

[10] Dryden's later reshaping of the truth is even more evident as he talks in an entry dated July 24 about the fact that Team Canada would be hurt by being forced to play in hot weather, which nobody anticipated until the players started returning to their bench dripping and exhausted as period one wore on in Montreal.

[11] "You may be the biggest hockey fan in Boston or New York or Chicago or Los Angeles, but I'm certain that you don't understand this [Russian challenge]. You must be a Canadian," Dryden claims (11).

[12] Recall that the change came in game six, but here Dryden describes it as working perfectly late in period two of game eight.

Works Cited

Abelson, Donald E. "Politics on Ice: The United States, the Soviet Union, and a Hockey Game in Lake Placid." *Canadian Review of American Studies* 40, no. 1 (2010): 63–94.

Bidini, Dave. *A Wild Stab for It: This Is Game Eight from Russia*. Toronto: ECW, 2012.

Clayton, Deidre. *Eagle: The Life and Times of R. Alan Eagleson*. Toronto: Lester & Orpen Dennys, 1982.

Coleman, Jim. *Hockey Is Our Game: Canada in the World of International Hockey*. Toronto: Key Porter, 1987.

"Conditioning Should Be Long Range, Not Crash Program." *Toronto Sun*, September 2, 1972.

Department of External Affairs, Government of Canada. *Ice Hockey in Canada*. Ottawa: External Information Programs Division, 1979.

Dryden, Ken. *Face-Off at the Summit*. With Mark Mulvoy. Toronto: Little, Brown, 1973.

Ellis, Ron. Personal interview with the author. Toronto: D. K. "Doc" Seaman Hockey Resource Centre, July 25, 2012.

Henderson, Paul. *How Hockey Explains Canada: The Sport that Defines a Country*. With Jim Prime. Chicago: Triumph, 2011.

Holland, Dave. *Canada on Ice: The World Hockey Championships 1920–2008*. Calgary: Canada on Ice Productions, 2008.

Holman, Andrew C. "The Canadian Hockey Player Problem: Cultural Reckoning and National Identities in American Collegiate Sport, 1974–80." *The Canadian Historical Review* 88, no. 3 (September 2007): 440–68.

Jokisipilä, Markku. "Maple Leaf, Hammer, and Sickle: International Ice Hockey during the Cold War." *Sport History Review* 36 (2006): 36–53.

Martin, Lawrence. *The Red Machine: The Soviet Quest to Dominate Canada's Game*. Toronto: Doubleday Canada, 1990.

Podnieks, Andrew. *Team Canada 1972: The Official 40th Anniversary Celebration of the Summit Series*. Toronto: Fenn/McClelland & Stewart, 2012.

Popovic, Megan L. "A Voice in the Rink: Playing with Our Histories and Evoking Autoethnography." *Journal of Sport History* 37, no. 2 (Summer 2010): 235–55.

Sinden, Harry. *Hockey Showdown: The Canada-Russia Hockey Series*. Toronto: Doubleday, 1972.

Terroux, Gilles. *Face-Off of the Century: Canada-USSR, the New Era*. Toronto: Collier-MacMillan Canada, 1972.

Tretiak, Vladislav. *The Hockey I Love*. With V. Snegirev. Translated by Anatole Konstantin. Toronto: Fitzhenry & Whiteside, 1977.

Wilson, J.J. "27 Remarkable Days: The 1972 Summit Series of Ice Hockey between Canada and the Soviet Union." *Totalitarian Movements and Political Religions* 5, no. 2 (Autumn 2004): 271–80.

What
about
Now?

Reflections on Canadian Moral Nation-Making on the Occasion of the Summit Series' Seventy-Fifth Anniversary

✦

TIM ELCOMBE

September 28, 2047[1]

Seventy-five years ago today the iconic voice of twentieth-century hockey broadcasting, Foster Hewitt, exclaimed "Henderson has scored for Canada!" across English CBC television airwaves. Paul Henderson's goal with thirty-four seconds remaining proved the difference in Team Canada's 6–5 victory over their Soviet Union ice hockey adversaries. Delirium swept across an estimated seventy per cent of Canadians simultaneously watching on crude two-dimensional televisions and listening to radios at home and elsewhere, along with the players, officials and three thousand Canucks attending the game in Moscow. Henderson's goal secured victory in an eight-game exhibition known as the "Summit Series," reaffirming for a time Canada's international hockey superiority over the emergent Soviet challenge.

Philosopher Thomas Alexander argued in the latter years of the twentieth century that "culture is transmitted in its stories and ceremonies, its images and dramas, which form the prereflective tapestry of a people.... To understand the political history of a nation one might well begin by examining the stories told to its children" (271). But why nations revise or stop telling certain stories similarly helps us understand the sociopolitical trajectory of a nation like Canada. Over the past seventy-five years, the use of the Summit Series, and hockey more generally, as a feature of Canadian identity and, relatedly, moral narratives have ebbed and flowed. So with the remaining members of Team Canada gathered today in Ottawa to celebrate the event's diamond anniversary, it seems appropriate to consider the fluid significance of the Summit Series to Canada's identity, particularly its cultural and moral identity, over the past seventy-five years.

Remembering: 1972

One of the world's two superpowers in 1972, the Soviet Union (centralized in Moscow) and its Communist allies challenged those aligned with the United States and free market democracy (including Canada) for political, cultural and economic control of the world. As the Cold War escalated in the years following World War II, both the Soviet-led Communist Bloc and the "Western capitalists" turned to elite athletics as a means to demonstrate moral superiority through international sport success.

Hockey in 1972, the one place Canadians viewed themselves as a world power, served as perhaps Canada's most significant contribution to the ideological battle with the communists. Consequently, when the nation's dominance in amateur competitions waned with the rapid evolution of elite Soviet hockey throughout the 1960s, Canada recoiled from participating in international tournaments. Critics claimed Soviet athletes violated the code of amateurism governing international sport at the time; thus most Canadians viewed Soviet successes in world hockey as a sham, maintaining a belief that the nation's best professional players would dominate any Soviet team.

This led to the creation of the eight-game exhibition with the Soviets. The timing was perfect from Prime Minister Pierre Trudeau's perspective; Justin's father viewed international sport success as a means to build a sense of national identity and unity – his central platform in a looming election. Consequently, the federal government's Department of External Affairs assisted the newly formed Hockey Canada board (led by NHLPA president Alan Eagleson) in the negotiations and handling of the eight-game tournament. For the first time, the nation's best players (minus World Hockey Association defectors, including

Bobby Hull, despite protestations from Prime Minister Trudeau) assembled to represent Canada on the ice against the Soviets.

On September 2, 1972, the series opened at the hallowed Montreal Forum. Leading up to the series, experts, including top NHL scouts and head coach Harry Sinden, suggested Team Canada could win all eight games. After a lengthy opening ceremony where even the ceremonial faceoff turned testy,[2] Canada scored thirty seconds into the "friendly" to lead 1–0, then tallied a second goal six minutes later to provide fodder for the sweep prognosticators. Canada's 2–0 lead remained for another five minutes before the Soviets scored the first of their seven goals to handily win game one 7–3. Forced to acknowledge the Soviets' skill and ability, as well as the genuine possibility that Canada might actually lose, the nation's citizenry nervously settled in for a tense and contentious series. Game two in Toronto ended with a 4–1 Team Canada victory, followed by a 4–4 game three tie in Winnipeg. In the final game played on Canadian soil, the hosts lost 5–3 and heard boos emanating from the Vancouver crowd even before the contest's initial faceoff. Following the loss, captain Phil Esposito expressed Team Canada's "disappointment" in the treatment of the players.

After a two-week hiatus in Stockholm that included a 4–1 win and 4–4 tie against the Swedish national team, Team Canada flew to Moscow for the final games of the series. After losing game five 5–4, the team needed victories in all three remaining games in Moscow's Luzhniki Ice Palace to win the tournament and retain the mantle of hockey supremacy. Team Canada dramatically came from behind to win both game six (3–2) and game seven (4–3), and in the epic game eight, Henderson's late heroics sealed the victory despite Team Canada trailing by two goals at the start of the final period.

At home, the telecast employing emerging (and raw) satellite technology gave the largest audience ever in Canada the opportunity to view the game. Schools cancelled classes and wheeled televisions into libraries and gymnasiums for students to watch. Businesses and workers paused to follow the action on transistor radios. In the middle of a Stratford, Ontario, theatrical performance of *King Lear*, the lead actor finished a dramatic speech to a capacity crowd of students by announcing Canada's 6–5 victory. Following the win, Prime Minister Trudeau and his main political rival Robert Stanfield wired congratulatory notes to the team. Trudeau indicated in his message that election campaigning halted despite entering into the final month of stumping. It was a time for all Canadians, no matter their differences, to come together as one nation. As Team Canada goaltender, author and early twenty-first-century federal politician Ken Dryden penned in his (along with Roy MacGregor) aptly named 1989 book *Home Game*, "It is rare that a Canadian event has made time stand still, even for Canadians.... There is only one wholly Canadian event that has left a similar trail of memory: Henderson's goal in Moscow" (193).

Legendizing: 1973–92

The cultural significance of Henderson's goal and Team Canada's victory only grew in stature as time passed. Author Will Ferguson fondly remembered being "seven years old, and for the first time...aware of belonging to this group, this *thing* called Canada" (76). The victory over the Soviets not only reaffirmed Canadian ice hockey supremacy but also signified ideological, political and, importantly, moral superiority over their communist foes. Most, Gruneau and Whitson argued in 1993, pointed to "Canadian virtues" as the reason for Team Canada's victory – a triumph grounded in individual accountability, a commitment to teammates, passion, flair and, most of all, character and heart, in contrast to stereotypical views of the mechanistic, emotionless and morally dubious Soviet "system."

In the years following the Summit Series, elite sport competitions continued to serve as a source of moral and political capital.[3] But despite victory in 1972, as well as heightened sociopolitical yearnings for global hockey superiority, on-ice results elicited nonpartisan skepticism regarding Canada's perceived ice hockey reign. The Soviets continued to rule elite international competitions, including four Olympic victories (and one famous silver in 1980) in the five Winter Games from 1976–92. At the International Ice Hockey Federation (IIHF) World Championships, the Soviets won gold in eleven and medalled in all sixteen competitions from 1973 to 1991. In contrast, Canada won only a single Olympic medal (silver) in four Winter Games following the nation's return to ice hockey competitions (in 1980, 1984, 1988 and 1992); at the IIHF World Championships, Canadian professional players captured only six medals (none gold) in twelve events from 1977 to 1992.[4] The Soviets also defeated a team of WHA stars in a 1974 reprisal of the Summit Series, with four wins and three ties in the eight games. In 1976, two touring Soviet clubs travelled to North America to battle NHL clubs in mid-season form in Super Series '76, winning five of eight games.

Decisive victories by the Buffalo Sabres (over the Soviet Wings) and Philadelphia Flyers (over the Central Red Army), as well as perceptions of domination by the Montreal Canadiens in their "epic tie" with the Red Army in Super Series '76, however, cemented in Canada's collective consciousness the nation's *true* place at the pinnacle of international ice hockey.[5] Canada's hockey defenders pointed to these "victories" (by USA-based franchises comprised almost exclusively of Canadian skaters), as well as triumphs featuring the best players from world hockey powers at the newly created Canada Cup competitions in 1976, 1984, 1987 and 1991, as affirmations of the nation's on-ice dominance and higher moral status following the Summit Series. Soviet victories over professional players, such as at the 1981 Canada Cup, were viewed as merely blips in Canadian demonstrations of "genuine" hockey supremacy.

On the home front, hockey in Canada thrived. Although most teams in the NHL represented American cities, Canadian players dominated the rosters. In 1979, three Canadian teams – the Edmonton Oilers, Quebec Nordiques and Winnipeg Jets – joined the NHL out of the defunct WHA. From 1973 to 1990, Canadian-based clubs won twelve of eighteen Stanley Cups, while Canadian stars led the two teams – the Philadelphia Flyers and New York Islanders – that captured the remaining six championships. Hockey was Canada's unquestioned "national sport" in terms of viewership, participation and, most importantly, moral and cultural significance.

On the occasion of its twentieth anniversary, the memories of the Summit Series served to reaffirm Canada's historical place as the birthplace and rightful home of ice hockey; the Canadian collective also "legendized" the Summit Series as a pivot from which the nation reasserted its superiority on and off the ice in a new world (hockey) order. Canada's Summit Series victory at once celebrated the nation's hockey past and represented its bright future. It also confirmed, for a time, proclamations that hockey functioned as Canada's national religion were not outrageous. This period also marked the last time international hockey success uncritically reflected the moral status of the "Canadian way."

Problematizing: 1992–2012

While sentiments about hockey as an organic component of Canada's moral identity within the collective consciousness remained mostly unchecked in the first twenty years following the Summit Series, geopolitical, cultural and economic changes chipped away at the event's legendary status. In particular, the end of the Cold War in the early 1990s dramatically changed the world and, important to Canada, elite hockey.

With the Fall of Communism in 1991, the Canada–Soviet Union hockey rivalry softened as the NHL globalized at the expense of Canadian player domination. Unheard of prior to the 1990s, former rivals, hated outsiders and moral infidels became teammates and heroes in cities across North America. By the 1992–93 season, the NHL's best included Russian players Pavel Bure, Sergei Fedorov and Alexander Mogilny, along with numerous other European and American stars. Of the twelve players named to the all-star teams that season, only five represented the birthplace of hockey (and only one, Finland's Teemu Selanne, played for a Canadian-based NHL franchise, in Winnipeg).

On a pro-nationalistic side, the Montreal Canadiens secured yet another Stanley Cup championship at the end of the 1993 season, with goalie Patrick Roy's Habs defeating Wayne Gretzky's Los Angeles Kings in the finals. But even victory by a Canadian-based team in the Stanley Cup – the thirteenth over a nineteen-year span – symbolized challenges to the nation's self-identity and the unquestioned place of hockey as an organic part of the Canadian culture. Gretzky, leading a Southern Californian club to the Stanley Cup final following his dramatic trade from Edmonton in 1988, represented anxieties about the growing "Americanization" and subsequent moral neutering of the sport. Although Kidd and Macfarlane had expressed similar concerns in a book titled *The Death of Hockey*, published the same year as the Summit Series, only now did whispers of an American economic takeover of hockey instigate mainstream conversations. "The 'loss' of Wayne Gretzky," Jackson explained, "came to embody many Canadians' worst fear regarding this American influence and domination" (172).

Despite living next to such a cultural, economic and political behemoth, Canadians in the 1970s and 1980s mostly viewed Americans as "one of us," spearheading the morally infused ideological battle against the evil Communist Bloc. Canadians cheered American successes against the Soviets as if they were their own moral victories, including the 1980 "Miracle on Ice" Olympic hockey gold captured by an underdog collection of American players. With the Cold War over, however, the United States remained the world's lone superpower in the early 1990s. As a result, the USA was increasingly perceived as an international bully, even by former allies. With European (including Soviet) players fully integrated into the NHL and the Soviet Union no longer a physical or political threat, Canadians joined the rest of the world in adopting anti-American sentiments. Gradually, the meaning of "Canadianness" boiled down to highlighting features of the Canadian experience that differentiated the nation from its neighbours to the south. "As a part of the general, though non-violent antagonism towards some things American," Hayes asserted in his mid 1990s analysis of the national identity project, "Canada attempted to develop as a nation that was – if nothing else – not American" (164).

As a result, Millard, Reigel and Wright argued that Canadians more readily resorted to American-style exhibitions of "loud nationalism" to assert the nation's sense of moral superiority over the United States. Several commentators, including Jackson, Kennedy, and Millard et al., pointed to the use of Molson beer commercials where a character named Joe loudly declares "I am Canadian" against a backdrop of beavers, untarnished natural wilderness, polite citizens, "real" beer and (of course) rugged yet virtuous hockey players to take aim at American shortcomings in relation to the Canadian experience. More and more, Canadians self-consciously portrayed themselves as stock characters to carve out their unique place in a rapidly globalizing world while simultaneously being culturally and economically dominated by the superpower next door. Canadians who were willing to overtly tout Canada's cultural and moral greatness, exemplified by Don Cherry every Saturday night on "Coach's Corner" during CBC's *Hockey Night in Canada* telecasts, garnered cult hero status (Elcombe, "Moral Equivalent," 205).[6] Successes by Canadians in American contexts, including by actors, musicians and athletes, took on heightened significance. Hayes, for instance, summarized the prevailing Canadian attitude after the Toronto Blue Jays' World Series titles in 1992 and 1993 as "'We' beat America at their own game" (164). Such overt displays of Canadian superiority symbolized the growing affinity for national chest pounding in the years following the Summit Series victory.

But despite the emerging jingoism of the Canadian identity project in the 1990s, highlighted by Millard et al., it clearly faced new challenges. Within the nation, Canada wrestled with diverse economies, cultures and political ideologies from coast to coast. Prior to the 1990s, challenges to a unified nation tended to focus exclusively on Quebec. A second failed Quebec sovereignty referendum held in 1995 did little to stem the tide of political and cultural fragmentation spreading across Canada, while a wider implementation of the North American Free Trade Agreement (NAFTA) in 1994 highlighted the inevitability of global economic (and political) influences. By the mid 1990s, Canada's collective identity found itself simultaneously stretched at the core through Quebec separatist threats and fraying around the edges as, Robertson Davies argued, politicians "signed away Canada's soul" with the NAFTA legislation (43).

Despite these sociopolitical realities, hockey still mattered to "Joe Canadian" in the 1990s. Still reeling from Gretzky's trade to Los Angeles in 1988, the relocation of the Quebec Nordiques to Denver in 1995 and the Winnipeg Jets to Phoenix in 1996 rocked the national hockey psyche. While Canada gained a new franchise in Ottawa in 1992, other expansion clubs found homes in very "un-Canadian" markets across the southern USA during the 1990s for economic reasons. When the Winter Olympics opened up for NHL player participation in 1998, Canada failed to even win a medal. All of these challenges led to a collective hand-wringing by those who felt the game symbolized Canada's place in the world – evidenced by the public attention paid to a three-day "Open Ice" conference organized in 1999 to address concerns that Canada no longer dominated the game ("1999: Summit Hopes"). Removing hockey as a piece of the "I am Canadian" narrative, many traditionalists like Don Cherry believed, would weaken the nation (Elcombe, "Moral Equivalent").[7]

Increasingly hockey in Canada came under scrutiny not only by virtue of changes in the professional/international landscape but also in terms of its deeper cultural and moral meanings. Gruneau and Whitson, in particular, critically analyzed hockey in Canada in their 1993 volume *Hockey Night in Canada*. As Holman opined, "the brilliance of Gruneau and Whitson's work is in its ability to problematize hockey. To understand hockey in a scholarly way is to see it as a series of historical struggles that emanate from its central position in Canadian culture as national icon, as work and entertainment, as pastime, as enterprise, as privilege, and as a class-, race- and gender-based locus of identity" (6). The more critical lenses turned to examine hockey, including the Summit Series, the less "Canadian" it looked. Just as "I-Am-Canadian Joe," upon closer examination, seemed to represent mostly twenty-something English white Canadians with cottages in Muskoka and the means to backpack across Europe, "Hockey Joe," too, seemed unable to thickly represent the changing face of Canada. As Adams pointed out in 2006, the idealized image of Canada portrayed through hockey failed to resonate with most women, non-whites, and the growing legions of disinterested men (71).

With the national identity project in flux, Canada's "moral victory" over the evil Soviets in the Summit Series likewise came into question. As George Orwell argued in his essay "Notes on Nationalism," "all nationalists have the power of not seeing resemblances between similar sets of facts.… Actions are held to be good or bad, not on their own merits, but according to who does them, and there is almost no kind of outrage…which does not change its moral colour when it is committed by 'our' side.… The nationalist not only does not disapprove of atrocities committed by his own side, but he has a remarkable capacity for not even hearing about them." Critics, particularly in intellectual circles, pointed to controversial activities on and off the ice in 1972 to challenge the assumed nation-unifying elements and shaded the depth of moral character generally accepted as embodied by Team Canada's Summit Series win.

The CBC, for instance, heightened Quebec-English Canada tensions through the selection of the retired, Toronto-based Foster Hewitt over Montreal's Danny Gallivan to provide television play-by-play (Auf der Maur). Also, Team Canada players regularly exhibited selfish behaviours that belied the national heroes designation assigned them, including suggesting they ought to receive payment to play, showing up to training camp in poor physical condition, and referring to themselves as "Team 50" (the number of players, officials and support staff) rather than Team Canada in response to being booed in Vancouver (Pelletier). Alan Eagleson, later convicted of defrauding players through NHL and international event dealings, regularly engaged in backroom power plays, including threatening to pull out of game eight due to the referee selection (Young). In the final contest, Canadian players pulled Eagleson onto the ice after a confrontation with Soviet police officers. While on the ice, he directed strange "up yours" gestures to the Soviet spectators as two other Canadian team staffers gave the Moscow crowd the middle finger. This scene was repeated after Henderson's iconic series-winning goal, where an official standing on the Team Canada bench rotated around, giving the crowd the middle finger and screaming, "Fuck you!" On the ice in 1972, Canadian players regularly delivered shots to the heads and crosschecks to the backs of Soviet players during play and following the whistle (and rarely with penalties assigned). J. P. Parise skated across the ice and threatened to swing his stick at the head of a referee after receiving an interference penalty. Players routinely directed throat-slashing gestures toward the Soviets while overtly stalling between plays and between periods to offset their conditioning disadvantage.[8] The most infamous on-ice incident occurred in game six when Bobby Clarke, urged on by assistant coach John Ferguson, intentionally slashed the Soviets' best player, Valery Kharlamov, across the ankle, rendering him ineffective for the remainder of the series (and out of game seven altogether).[9]

In light of this more problematic analysis, a growing sense of ambivalence towards the moral meaningfulness of the 1972 Summit Series (and, importantly, hockey more generally) to the Canadian experience marked the period from 1992 to 2012. On one hand, the Summit Series continued to stand as a cherished and significant event in Canadian history. Citizens fondly (and selectively) "remembered" the great comeback of Team Canada, the players' embodiment of Canadian "virtue" and the single moment when virtually an entire nation watched Henderson *score for Canada*. Regularly listed among the greatest moments in Canadian history up until 2012, the Summit Series' significance to late twentieth- to early twenty-first-century Canada resulted in numerous awards and recognition for the players, team and series in general. Hockey still mattered to many Canadians invested in the national identity project, and Olympic victories in Salt Lake City in 2002 and on home ice in Vancouver in 2010 reinvigorated the game's place in the national consciousness. Stephen Brunt, capturing the nationalistic sentiments felt in the final days of the Vancouver Olympics, stated, "It was though an entire country was given permission to feel something it needed to feel.... The story was supposed to be all about winning, about finishing first, about putting a new swagger in our step. Turns out, the swagger was already there – it was just waiting for the right stage." These feelings crescendoed following Sidney Crosby's gold-medal-winning overtime goal to defeat the Americans at the close of the 2010 Games.

On the other hand, despite the nostalgic fervour of national collectivity reignited by international hockey successes early in the twenty-first century, the game also represented the slow disintegration of Canada as a unified citizenry. Hockey as an organic feature of the Canadian experience faced growing critical challenges in terms of its cultural and moral significance. The game invigorated the general public only sporadically, participation rates for youth players declined,[10] and hockey players touted as "ideal Canadians" increasingly looked less like the typical Canadian as immigration patterns continued to reconstruct the face of the country and a wider range of recreational opportunities beckoned the nation's youth. On the ice, Canadian domination waned both in professional play and on the international stage (despite the two Olympic gold medals). Hockey fans cared less about the nationality of NHL players and more about their contributions to the successes (and style) of their favourite clubs, evidenced by the fact that in 2000 only one team captain (the player often most beloved by the club's fan base) from the six Canadian NHL franchises hailed from Canada. Players from the former Soviet Union were increasingly humanized and celebrated in Canadian culture. Quietly the Summit Series looked less like a moral victory, and the event's significance to the nation's identity slowly receded.

Forgetting: 2012–37

From 2012 to 2037, widening fissures and inequality overtly marked the Canadian experience.[11] As a result, the citizenry emphasized protective individual rights in a nation and world focused on short-term economic instrumentality. Immigration and an aging population strained the country's ability to provide a state safety net. The increasingly diverse populace seemed to share less and less in common with one another. Polls regularly revealed a deep distrust in the nation's leaders, with CEOs near the bottom and federal politicians dead last (behind car salespeople) when considering the trustworthiness of various professions.[12] Quebec's aspirations for political independence continued, but it was now joined by Alberta and Saskatchewan as a distrust of Ottawa's distribution of their energy wealth grew. Political apathy, already a problem in most Western democratic nations, reached an all-time low in 2025 with only a twenty-five per cent voter turnout for the federal election. Community engagement, like everything else, was reduced to special and relativistic interests. Canada existed only in narrowly functional terms, and the nation considered a future as independent regions bound together by a European Union–like alliance. Consequently, Canadians turned away from the idea of a unified nation embodied by the collective memory of Henderson's goal.

In terms of hockey, the delayed start to the 2012–13 NHL season due to the second labour dispute within nine years strained residual nationalistic connections to the game Canadians re-established following the Vancouver Olympics. While enthusiasts returned to support the NHL in full force, Canadian franchises now generated mostly tribal support; even the Montreal Canadiens, as noted by Harvey, no longer served as an iconic symbol of French Canada (49). Fans of the Toronto Maple Leafs, for instance, were as likely (or even more likely, due to growing regional tensions) to cheer for the Boston Bruins if playing the Vancouver Canucks.[13] Even the nationalistic shine emanating from the relocation of the Atlanta Thrashers to Winnipeg in 2011 quickly faded outside of Manitoba as the NHL appealed less and less to an increasingly complex and diversified Canadian citizenry. The NHL remained an economic force in big-city Canada, but the game was devoid of the moral and cultural capital generated by the Summit Series.

The symbolic "death of Canadian hockey" as a "national religion" forecasted in 1972 by Kidd and Macfarlane subtly continued in the lead up to the 2014 Winter Olympics in Sochi, Russia. Despite Canada's gold medal victory in men's hockey, drawn out negotiations to include NHL players reflected the athletes' and officials' primary allegiance to the professional game in contrast to national representation; owners and management expressed concerns about shutting down the NHL for two weeks while players haggled over personal insurance coverage (Harrison). With several star players (including Canadian John Tavares of the New York Islanders) suffering serious injuries in Sochi, and with 2018 host Pyeongchang, South Korea, offering the league little in terms of marketing incentives, most assumed the 2014 Winter Games represented the final opportunity for fans to watch NHL stars compete for Olympic gold.

Even the great defender of the monolithic Canadian identity project, Don Cherry, realized the futility of his cause. For years, a large swath of the population regularly parroted Cherry's rants intended to protect (through hockey discourse) the traditional values and ideologies of a certain Anglo Saxon view of Canada (Elcombe, "Moral Equivalent," 200). Starting in 2013, however, Cherry regularly prefaced his diatribes by saying, "I know most of you won't agree with me, but..." NHL rules requiring incoming players to don visors, the eventual removal of implicitly sanctioned fighting at all levels, and the de-emphasis of bodychecking in youth hockey all came to pass with little resistance, save for a few "old school" hockey traditionalists. Relative to the Summit Series, the game arrived at an ironic full circle, emphasizing a vision of elite hockey first introduced to Canadians by the Soviets at the Montreal Forum on September 2, 1972.

Hockey no longer looked "Canadian" in the traditional sense. In fact, Don Cherry's worst nightmare came to fruition as soccer looked more and more "Canadian" than hockey in terms of representing the populace, while an emerging coterie of NBA stars from the country drew as much urban acclaim as the nation's best hockey players. All of this took place against the backdrop of a citizenry apathetic to grand state narratives, emphasizing instead cultural enclaves and selective/regionalized sociopolitical attention. Canada as a cultural and moral idea stalled, simply reduced to a legal and political entity functioning to keep the economy from collapsing and provinces able to transact with one another. The complex and seemingly insurmountable challenges to the Canadian identity project, captured in Irvin Studin's 2006 edited volume *What Is a Canadian?*, overwhelmed the nation.[14] Roy MacGregor in his contribution argued that "[Canada], in fact, is a society that has changed so rapidly that even if you could properly say 'A Canadian is...' your definition would be out of date before the sentence could be completed" (98). In such a fluid nationalistic context, previously iconic historical moments like the Summit Series were rendered relatively meaningless; the moral worth previously accrued by the nation through international hockey success bankrupted.

Remaking: 2037–47

Mark Kingwell accurately predicted in 2008 that Canada by the year 2020 would exist in a contemporary "Dark Age" as a result of political apathy, cultural banality and relativistic morality (95–96). Over the past ten years, however, Canadians' view of their national identity, as well as of the game of hockey and the significance of the Summit Series, reemerged from this sociopolitical and moral "darkness." Many factors converged to initiate these changes, including the inability of federal political parties to function in regionally biased minority government scenarios, the resultant dwindling voter turnout, and a proposal to rename "Canada Day" as "People Day" on the occasion of the nation's 170th birthday (Cohen, 15). Canadians no longer genuinely and meaningfully engaged with one another culturally and politically. Yet citizens new and old increasingly expressed a desire to feel more deeply about belonging in their homeland, to identify themselves as "Canadians" first and foremost.

Morgan in the latter years of the twentieth century argued that people take their moral cues, their sense of how to live well with one another, most often from the nation (50) – a sentiment echoed by Saul in 2005. Yet Canadians throughout the twenty-first century lost the all-important sense of "us" when it came to nationalism. Despite the best efforts at the turn of the century for the "Joe Canadians" and "Don Cherrys" to loudly proclaim moral superiority and cultural distinctiveness, the emphasis on the promotion of a single, static, exclusionary version of what it meant to be a true Canadian backfired. As the fixed image of "being Canadian" reflected fewer and fewer of the nation's citizens over the years, and the more we defined ourselves morally in opposition to others – first the Communists, and later the United States – the more the nation was thrown into an existential identity crisis. Canadians also suffered, Hurka lamented in 2006, from a "distinctiveness fetish." Thus, in the latter years of the twentieth and early years of the twenty-first centuries, we thought we had a clear essence, we knew who we were and who we were not. The Summit Series supposedly confirmed this reality for us. Canadians were Henderson, Esposito, Clarke and Cournoyer. Kharlamov, Yakushev and Tretiak represented the "others." We were one; we were better on and off the ice; we were Canadians.

Dialogue initiated in the academic realm about nationalism, morality and belonging spilled into the public space. Town hall–style discussions in various formats became the norm coast to coast. Realizing the centrality of "ideas" to the making and remaking of Canada and the flourishing of genuine democracy, humanities returned to the forefront in education. New and old generations of diverse Canadians, applying the lessons of philosophy, history and the arts in general, moved the nation beyond the stagnation engendered by decades of devotion to Enlightenment reductionism, radical individualism, political apathy and short-term economic instrumentality. Sociopolitical language replaced the dominant language of economics with the emerging language of ecology. Rather than emphasize "efficiency," "deficits" and "cost-benefit analysis," politicians and cultural leaders spoke in terms of "evolution," "transformation," "growth" and "adaptability."

Canada today derives its identity from the *process* by which the nation's institutions and its citizens weave and reweave the country's *unique confluence of features* (physical, cultural, political) to constantly recreate a meaningful Canadian tapestry. The reconstruction that commenced in 2037 expanded the sense of "we" embodied by the idea of nation making rather than nation fixing.[15] Effectively this nation-making process is a moral one: Canadians, while still acknowledging our shared history, continually negotiate how we ought to live and what we ought to value in *this* place at *this* time. And it is this collective moral process Canadians engage in through formal institutions and informal conventions better than any other lasting nation in history (save for the years when the country effectively gave up the project). The tide of isolated regionalism and national xenophobia has thus turned. Canadians now use the vast "otherness" of the country's citizenry to generate a vibrant and transformative sense of "we" rather than blame diversity and physical expanse for undermining the nation's cultural foundation.

The Summit Series seventy-five years later contributes to this reinvigorated Canada and the ongoing moral process of nation making. Hockey, in general, reemerged from a slow decline in interest to now function as a tool in which citizens discuss and contextualize topics such as ethics, otherness and nation. The game once again serves as a shared "Canadian experience" – not merely as a powerful symbol of the history and geography of the land but also as an instrument for making and remaking the nation. The hockey series of 1972, in particular, reassumed a place of significance, albeit now considered a "moral spectacle" rather than a referendum on the nation's moral stature.[16] As a moral spectacle, our relation to the Summit Series as a cultural narrative over the years shined a collective spotlight on the nation's values and moral codes, rather than a moment cementing Canada's ideology or affirming its moral superiority over others. The Summit Series thus demanded attention, clarification and dialogue – a continual critical process to conceptualize what the event meant to Canada in the context of yesteryear as well as Canada today.

Nationalism, Hurka explained early in the twenty-first century, "is a form of partiality, of caring more about some people than about others.... What ties [a Canadian nationalist] to his fellow Canadians is something historical; that they grew up with him here, experiencing the same weather and TV shows, electing and then despising the same politicians" (359–60). Capturing the significance of the Summit Series' contribution to the collective history and moving present of Canada, Ken Dryden, on behalf of the remaining players in attendance at the seventy-fifth anniversary gala in Ottawa, recited a passage he first shared on the occasion of Team Canada's selection as the nation's Team of the Century in 2000:

> You are always looking for shared memories...for a shared experience. They don't happen very often. And you're never sure what is going to create one. You don't want it to be an assassination of a president. You might want it to be the first man on the moon. You don't expect it is going to be a goal that ends a series. You can't predict it. You can't know it. And one isn't more important than another. Because one is a sporting event and one is a political event and one is a scientific event, there [are] no hierarchies here. It is the event. It is the effect of the event. It's the common experience that counts. It's whatever generates it that counts. (*Canada's Team of the Century*)[17]

Echoing Hurka and Dryden, Stephen Brunt narrated the following text for his 2010 Vancouver Olympics video essay: "Cynicism is easy; so is retreating into historic grudges; so is looking at a world in which what were once borders are now dotted lines at best. And believing it doesn't really matter what you call yourself or where you live. It does matter, or at least it can. It *is* important to have a shared history; there *is* power in the collective experience. And, admit it: it feels good. It feels good to let your heart show" (*Globe and Mail*).

There is a renewed interest across Canada in hockey as we move to the last half of the twenty-first century. The awareness of hockey's moral place in the nation's collective history, its cultural representations and the game's ability to engage Canadians in sociopolitical dialogue is at an all-time high in 2047. With the reemergence of hockey within the national consciousness, associations across the country report the highest participation rates for boys and girls since the turn of the century. Although the game looks quite different seventy-five years after the Summit Series, we now recognize the transformations in hockey underscore, rather than detract from, its truly Canadian nation-making process. The idea that hockey ought to be played one way for all of time misrepresented the always evolving Canadian experience. Today we recognize the nation's ability to address the complex confluence of factors that lead to hockey's ongoing transformations as truly representative of the history and trajectory of Canada.

In important ways the 1972 Summit Series, now viewed as a moral spectacle, set in motion a deeper national self-understanding arrived at seventy-five years after Henderson scored for Canada. Today we embrace the complex, messy and ongoing process of "being Canadian" in a moral, shared sense. As a result of this newfound appreciation of our national identity and for the Summit Series as part of this project, hockey once again plays a meaningful role in the making and remaking of Canada.

---

[1] I am using Richard Rorty's essay "Looking Backwards from the Year 2096" as a model for this chapter.

[2] Prime Minister Trudeau dropped the puck for a ceremonial faceoff as part of a lengthy opening ceremony. Team Canada captain Phil Esposito felt he had to win the faceoff.

[3] For example, Canada joined other "anti-communist" crusaders in a boycott of the 1980 Olympic Summer Games in Moscow, while the Soviet Union and many allies returned the insult by sitting out the 1984 Summer Games in Los Angeles.

4   Canada returned to IIHF World Championship competitions only once professional players were permitted to compete in 1977, following a boycott initiated in 1970.

5   For an analysis of the 1976 Super Series, see the author's essay "Hockey New Year's Eve in Canada."

6   For a discussion on the idea of Don Cherry's sociopolitical significance to Canada, see the author's essay "The Moral Equivalent of 'Don Cherry.'"

7   See the author's comparison of Don Cherry to the character Colonel Nathan Jessup from the motion picture *A Few Good Men* as to the need to be left to "protect" the nation without interference ("The Moral Equivalent of 'Don Cherry,'" 207–8).

8   Descriptions of the on-ice incidents are from the author's DVD viewing of *Canada's Team of the Century: 1972 Canada vs. USSR*.

9   Ferguson, years after the Summit Series (and in response to criticism from Paul Henderson about Canada's dirty play), acknowledged his role in the Kharlamov incident: "I called Clarke over to the bench, looked over at Kharlamov and said: 'I think he needs a tap on the ankle.' I didn't think twice about it. It was Us vs. Them. And Kharlamov was killing us. I mean, somebody had to do it, and I sure wasn't going to ask Henderson." See Fisher, "Summit Series 40th Anniversary."

10 Only ten per cent of families surveyed in a 2013 study commissioned by Bauer, Inc., and Hockey Canada reported participating in hockey. See CNW Group, "Bauer Hockey, Hockey Canada Research Shows Growing the Game is Achievable," August 1, 2013, http://www.newswire.ca/en/story/1205789/bauer-hockey-hockey-canada-research-shows-growing-the-game-is-achievable.

11 The "predictions" of Canada's future come primarily from a collection of essays found in Rudyard Griffiths edited volume Canada in 2020. In particular, essays from Clarke, Cohen, Fortin, Griffiths, Kingwell and Stoffman are used. Works by Rorty ("Looking Backwards from the Year 2096") and Taylor (*The Ethics of Authenticity*) also informed this section.

12 These results are from a 2003 Ipsos Reid survey as well as a 2005 Angus Reid poll.

13 Gare Joyce, in a 2013 *Sportsnet Magazine* article examining why Canadian teams continually fail to win the Stanley Cup, recounts a story whereby an American ESPN producer asked him to find a locale in Toronto filled with fans cheering for the Vancouver Canucks in the 2011 Stanley Cup final against the Boston Bruins. Joyce's response: "You're more likely to go down to the Metro Convention Centre and find a congress of sasquatches than you are a bar full of Vancouver fans in Toronto or anywhere outside the Pacific time zone."

14 See Studin's afterword to *What Is a Canadian?* for a summary of the multiple ways the "Canadian identity" project is conceptualized.

[15] See the author's introduction of the concept of nation making in his analysis of the 1976 Super Series game between the Soviet Central Army and Montreal Canadiens ("Hockey New Year's Eve in Canada").

[16] The term "moral spectacle" comes from Richard Rorty's essay titled "Failed Prophecies, Glorious Hopes" (206), where he uses it to discuss the New Testament and the *Communist Manifesto.*

[17] This passage is found following an interview with Dryden after the presentation of game six in the *Canada's Team of the Century* DVD collection.

Works Cited

Adams, Mary Louise. "The Game of Whose Lives? Gender, Race, and Entitlement in Canada's 'National' Game." In *Artificial Ice: Hockey, Culture, and Commerce*, edited by David Whitson and Richard Gruneau, 71–84. Peterborough: Broadview, 2006.

Alexander, Thomas M. *John Dewey's Theory of Art, Experience, and Nature: The Horizons of Feeling*. Albany, NY: State University of New York Press, 1987.

Angus Reid. "Fire Fighters, Nurses Are Canada's Most Trusted," March 22, 2005. http://www.angus-reid.com/polls/19433/fire_fighters_nurses_are_canadas_most_trusted.

Auf der Maur, Nick. "Foster Hewitt 'the Fossil'." By Danny Finkleman. *This Country in the Morning*, Radio, September 2, 1972. CBC Digital Archives. Last modified November 23, 2012. http://www.cbc.ca/archives/categories/sports/hockey/canada-soviet-hockey-series-1972/foster-hewitt-the-fossil.html.

Brunt, Stephen. "Brunt's Olympic Essay." *Globe and Mail*. Created February 2010. Video, 4:08. Posted February 11, 2011. http://www.theglobeandmail.com/sports/sports-video/brunts-olympic-essay/article602543/.

Canada's Team of the Century: 1972 Canada vs. USSR. DVD. Produced by Robert MacAskill. Willowdale, ON: Universal Studios Canada, 2002.

Clarke, George E. "Two 2020 Scenarios." In Griffiths, *Canada in 2020*, 83–91.

Cohen, Andrew. "Imagining Canada's 153rd Birthday." In Griffiths, *Canada in 2020*, 13–20.

Davies, Robertson. "Signing Away Canada's Soul: Culture, Identity, and the Free Trade Agreement." *Harper's*, January 1989.

Dryden, Ken, and Roy MacGregor. *Home Game: Hockey and Life in Canada*. Toronto, McClelland & Stewart, 1989.

Elcombe, Tim. "Hockey New Year's Eve in Canada: Nation-Making at the Montreal Forum." *International Journal of the History of Sport* (May 2010): 1287–312.

———. "The Moral Equivalent of 'Don Cherry.'" *Journal of Canadian Studies* (Spring 2010): 194–218.

Ferguson, Will. *Why I Hate Canadians*. Vancouver, BC: Douglas & McIntyre, 1997.

Fisher, Red. "Summit Series 40th Anniversary: Clarke's Game 6 Slash on Kharlamov was Turning Point for Team Canada." *The Gazette* (Montreal), September 24, 2012. http://www.montrealgazette.com/sports/Summit+Seri es+40th+anniversary+Clarke+Game+slash+Kharlamov+turning+point+Team +Canada/7287054/story.html

Fortin, Pierre. "The Baby Boomers' Tab: Already $40 Billion in 2020." In Griffiths, *Canada in 2020*, 39–47.

Griffiths, Rudyard, ed. *Canada in 2020: Twenty Leading Voices Imagine Canada's Future*. Toronto: Key Porter, 2008.

Gruneau, Richard, and David Whitson. *Hockey Night in Canada: Sport, Identities and Cultural Politics*. Toronto: Garamond, 1993.

Harrison, Doug. "NHL Players to Compete at 2014 Sochi Olympics." CBC Sports, July 19, 2013. http://www.cbc.ca/sports/hockey/nhl/story/2013/07/19 /sp-olympics-nhl-sochi-russia-gary-bettman.html.

Harvey, Jean. "Whose Sweater Is This? The Changing Meanings of Hockey in Quebec." In *Artificial Ice: Hockey, Culture, and Commerce*, edited by David Whitson and Richard Gruneau, 29–52. Peterborough, ON: Broadview, 2006.

Hayes, Sean. "America's National Pastime and Canadian Nationalism." *Culture, Sport, Society* (2001): 157–84.

Holman, Andrew C., ed. Introduction to *Canada's Game: Hockey and Identity*, 3–8. Montreal: McGill-Queen's University Press, 2009.

Hurka, Thomas. "Canadian Nationalism and the Distinctiveness Fetish." In *In the Agora: The Public Face of Canadian Philosophy*, edited by Andrew D. Irvine and John S. Russell, 359–62. Toronto: University of Toronto Press, 2006.

Ipsos Reid. "So, Whom Do We Trust?" January 22, 2003. http://www.ipsos-na. com/news-polls/pressrelease.aspx?id=1716.

Jackson, Steven J. "Gretzky Nation: Canada, Crisis and Americanization." In *Sport Stars: The Cultural Politics of Sporting Celebrity*, edited by David L. Andrews and Steven J. Jackson, 164–86. London: Routledge, 2001.

Joyce, Gare. "Man, This Hurts." *Sportsnet Magazine*, June 2013. http://www. sportsnet.ca/magazine/man-this-hurts.

Kennedy, Brian. "Confronting a Compelling Other: The Summit Series and the Nostalgic (Trans)Formation of Canadian Identity." In *Canada's Game: Hockey and Identity*, edited by Andrew C. Holman, 44–62. Montreal: McGill-Queen's University Press, 2009.

Kidd, Bruce, and John Macfarlane. *The Death of Hockey*. Toronto: New Press, 1972.

Kingwell, Mark. "The Future of Democracy." In Griffiths, *Canada in 2020*, 93–110.

MacGregor, Roy. "Roy MacGregor." In *What Is a Canadian? Forty-Three Thought-Provoking Responses*, edited by Irvin Studin, 95–100. Toronto: McClelland & Stewart, 2006.

Millard, Gregory, Sarah Riegel, and John Wright. "Here's Where We Get Canadian: English-Canadian Nationalism and Popular Culture." *American Review of Canadian Studies* (2002): 11–34.

Morgan, William J. "Patriotic Sports and the Moral Making of Nations." *Journal of the Philosophy of Sport* (1999): 50–67.

"1999: Summit Hopes to Restore Canada's Hockey Supremacy." *The National*. Toronto: CBC, August 25, 1999. http://www.cbc.ca/archives/categories /sports/hockey/general-20/summit-hopes-to-restore-canadas-hockey-supremacy.html.

Orwell, George. "Notes on Nationalism." Dag's Orwell Project. http://orwell. ru/library/essays/nationalism/english/e_nat. First published October 1945 by *Polemic* magazine.

Pelletier, Joe. "1972 Summit Series Game Recaps." *Sports Illustrated*, September 27, 2003. http://sportsillustrated.cnn.com/hockey/news/2002/09/27/summitseries _recaps/. First published www.1972summitseries.com.

Rorty, Richard. "Failed Prophecies, Glorious Hopes." In *Philosophy and Social Hope*, 201–9. Toronto: Penguin, 1999.

———. "Looking Backwards From the Year 2096." In *Philosophy and Social Hope*, 243–51.

Saul, John Ralston. *The Collapse of Globalism: And the Reinvention of the World*. Toronto: Penguin, 2005.

Studin, Irvin, ed. Afterword to *What Is a Canadian? Forty-Three Thought-Provoking Responses*, edited by Irvin Studin, 262–71. Toronto: McClelland & Stewart, 2006.

Stoffman, Daniel. "Sao Paolo of the North: The Effects of Mass Immigration." In Griffiths, 29–38.

Taylor, Charles. *The Ethics of Authenticity*. Cambridge: Harvard University Press, 1992.

Young, Scott. *War on Ice: Canada in International Hockey*. Toronto: McClelland & Stewart, 1976.

Do the Young People Still Believe?
The Rise and Shift of Mythic Tradition

🍁

RICHARD LEHMAN

I remember the first time I heard my father, uncle and grandfather discussing where they watched game eight of the 1972 Summit Series. I could tell you each of their stories as if I had been there. In my family, "Where were you when Henderson scored?" is a question that's asked at least once per gathering. I've never heard where any of them were when Neil Armstrong walked on the moon three years earlier, and to be honest, I don't really care. I've always had the impression that the Henderson goal was bigger. It sounds ridiculous, because it is, but that's the way diehard Canadian hockey fans who watched the series live seem to have felt. As a self-proclaimed hockey historian, I've always felt a connection to the Summit Series, but that connection has always been tied more to the accounts of the fans than to the games themselves. Before sitting down at about fifteen years old and actually watching the series on tape, I had imagined an epic contest between two powerhouse teams. And I remember, after watching all eight games, thinking, "Wow…that was it?" But, I trusted everyone when they told me that I couldn't appreciate the games because I was not caught up in the emotion of the series. Until I watched the tape of the three-game final of the 1987 Canada Cup. Now that was the best hockey ever played between the two best teams ever assembled. I didn't have to pretend it was live, or do a pile of research on the Cold War to "get it." I just watched and marvelled at the games. I wondered, as someone who did not live through the unrest of the political and military events leading up to the games, how the Summit Series could be spoken of so highly when I had barely heard anything about the 1987 Canada Cup, and I was left to ponder whether the quality of the hockey alone was what made a series memorable.

After the 2002 Olympics, I saw *TSN* magazine's Team Canada Collector's Edition in an airport. Of course I bought it, and it was at that point that I began to get closer to understanding what the Summit Series actually stood for. I read that "Ken Dryden, Team Canada '72 goalie and hockey philosopher king, says the true measure of historic events is twofold – the original sound made by the event and the echo that reverberates for years to come. On that scale, the 1972 Summit Series is a perfect 10 for the sonic boom it made in September, 1972, and the fact it continues to ring loud and clear some three decades later" (Dryden, 7). If this is in fact true, and the sound made by the series continues to echo today, what makes it accessible to young people?

It is undeniable that the mythos surrounding the Summit Series remains impressive today. In order for something as seemingly trivial as a hockey game to survive, it must be passed on to the next generation, and it is not unreasonable to suggest that the 1972 Summit Series has become a form of mythology to the younger generations in Canada. As such, it has been passed down through the oral tradition that has played a hand in creating so many other mythological stories we have heard. Through the oral tradition, men can become larger and more important than they actually were. They serve as a vessel for the greater story. They become giants. Phil Esposito becomes the military-like leader who rouses an entire country with one speech. Valery Kharlamov becomes the tragic hero, infallible and immortal but for a wobbly ankle. The story of the Summit Series can be packaged up nicely and fit into Joseph Campbell's monomyth, where "a hero ventures forth from the world of common day into a region of supernatural wonder: fabulous forces are there encountered and a decisive victory is won: The hero comes back from this mysterious adventure with the power to bestow boons on his fellow man" (30).

The Summit Series can be paralleled to other pieces of mythology, where figures like Esposito, Kharlamov, Tretiak, Henderson and Eagleson become characters of epic comparable to Achilles, Agamemnon, Hector and Aeneas.

True hatred runs rampant amongst our characters. Achilles drags Hector's lifeless body back to his tent, because simply murdering him is not enough. And Phil Esposito writes the following in his somewhat hyperbolic autobiography:

"I often wondered if I could kill someone, to actually get a gun, get someone in my sights, and shoot. I've been in a few hockey fights, but I never wanted to kill anyone.... When I think about it, if I had to kill the [Soviet] players to beat them, I'd have done that too. That's how much we wanted to beat them. It wasn't just two teams. It was two ways of life battling to prove which was superior" (137).

Bobby Clarke remembers:

> Defenceman Valery Vasiliev grabbed me and said, "Toast." I nodded yes, so he found a bottle of vodka and filled up a water glass for him and another for me. I took a little sip and he just looked at me and shook his head. "No, no, no," he said before guzzling down about 10 straight ounces. I had no choice but to match him gulp for gulp.... It almost killed me. But after 27 days and eight games of battling these people for world hockey supremacy that was very nearly taken away from us, the last thing I was going to do was give one of these guys the satisfaction of knowing he could out-drink me. (11)

So what can we learn from firsthand accounts like these, other than what we already might have suspected – that Esposito and Clarke are a little nuts? We learn that passing stories down through the oral tradition depends not only on the quality and content of the story but also on the quality of the storyteller. Homer may have been the greatest storyteller the world has ever seen, so the mythology that he created has continued to be passed down and continues to resonate today. But can the great Canadian myth, the story of the 1972 Summit Series, continue to survive through this method? With the games themselves so accessible, coupled with the fact that the NHL and the Hockey Hall of Very Good do an extremely poor job of celebrating their history, I would argue that it cannot, will not and, by now, perhaps even has not survived. This is certainly not to say that the series has lost all meaning, but rather has lost the shiny "this was the most important hockey ever played" tag that it once had.

It does not require a stretch of the imagination to envision future hockey fans being perplexed by the Summit Series team's title of "Team of the Century." It seemed only right when, as a team, they were honoured by the Hockey Hall of Fame. And in 2012 they received a star on Canada's Walk of Fame. The team's write-up at the Hall refers to the Summit Series myth by stating that "for Canadians, it was the greatest hockey victory in the history of the nation. The series has taken on mythical proportions. Paul Henderson's series-winning goal has become known as the 'Goal of the Century,' and was named one of the top ten events of the 20th century in Canadian history" (Shea). Team Canada forward Rob Ellis continues in the same piece, "We knew at the time that we were involved in a wonderful series, a unique series, but I don't think any of us expected (the Summit Series) to live as long as it has. I am so grateful that I was able to represent my country and our way of life in the Series of the Century" (Shea).

Yet the constant reference to "our way of life" by the players points to exactly why the Summit Series cannot survive in the Canadian psyche in its current form. The threat of the unknown has to exist in order to breed this type of thinking, and it does not, for modern-day observers. The heroes of our myth are simply not accessible as heroes anymore, and perhaps too accessible as people.

What separates the Summit Series from other, more successful myths is the fact that it definitively happened. We know exactly when it happened, why it happened and who set it up. We can watch the videos and read the books; we don't simply have to take our elders' word for it. Unlike classical-age Greeks hearing tales of the Trojan War, we can form our own opinions based on the facts that we have in front of us. We know that the early 1970s was a transitional period for the NHL. We know that Bobby Orr, the best player in the game at the time, was injured and unable to play. We know that Alan Eagleson, the man who set the series up, had blackballed the World Hockey Association players from participating, eliminating Bobby Hull and the hardest slapshot in the world from the selection pool. But what is not often acknowledged is that this move also meant that Gerry Cheevers, the reigning Stanley Cup champion goaltender and one of the best big-game players of all time, could not play. Canada would use Ken Dryden, who would prove time and time again that he was ineffective against the Soviets, and Tony Esposito, one of the worst playoff chokers of that era.

Further, we know that most of the great stars of the 1970s – Guy Lafleur, Marcel Dionne, Larry Robinson and others – had not quite reached the level they would by 1976 when team Canada steamrolled the whole world in the Canada Cup. We know that the series took place in September, and that Team Canada was not at all prepared for an eight-game series against the Soviets. The hockey itself was nothing to write home about, especially early in the series. The simple fact that these truths are available to us has diluted the story of the Summit Series to the point that all we really have left is the hatred that Canadians felt toward the Soviets. We have the emotions, the absolute need to win. We have the fact that as a nation, we tend to live and die with our hockey teams. And all of that is great. It makes for wonderful storytelling. But perhaps having so much verifiable knowledge makes emotions exceedingly difficult to pass on, especially when they are directed toward an enemy that no longer terrifies us.

When we as Canadians study our own history, we tend to take great pride in our nation's contributions to global issues. The Battle of Vimy Ridge in the First World War and the storming of Juno Beach on D-Day in the Second World War are taught at an early age to Canadian youth, due in part to the major roles played by Canada's oft-underrated military. The legends of these battles have been passed down from generation to generation in schools, in songs and in countless television programs and movies, rightfully stirring the hearts of Canadians young and old. The Summit Series, for those Canadians who experienced it, was the major role that Canada played during the Cold War. The series has been dubbed the "Cold War on Ice" and was, as has been written about ad nauseam, a much more political and historic event than merely eight hockey games. The series, however, cannot stand the proverbial test of time because it has become the epitome of "you had to be there" moments. As the tumultuous events of the 1970s fall farther away in our rearview mirrors, they begin to translate less poignantly as major events in our country's history. The idea of a hockey series symbolizing our great contribution to a war that never really happened is not a very exciting one.

I was six years old when the Iron Curtain fell. Some of my best hockey memories revolve around Pavel Bure, Sergei Fedorov, Igor Larionov and others from the first wave of Russian players in the NHL. Alexander Ovechkin and Pavel Datsyuk are two of the most exciting players in the game today. The current generation of Canadian hockey fans absolutely loves Canada-Russia games because of the exciting, fast-paced way the games are played. However, we tend to save our emotional responses to hockey games for games against the United States. Our two most recent triumphs in best-on-best tournaments came against the US, and our reaction has been akin to beating our big brother in a one-on-one game. When we unite as a country to hate another team, it's usually the one from our neighbours to the south. Whether or not it is fair to feel this way, the Summit Series represents (at least to today's young hockey fans) a fun story of a time when hockey was not quite the internationally developed sport that it is today. It represents a time when there really were only two countries that played the game, and the other country stood for everything we were scared of. This is in direct contrast to the way in which current Canadian hockey fans view the Olympic Games: as a high-stress, must-win tournament against the best hockey teams ever assembled. If you take away the political factors at play in 1972, it is clear that the Olympic tournament every four years is by all definitions a higher-quality hockey tournament than the Summit Series. And with the memory of the Cold War quickly fading, the hockey is all that is left.

Hockey fans now have access to books like Lawrence Martin's *The Red Machine* and Todd Hartje's *From Behind the Red Line* that humanize the Soviet players. The puck-possession game that those teams played was brought to the NHL, and we were all able to witness its dominance as the Red Wings of the late 1990s terrorized the league. The fear, uneasiness and outright must-win attitude that defined the Summit Series is simply not accessible to today's Canadian hockey fans, which has caused the reverberation of the series to die down to a whisper. A whisper of a series whose greatest contribution to the game is what it led to, rather than what it was. As time marches forward, and as the generation of hockey fans who truly *felt* the Summit Series loses touch with younger generations, there will be no more echo of what the series was. It will slowly turn into a very important, but certainly not earth-shattering, series that began the string of best-on-best tournaments that will always be fun to watch.

Works Cited

Campbell, Joseph. *The Hero with a Thousand Faces.* Princeton: Princeton University Press, 1968.

Canada Russia '72. DVD. Directed by T.W. Peacocke. Montreal: Maple Pictures, 2006.

Clarke, Bob. "Great Escape." *TSN* magazine, November 27, 2002, Team Canada Collector's Edition.

Dryden, Steve. "Victory: Canada's Hat-Trick." *TSN* magazine, November 27, 2002, Team Canada Collector's Edition.

Esposito, Phil, and Peter Golenbock. *Thunder and Lightning: A No-B.S. Hockey Memoir.* Toronto: McClelland & Stewart, 2003.

Hartje, Todd. *From Behind the Red Line: A North American Hockey Player in Russia.* With Lawrence Martin. Toronto: Warwick, 1996.

Martin, Lawrence. *The Red Machine.* Toronto: Doubleday, 1990.

Shea, Kevin. "Legends of Hockey: Team Canada '72." Hockey Hall of Fame, November 27, 2012. http://www.hhof.com/htmlSpotlight/spot_oneononeTeamCan72.shtml (accessed July 27, 2013).

Acknowledgements

♦

This book would not have been possible but for two acts of generosity. One was the sabbatical awarded to me by Pasadena City College during the 2012–13 academic year. The second was the fellowship given to me by the Centre for the Study of Sport and Health at Saint Mary's University in Halifax that same year. The people behind these benefits include my dean at PCC, Professor Amy Ulmer, and my friend and supporter Dr. Colin Howell, from Saint Mary's. I extend to them and the institutions they represent my heartiest thanks.

I would also like to thank Phil Pritchard, known to hockey fans as the Keeper of the Cup. He accommodated my wish to work in the Hockey Hall of Fame's D. K. "Doc" Seaman Hockey Resource Centre in Toronto, and he made it possible for me to interview Ron Ellis, who was a firsthand witness to the events of September 1972 as a member of Team Canada.

The writers who contributed to this volume amaze me. Their research is thorough, accurate and worthwhile as a witness to the events they describe. And their spirit in meeting deadlines and responding to every minute criticism of their work that I offered as editor was exemplary. Thanks to them for a book that, I believe, will continue to be read many years from now as an important window into this singular moment in hockey history and Canadian cultural life.

Three generations of my family also need to be acknowledged. My father, Hugh, taught me to love the game and watched with me the oddity that was the Soviet style of play in the Summit Series. My sister, Sandra, was on the same school bus I was when Henderson scored the goal. And my nephew and niece, Daniel and Sarah, have embraced the oddity of Uncle Bean (me) and daddy (their father, Phil), who always, no matter what, have to watch game eight when Uncle Bean is visiting at Christmas.

And to Gaby, my partner in everything, no thanks I could offer to you would ever be enough.

Contributors

✤

Michael Buma is a former faculty member in the English and kinesiology departments at Western University. He has written several articles and book chapters on the cultural meanings of sport and is the author of *Refereeing Identity: The Cultural Work of Canadian Hockey Novels*. He is currently working as an analyst at an IT research firm.

Iri Cermak is a media and film studies researcher with experience in film production. She was born to Czech-Hungarian parents in Lima, Peru. Cermak earned her Ph.D. in Communications from the University of Washington, Seattle. Her dissertation, "Seeing Red: Images of Soviet and Russian Hockey in US and Canadian Olympic Broadcasts," comprises three time periods. The first segment, retitled "Seeing Red: Mediasport Discourses of Soviet Olympic Hockey," was co-published by the Canadian Studies Center and the Henry M. Jackson School of International Studies at UW. The third segment also investigates portrayals of the Finnish national hockey team. She is currently working on a project about hockey in Canadian and US feature films.

Jamie Dopp is an Associate Professor of Canadian Literature at the University of Victoria. His articles, reviews, stories and poems have appeared in many journals over the years. He is also the author of two books of poetry and a novel. In 2009, he co-edited a collection of essays about hockey with Richard Harrison called *Now is the Winter: Thinking about Hockey* (Wolsak and Wynn).

Tim Elcombe, an Assistant Professor in Kinesiology & Physical Education at Wilfrid Laurier University in Waterloo, Ontario, received his Ph.D. from Penn State University. His research focuses on addressing ethical issues emerging in sporting contexts, exploring intersections between sport and culture, and examining uses of sport as a socio-political tool. Publishing in journals including the *International Journal of the History of Sport*, the *Journal of the Philosophy of Sport*, the *Journal of Canadian Studies* and the *SAIS Review of International Affairs*, he was awarded the British Philosophy of Sport Association's Developing Researcher Award in 2010.

Richard Harrison's *Hero of the Play*, poems in the language of hockey, was launched at both the Hockey Hall of Fame and the Saddledome. His essays on the game have appeared in various journals and in Andrew Holman's anthology *Canada's Game*. With Jamie Dopp, Richard edited *Now is the Winter*, essays from the "Canada and the League of Hockey Nations" conference at the University of Victoria. His commentaries on hockey have been published in the *Globe and Mail*, aired on CBC and presented at the Museum of Civilization's exhibit in honour of Maurice Richard.

Andrew C. Holman is Professor of History and Director of the Canadian Studies Program at Bridgewater State University in Massachusetts where he teaches courses in Canadian, American and sport history, and edits *Bridgewater Review*, the school's faculty magazine. He is editor of *Canada's Game: Hockey and Identity* (McGill-Queen's 2009), co-editor (with Robert Kristofferson) of *More of a Man* (University of Toronto Press, 2013) and author of several scholarly articles on sport and Canadian society.

Brett Kashmere is a Canadian-born, Pittsburgh-based filmmaker, writer, curator and editor. Combining traditional research methods with materialist aesthetics and hybrid forms, Kashmere's experimental documentaries explore issues of history and (counter-) memory, popular culture, geographies of identity and the politics of representation. His 2006 video essay, *Valery's Ankle*, which examined the spectacle of hockey violence in North American media, has screened internationally at festivals, museums, microcinemas and galleries. Kashmere's follow-up, FROM DEEP (2013), continues his foray into the skein of sports, identity, nationality and fandom, focusing on the merger of basketball and hip hop in the mid 1980s and the rise of Michael Jordan as the world's first corporate branded athlete.

Brian Kennedy, Ph.D., teaches at Pasadena City College as Associate Professor of English. A Canadian, he writes about contemporary British and post-colonial literature, as well as hockey. He has previously published six books, including a memoir, *Growing Up Hockey* (Folklore, 2007); a critical look at Canada's favorite sport, *My Country Is Hockey* (Argenta, 2011); and a novel, *Pond Hockey* (Argenta, 2013). He is currently finishing *Mixing Memory and Desire: The Great War in Contemporary Commonwealth Fiction*. He has been interviewed on CBC radio and television, and is a frequent guest on NHL-related radio shows in both Canada and the US. He also appeared in the recent PBS documentary film *More Than a Game*.

Alexander Kubyshkin received his M.A. from Ivanovo State University, his Ph.D. in History from Saint Petersburg State University and a doctorate of Sciences in History from the Institute of World History, Russian Academy of Sciences.

His research is concentrated on International Relations and American Studies. He has led a research centre for American Studies (1994–2008) and was editor-in-chief of the journal *Americana* (1995–2013). He is the author of one hundred fifty publications, including five monographs.

Since 2008 he has been a professor in the Department for American Studies (School of International Relations, Saint Petersburg State University) and Smolny College of Liberal Arts and Sciences. He lives in Saint Peterburg.

Anna H. Lathrop is the Vice-Provost, Teaching and Learning, at Brock University, and a professor in the Department of Kinesiology in the Faculty of Applied Health Sciences. Her areas of research include the history of physical education and sport, children and physical activity and pedagogy in higher education. Her distinctions include the Brock University Distinguished Teaching Award (2000); the Ontario Confederation of University Faculty Association Award for Outstanding University Teaching (2000); the 3M Teaching Fellowship Award of Canada (2001); the Ontario Leadership in Faculty Teaching Award (MTCU) (2007–8) and the Brock University Chancellor's Chair for Teaching Excellence (2012).

Daryl Leeworthy hails from south Wales and is currently a lecturer in modern history at the University of Huddersfield in Yorkshire, England, where he teaches American history, British history and European history, often peppered with a little sports history. His first book, *Fields of Play: The Sporting Heritage of Wales*, was published in 2012, entirely coincidental with a large sporting event held in London that year, and he is currently writing a book on American and Canadian sports in Britain since 1870. His first memory of hockey is watching *The Mighty Ducks* aged six.

Rich Lehman grew up in Dartmouth, Nova Scotia, and received a B.A. in English from the University of Victoria where he competed with the Varsity Track and Cross Country teams, twice being named as a First Team All-Canadian. After completing his degree and athletic career, he returned to his hometown of Dartmouth to pursue a career in coaching. He is a certified level 3 track and field coach and currently works as the Head Coach of the Dalhousie Track and Field and Cross Country Teams, having won three Atlantic University Sport Coach of the Year Awards.

Dr. Don Morrow is a Full Professor in the Faculty of Health Sciences, School of Kinesiology and the Graduate School of Health and Rehabilitation Sciences, Western University Canada. He teaches a broad spectrum of courses related to: Exercise, Health, Sport, and the Body in Western Culture; Sport Literature; Integrative (Alternative/Complementary) Health; Sport History; Health Promotion; and he is keenly interested in teaching methods. The author of a wide variety of research articles and eight books (the most recent is *Sport in Canada: A History*, Oxford, 2013), his research focuses on narrative writing and narrative critical inquiry; fiction and non-fiction related to sport and exercise; and Canadian sport history.

J. Andrew Ross is a postdoctoral fellow in the departments of history and economics at the University of Guelph. His first book, *Joining the Clubs: The Business of the National Hockey League to 1945*, is forthcoming from Syracuse University Press, and he is currently working on a second concerning on the NHL's operations in the postwar era.

Tobias Stark is an Associate Professor in the Department of Sport Sciences at Linnaeus University in Växjö, Sweden, where he teaches sport history and sport sociology. He is the author of *Folkhemmet på is: Ishockey, modernisering och nationell identitet i Sverige 1920–1972* (*The People's Home on Ice: Ice Hockey, Modernization and National Identity in Sweden 1920-1972*) (2010), as well as numerous book chapters and journal articles on Swedish and European ice hockey.

Dr. Julie Stevens is an Associate Professor in the Department of Sport Management at Brock University. Dr. Stevens is an active hockey scholar. Her insight on the history and development of female hockey in Canada and abroad generated a co-authored work titled, "Too many men on the ice: Women's hockey in North America," which is a definitive source about the female game. She explores critical hockey issues, particularly the community-commercial tensions within the sport. Her collaborative research on men's professional hockey, ethics and head shots includes an editorial in the *Toronto Star*. She coached at the Canada Winter Games and played varsity for Queen's University.

Index

♦